Starting and Running an Online Business For Dummies

D0539431

Contact Information to Keep Close at Hand

Nobody runs a business alone. You need to know where to go for help if problems arise. Take a moment to jot down the following names and phone numbers/e-mail addresses so that you have them when you need them:

- ✔ Your ISP's technical support number (where to call if you can't connect or access your e-mail) and your Internet access account's username and password:

  _____

- ✔ Your Web hosting service's number (the company that posts your Web site on its server — may be the same as your ISP), plus your Web hosting service's username and password, your Domain Name Service server names and IP addresses:

  _____

  _____

- ✔ Your Web site designer's number (a friend or a firm that you hired to help you build your Web site):

  _____

- ✔ Your technical support contact (a neighbour, a free computer support company, or a paid service):

  _____

- ✔ Your employees' or business partners' numbers:

  _____

  _____

  _____

- ✔ Your credit card network's number (where to call when you want to process a credit card order):

  _____

- ✔ Your accountant's number:

  _____

- ✔ Your Internet service provider's (ISP's) access number (the number you usually dial to connect to the Internet):

  _____

- ✔ Other contacts:

  _____

  _____

For Dummies: Bestselling Book Series for Beginners

Starting and Running an Online Business For Dummies®

Cheat Sheet

Web Site Checklist

You can put almost anything you want on your Web site, but here are some essential things that you need to be sure you include:

- ❏ Your contact information
- ❏ Your company name and logo, if you have one
- ❏ Your business mission statement
- ❏ Titles that match each Web page's contents
- ❏ <META> tags that help search services index your site
- ❏ Copyright notice
- ❏ Links to main areas of your business Web site
- ❏ Feedback form or guest book

- ❏ Endorsements from satisfied customers/clients
- ❏ Clear photos of your merchandise for sale
- ❏ Online order form
- ❏ A Frequently Asked Questions (FAQ) page
- ❏ Customer service information
- ❏ Payment options (credit card, cheque, online payment)
- ❏ Posting/shipping options (special delivery, courier, first class, air-mail)

Referral List

Smart businesspeople build goodwill and develop loyalty by referring customers to other sources when they can't provide what is needed. Keep a list of the names, e-mail addresses, Web site URLs, or phone numbers of companies or individuals that you can personally recommend:

Name _____ Contact info. _____

Name _____ Contact info. _____

Name _____ Contact info. _____

Name _____ Contact info. _____

Name _____ Contact info. _____

Legal and Business Requirements

- ✔ **Decide what type of business you're going to be:** Are you going to be a sole trader, a partnership, or are you going to become a statutory business entity?

- ✔ **Register with HMRC:** You're required to register your business with Her Majesty's Revenue and Customs, and you'll probably have to register for VAT as well.

- ✔ **Choose an accounting method:** You can either use cash-basis or accrual-basis accounting.

- ✔ **Choose an accounting period:** The calendar year is simple, but you can also choose a fiscal year.

- ✔ **Record your revenue:** Write down the amount you receive, the form of payment, the date, the name of the client, and the goods or services you provided in exchange for the payment.

- ✔ **Keep track of expenses:** Write down the date the expense occurred, the name of the person or company that received payment, and the type of expense incurred.

- ✔ **Be aware of Health and Safety restrictions:** As soon as you set up and register your online business, you must create a safe and risk free environment for your employees (even if the only employee is you!).

- ✔ **Research your trade name:** Do a search on the Internet followed by a search of Companies House (www.companieshouse.co.uk).

Starting and Running an Online Business

FOR DUMMIES®

Starting and Running an Online Business

FOR DUMMIES®

by Dan Matthews and Greg Holden

John Wiley & Sons, Ltd

Starting and Running an Online Business For Dummies®

Published by
John Wiley & Sons, Ltd
The Atrium
Southern Gate
Chichester
West Sussex
PO19 8SQ
England

E-mail (for orders and customer service enquires): cs-books@wiley.co.uk

Visit our Home Page on www.wiley.com

For general information on our other products and services, please contact our Customer Care Department within the U.S. at 800-762-2974, outside the U.S. at 317-572-3993, or fax 317-572-4002.

For technical support, please visit www.wiley.com/techsupport.

Wiley also publishes its books in a variety of electronic formats. Some content that appears in print may not be available in electronic books.

British Library Cataloguing in Publication Data: A catalogue record for this book is available from the British Library

ISBN: 978-0-470-05768-1

Printed and bound in Great Britain by Bell & Bain Ltd., Glasgow

10 9 8 7 6 5 4 3 2 1

WILEY

About the Authors

Dan Matthews is Group Online Editor of Caspian Publishing, which produces magazines, Web sites, and events for an audience of UK entrepreneurs. Primarily working on realbusiness.co.uk, Dan writes about stellar business success stories as well as up-and-coming start-ups.

He was previously Group Online Editor of Crimson Business Publishing, with responsibility for sites such as startups.co.uk and growingbusiness.co.uk. He has contributed to a range of business magazines, including being contributing editor of *Real Business* magazine and *Growing Business* magazine, and is the co-author of *Starting a Business on eBay.co.uk For Dummies*.

Greg Holden started a small business called Stylus Media, which is a group of editorial, design, and computer professionals who produce both print and electronic publications. The company gets its name from a recording stylus that reads the traces left on a disk by voices or instruments and translates those signals into electronic data that can be amplified and enjoyed by many. He has been self-employed for the past ten years. He is an avid user of eBay, both as a buyer and seller, and he recently started his own blog.

One of the ways Greg enjoys communicating is through explaining technical subjects in nontechnical language. The first edition of *Starting an Online Business For Dummies* was the ninth of his more than 30 computer books. He also authored *eBay PowerUser's Bible* for Wiley Publishing. Over the years, Greg has been a contributing editor of *Computer Currents* magazine, where he writes a monthly column. He also contributes to *PC World* and the University of Illinois at Chicago alumni magazine. Other projects have included preparing documentation for an electronics catalogue company in Chicago and creating online courses on Windows 2000 and Microsoft Word 2000.

Greg balances his technical expertise and his entrepreneurial experience with his love of literature. He received an M.A. in English from the University of Illinois at Chicago and also writes general interest books, short stories, and poetry. Among his editing assignments is the monthly newsletter for his daughters' grade school.

After graduating from college, Greg became a reporter for his hometown newspaper. Working at the publications office at the University of Chicago was his next job, and it was there that he started to use computers. He discovered, as the technology became available, that he loved desktop publishing (with the Macintosh and LaserWriter) and, later on, the World Wide Web.

Greg loves to travel, but since his two daughters were born, he hasn't been able to get around much. He was able to translate his experiences into a book called *Karma Kids: Answering Everyday Parenting Questions with Buddhist Wisdom*. However, through the Web, he enjoys traveling vicariously and meeting people online. He lives with his family in an old house in Chicago that he has been rehabbing for – well, for many years now. He is a collector of objects such as pens, cameras, radios, and hats. He is always looking for things to take apart so that he can see how they work and fix them up. Many of the same skills prove useful in creating and maintaining Web pages. He is an active member of Jewel Heart, a Tibetan Buddhist meditation and study group based in Ann Arbor, Michigan.

Dedication

Greg: To my best friend Ann Lindner, who makes everything possible.

Authors' Acknowledgements

Dan: Dan would like to thank Simon, Sam, Kelly, and Wejdan at John Wiley for their guidance, support, and ultimately patience in producing this book. He'd also like to thank Gemma for her patience and serenity, and Charles, Rebecca, and Kate at Real Business for being all-round good eggs!

Greg: One of the things I like best about this book is that it's a teaching tool that gives me a chance to share my knowledge – small business owner to small business owner – about computers, the Internet, and communicating your message to others in an interactive way. As any businessperson knows, most large-scale projects are a team effort.

The most successful entrepreneurs also tend to be the ones who were the most generous with their time and experience. They taught me that the more helpful you are, the more successful you'll be in return.

I want to thank all those who were profiled as case studies, particularly John Moen of Graphic Maps, who pops up all through the book.

I would also like to acknowledge some of my own colleagues who helped prepare and review the text and graphics of this book and who have supported and encouraged me in other lessons of life. Thanks to Ann Lindner, whose teaching experience proved invaluable in suggesting ways to make the text more clear, and to my assistant Ben Huizenga.

For editing and technical assignments, I was lucky to be in the capable hands of the folks at Wiley Publishing.

Thanks also to Neil Salkind and David and Sherry Rogelberg of Studio B, and to Terri Varveris of Wiley Publishing for helping me to add this book to the list of those I've authored and, in the process, to broaden my expertise as a writer.

Last but certainly not least, the future is in the hands of the generation of my two daughters, Zosia and Lucy, who allow me to learn from the curiosity and joy with which they approach life.

Publisher's Acknowledgements

We're proud of this book; please send us your comments through our Dummies online registration form located at www.dummies.com/register/.

Some of the people who helped bring this book to market include the following:

Acquisitions, Editorial, and Media Development

Project Editor: Kelly Ewing and Simon Bell

Content Editor: Steve Edwards

Commissioning Editor: Samantha Clapp

Technical Editors: Dr Stephen Small, marketing copywriter and communications consultant (www.top-copywriting.com), and James Connolly.

Executive Editor: Jason Dunne

Executive Project Editor: Martin Tribe

Cover Photos: GettyImages/Jamie Grill

Cartoons: Ed McLachlan

Composition Services

Project Coordinator: Jennifer Theriot

Layout and Graphics: Joyce Haughey, Stephanie D. Jumper, Laura Pence, Heather Ryan, Julie Trippetti

Anniversary Logo Design: Richard Pacifico

Proofreaders: Cynthia Fields, Susan Moritz, Charles Spencer

Indexer: Aptara

Publishing and Editorial for Consumer Dummies

Diane Graves Steele, Vice President and Publisher, Consumer Dummies

Joyce Pepple, Acquisitions Director, Consumer Dummies

Kristin A. Cocks, Product Development Director, Consumer Dummies

Michael Spring, Vice President and Publisher, Travel

Kelly Regan, Editorial Director, Travel

Publishing for Technology Dummies

Andy Cummings, Vice President and Publisher, Dummies Technology/General User

Composition Services

Gerry Fahey, Vice President of Production Services

Debbie Stailey, Director of Composition Services

Contents at a Glance

Table of Contents

Introduction

● ●

You've been thinking about starting your own business, but until now, it was just a dream. After all, you're a busy person. You have a full-time job, whether it's running your home or as part of the rat race. Perhaps you've been through a life-changing event and are ready to move in a new direction.

Well, we have news for you: *Now* is the perfect time to turn your dream into reality by starting your own Web-based business. People just like you are making money and enriching their lives by starting up online. Opening hours don't exist, but you can work when you need to, and the location of your business makes no difference. Anyone can run a small business from the comfort of a home office – even if it's just your spare bedroom. And there's an ever increasing number of ways you can make money online, such as running your own blog, starting a business on eBay, or dreaming up something entirely unique.

If you like the idea of being in business for yourself, but you don't have a particular product or service in mind at the moment, keep a look out for openings and ideas: What could you put online that isn't there already? The Internet is home to many diverse businesses that have 'made it' in their own way. Among the entrepreneurs we interviewed for this book are a woman who sells her own insect repellent, a housewife who sells sweetener and coffee on eBay, a sculptor and painter, and a young man who started selling electronics online at age 16. With help from this book, you can transform a simple idea into your very own online empire.

About This Book

You say you wouldn't know a merchant account, domain name, or click-through if you sat next to one on a train? Don't worry: The Internet (and this book) levels the playing field, so a novice has almost as good a chance at succeeding as the MBA-clutching whiz kids you hear about.

The Internet is a vital part of what makes a business these days. Whether you've been in business for 20 years or 20 minutes, the keys to success are the same:

▶ **Having a good idea:** If you have something to sell that people have an appetite for, and if your competition is thin on the ground, your chances of success are good.

- ✔ **Working hard:** When you're your own boss, you can make yourself work harder than any of your former bosses ever could. If you put in the effort and persevere through the inevitable ups and downs, you'll come up smiling.

- ✔ **Preparing for success:** One of the most surprising and useful things we can discover from online businesspeople is that if you believe that you will succeed, you stand a much better chance of doing so. Believe in yourself and go about your plans like they're dead certs. Together with your good ideas and hard work, your confidence will pay off.

If you're the cautious type who wants to test the waters before you launch your new business on the Internet, let this book lead you gently over the learning curve. Once you're online, you can master techniques to improve your presence. Even if you aren't among the lucky small business owners who make a fortune by connecting to the Net, the odds are very good that you will make new friends, build your confidence, and have fun, too.

Conventions Used in This Book

In this book, we format important bits of information in special ways to make sure that you notice them right away:

- ✔ **In This Chapter lists:** Chapters start with a list of the topics that we cover in that chapter. This list represents a kind of table of contents in miniature.

- ✔ **Numbered lists:** When you see a numbered list, follow the steps in a specific order to accomplish the task.

- ✔ **Bulleted lists:** Bulleted lists (like this one) indicate things that you can do in any order or list related bits of information.

- ✔ **Web addresses:** When we describe activities or sites of interest on the World Wide Web, we include the address, or Uniform Resource Locator (URL), in a special typeface like this: `http://www.wiley.com/`. Because popular Web browsers such as Microsoft Internet Explorer and Mozilla Firefox don't require you to enter the entire URL, this book uses the shortened addresses. For example, if you want to connect to the Wiley Publishing site, you can get there by simply entering the following in your browser's Go To or Address bar: `www.wiley.co.uk`.

Don't be surprised if your browser can't find an Internet address you type or if a Web page that's depicted in this book no longer looks the same. Although the sites were current when the book was written, Web addresses (and sites themselves) can be pretty fickle. Try looking for a missing site by using an Internet search engine. Or try shortening the address by deleting everything after the `.co.uk` (or `.com` or `.org.uk`).

Foolish Assumptions

This book assumes that you've never been in business but that you're interested in setting up your own commercial site on the Internet. We also assume that you're familiar with the Internet and have been surfing for a while.

We also assume that you have or are ready to get the following:

- ✔ **A computer and a modem:** Chapter 2 explains exactly what kind of stuff you need.

- ✔ **Instructions on how to think like a businessperson:** We spend big chunks of this book encouraging you to set goals and do the sort of planning that successful businesspeople need to do.

- ✔ **Just enough technical know-how:** You don't have to do it all yourself. Plenty of entrepreneurs decide to partner with someone or hire an expert to perform design and technical work. This book gives you your options, as well as a basic vocabulary, so that you can work productively with the consultants you hire.

How This Book 1s Organised

This book is divided into five parts. Each part contains chapters that discuss stages in the process of starting an online business: designing the Web site, getting it hosted, choosing what shape your business will take, and figuring out what you plan to sell.

Part 1: Strategies and Tools for Your Online Business

In Part I, we describe what you need to do and how you need to *think* in order to start your new business. Throughout the part, you find case studies profiling entrepreneurs and describing how they started their online businesses. Within these pages, we tell you what software you need to create Web pages and perform essential business tasks, along with any computer upgrades that will help your business run more smoothly. You also discover how to choose a Web host and find exciting new ways to make money online.

Part II: Establishing Your Online Presence

This part explains how to create a compelling and irresistible Web site, one that attracts paying customers around the world and keeps them coming back to make more purchases. This part also includes options for attracting and keeping customers, making your site secure, and updating and improving your online business.

Part III: Running and Promoting Your Online Business

Your work doesn't end after you put your Web site online or start to make a few sales. In fact, what you do after you open your virtual doors for business can make the difference between a site that says, 'Buy from me!' and one that says, 'Get out quick!' In this part, we describe cost-effective marketing and advertising techniques that you can do yourself to increase visibility and improve customer satisfaction. You discover how to create a smooth shopping experience for your customers, how to accept payments, and how to provide good customer service. You also find out about ways to increase visibility with search services.

Part IV: The Necessary Evils: Law and Accounting

This part delves into some less-than-sexy but essential tasks for any online business. You find out about general security software designed to make commerce more secure on the Internet. We also discuss copyrights, trademarks, and other legal concerns for anyone wanting to start a company in an increasingly competitive atmosphere online. Finally, you get an overview of basic accounting practices for online businesses and suggestions of accounting tools that you can use to keep track of your e-commerce activities.

Part V: The Part of Tens

Filled with tips, cautions, suggestions, and examples, the Part of Tens presents many titbits of information that you can use to plan and create your own business presence on the Internet, including ten hot new ways to make money on the Web.

Icons Used in This Book

Starting and Running an Online Business For Dummies also uses special graphical elements called *icons* to get your attention. Here's what they look like and what they mean:

This icon flags practical advice about particular software programs or about issues of importance to businesses. Look to these tips for help with finding resources quickly, making sales, or improving the quality of your online business site. This icon also alerts you to software programs and other resources that we consider to be especially good, particularly for those new to the industry.

This icon points out potential pitfalls that can develop into major problems if you're not careful.

This icon alerts you to important facts and figures to keep in mind as you grow your online business.

This icon calls your attention to interviews we conducted with online entrepreneurs who provide tips and instructions for running an online business.

This icon points out technical details that may be of interest to you. A thorough understanding, however, isn't a prerequisite to grasping the underlying concept. Non-techies are welcome to skip items marked by this icon altogether.

Where to Go from Here

We've made this book into an easy-to-use reference tool that you should be comfortable with, no matter what your level of experience. You can use this book in a couple of ways: as a cover-to-cover read or as a reference for when you run into problems or need inspiration. Feel free to skip straight to the chapters that interest you. You don't have to scour each chapter methodically from beginning to end to find what you want. The Web doesn't work that way, and neither does this book!

Want a snapshot of what it takes to get online and be inspired by one man's online business success story? Jump ahead to Chapter 1. Want to find out how to accept credit-card payments? Check out Chapter 11.

If you're just starting out and need to do some essential business planning, see Chapter 2. If you want to prepare a shopping list of business equipment, see Chapter 3. Part II is all about the essential aspects of creating and operating a successful online business, from organising and marketing your Web site to providing effective online customer service and security. Later chapters cover advertising, legal issues, and accounting. So start where it suits you and come back later for more.

Part I
Strategies and Tools for Your Online Business

In this part . . .

What all does starting an online business involve? In this part, we answer that question with a brief overview of the whole process. The following chapters help you set your online business goals, draw up a blueprint for meeting those goals, and explore new ways to market your goods and services.

And just as dentists prepare their drills and carpenters assemble their tools, you need to gather the necessary hardware and software to keep your online business running smoothly. So, in this part, we discuss the business equipment that the online store owner needs and suggest ways that you can meet those needs even on a limited budget.

Let the step-by-step instructions and real-life case studies in this part guide you through the process of starting a successful business online.

Chapter 1

Opening Your Own Online Business in Ten Easy Steps

. . . .

In This Chapter

▶ Finding a unique niche for your business

▶ Identifying a need and targeting your customers

▶ Turning your Web site into an indispensable resource

▶ Finding more than one way to market your business

▶ Evaluating your success and revising your site

. . . .

Starting an online business is no longer a novelty. It's a fact of life for individuals and established companies alike. The good news is that *e-commerce* – the practice of selling goods and services through a Web site – is not only here to stay, but it's thriving. More good news is that the steps required to conduct commerce online are well within the reach of ordinary people like you and me, even if you have no business experience. Constantly updated software and services make creating Web pages and transacting online business easier. All you need is a good idea, a bit of startup cash, computer equipment, and a little help from your friends.

One of our goals in this book is to be friends who provide you with the right advice and support to get your business off the ground and turn it into a big success. In this chapter, we give you a step-by-step overview of the entire process of coming up with and launching your business.

The Time Is Now

Now is the perfect time to start your online business. More and more people are shopping online and a growing number of businesses are seeing the unique value of advertising on the Web. We're happy to tell you that business opportunities are springing up all over the place and that the fragile dotcom bubble of 1998–2001 has been replaced by a stable – and sustainable – business medium. eBay is booming. Other well-known Web-based service providers like Yahoo!, PayPal, and Amazon are helping small entrepreneurs to energise their businesses. Bloggers are taking the Internet by storm, and some are making tidy sums from their online diaries. Google and Overture are making it easier than ever to build up advertising revenue.

The immense popularity of the Web and the wildfire spread of broadband Internet connections means you can offer more to your customers online. Once upon a time, jazzy Web sites took ages to upload and people got tired of them quickly; nowadays ultra-speedy connections mean that anything is possible. Still, you may have concerns about the future of e-commerce. We promise your fears will quickly evaporate when you read this book's case studies of our friends and colleagues who do business online. They're either thriving or at least treading water, and they enthusiastically encourage others to take the plunge.

It's still a great time to start an online business. People who are getting into e-commerce today have advantages over those who started out five or six years ago. Simply put, consumers and businesses are smarter. 'There are more experts in the field so that it is easier to make things happen,' says Sarah-Lou Reekie, an online entrepreneur. 'The world is far more *au fait* and switched on to the Web. The number of people able to access the Web and order products and services is far higher. People aren't as nervous as they were to put through credit cards. After an amazingly short time, the Web has changed from an unknown and somewhat scary medium to something as easy as ABC.'

Step 1: Identify a Need

The fact is, no matter how good you are, you always have room for improvement. Even those at the top of their business game, like Tesco, Topshop, and Innocent Smoothies, are always looking over their shoulder at the competition. But the chances are that someday someone else will come along and do it either cheaper or better or both. The same goes for the Web, and it's this fact that you should keep in mind when you're coming up with your business ideas.

From an everyday point of view, e-commerce and the Web have been around for more than a decade now. But new products and ways to sell them are being identified all the time. Think of the things that didn't exist when the first Web sites were created: MP3s, wireless modems, DVDs, eBay. Consider Dan's fledgling Web site InfoZoo.co.uk. He had the idea for a search engine that would allow small businesses to advertise their products and services cheaply and to a wide audience. Like many people in business, Dan's first thought was that the specific product didn't exist and that it may do a lot of good if it did. Will Dan succeed because he has the benefit of both business and online experience? Success is never guaranteed. It depends on you – your energy, dedication, and enthusiasm; as well as your initial business idea.

Your first job is to identify your market (the people who'll be buying your stuff or using your service) and determine how you can best meet its needs. After all, you can't expect Web surfers to flock to your online business unless you identify services or items that they really need. Who are you targeting and why? Is your market likely to splash out on what you're promoting? Is there a genuine need for your product? Ask around and gauge the reaction of your friends and family. Ask them to be honest (you can waste a lot of money if they're not) and listen out for any constructive feedback that may help develop your site into a better offering.

Getting to know the marketplace

The *Internet* is a worldwide, interconnected network of computers to which people can connect either from work or home, and through which you can natter via e-mail, learn new things from the Web, and buy and sell items using credit and debit cards.

A hotbed of commerce

The Internet is a hotbed of commerce – and it just keeps getting hotter. Read what the experts are saying:

✔ The Internet Media Retail Group (IMRG) found that in 2006, £80 billion-worth of shopping was either conducted online or heavily influenced by Internet advertising and offers. That's 10 per cent of all the stuff bought by UK consumers! It says the popularity of Internet has grown by a whopping 2,000 per cent since the year 2000.

✔ PayPal, the transaction service run by eBay, reckons we'll be spending £18.5 billion a year on Internet shopping by 2010, and that 25 million people (close to half the UK population) will be online – 10 million more than today. We'll be spending £2.27 billion a year on clothes and shoes alone.

✔ Research by credit-card company Visa shows that businesses are using the Internet to shop around and save money. More than half search online for travel arrangements, places to stay, and items such as IT equipment.

You'd be mad not to take advantage of this massive swing in consumer activity, but a word of warning in your ear: Online consultancy Empirix says 91 per cent of people would give up on a Web site if they experienced a technical hitch, and 99 per cent wouldn't bother to report the problem. So, your Web site has to work well if you're going to enjoy a slice of this expanding market.

The Internet is a perfect venue for individuals who want to start their own business, who can cope with using computers, and who believe that 'cyberspace' is the place to do it. You don't need much money to get started, after all. If you already have a computer and an Internet connection and can create your own Web pages (which this book will help you with), making the move to your own business Web site may cost as little as a few hundred pounds. After you're online, the overheads are pretty reasonable, too: You can get your Web site hosted online for as little as £5 a month.

With each month that goes by, the number of Internet users increases exponentially. In turn, this creates a vibrant money-making marketplace for the savviest Internet businesses. To illustrate, figures from the Internet Media Retail Group (IMRG) show that more than £5 billion was spent online in the 10 weeks before Christmas 2005; £1.7 billion more than the same period the previous year. Not convinced? Well how about the fact that around half the UK population shopped online last year, spending around £800 each on average? The Internet has become fertile ground for innovative businesses. Just look at Google; it has become one of the world's largest media companies and with a value of tens of billions of pounds.

Many people decide to start an online business with little more than a casual knowledge of the Internet. But when you decide to get serious about going online, it pays to know how the land lies and who's walking on it with you.

One of your first steps should be to find out what it means to do business online and figure out whether your idea fits in the market. For example, you need to realise that customers are active, not passive, in the way that they absorb information; and that the Net was established within a culture of people sharing information freely and helping one another.

Some of the best places to find out about the culture of the Internet are the blogs (or *Web logs:* they're online diaries usually written by people who aren't qualified writers), forums, newsgroups, chat rooms, and bulletin boards where individuals exchange ideas and messages online. Visiting Web sites devoted to topics that interest you personally can be especially helpful, and you may even end up participating! Also visit some leading commerce Web sites (in other words, where people buy and sell items online), such as eBay.co.uk, Amazon.co.uk, ASOS.com, and Play.com, and take note of ideas you like. Pay special attention to the design and the way you *drill down* through the Web site. Remember that appearance and function are as important as the stuff you're selling.

'Cee-ing' what's out there

The more information you have about the 'three Cs' of the online world, the more likely you are to succeed in doing business online:

- **Competitors:** Familiarise yourself with who's already out there. Work out whether there's space for you and how you plan to fill that space. Don't be intimidated by their existence – you're going to do it a lot better!

- **Customers:** Who's gonna visit your Web site, and how will you get them there? Just like with any business, you must encourage demand for your products and make potential customers aware that you exist.

- **Culture:** Every demographic has its own culture. If you're selling clothes to teenagers then your online business will look and feel very different than the site of someone selling stair lifts to the elderly. What's their style? How do they talk? What will they expect to see when they arrive at your site?

As you take a look around the Internet, notice the kinds of goods and services that tend to sell, as well as who's doing the selling. You have to be either different, better, or, at least, more talked about than these guys. Keep the four Cs in mind if you want achieve this goal:

- **Cheapness:** Items tend to be sold at a discount compared with high street shops in the real world – at least, that's what shoppers expect.

- **Customise:** Anything that's hard-to-find, personalised or, better yet, unique, sells well online.

- **Convenience:** Shoppers are looking for items that are easier to buy online than at a bricks-and-mortar shop – a rare book that you can order in minutes from Amazon.co.uk (`www.amazon.co.uk`) or an electronic greeting card that you can send online in seconds (`www.free-greetingcards.co.uk`).

- **Content:** Consumers go online to breeze through news and features available free or through a subscription, such as newspapers and TV channels, or that exist online only, such as blogs and online magazines *(sometimes called ezines)*.

Visit one of the tried-and-tested indexes to the Internet, such as Yahoo! (`www.yahoo.co.uk`), or the top search service Google (`www.google.co.uk`). Enter a word or phrase in the site's home page search box that describes the kinds of goods or services you want to provide online. Find out how many existing businesses already do what you want to do. Better yet, determine what they *don't* do and set a goal of meeting that need yourself.

Working out how to do it better

The next step is to find ways to make your business stand out from the crowd. Direct your energies toward making your site unique in some way. Can you provide things that others don't offer? The things that set your online business apart from the rest can be as tangible as half-price sales, contests, seasonal sales, or freebies. Or they can be features of your site that make it higher quality or make it a better user experience than your competitors. Maybe you want to concentrate on making your customer service better than anyone else.

What if you can't find other online businesses doing what you want to do? In this case, you've either struck gold (you've come up with an idea that no one else has thought of) or struck out (it doesn't exist because it's a bad idea). In e-commerce, being first often means getting a head start and being more successful than latecomers, even if they have more resources than you do. The Internet is getting more and more crowded, however, and genuinely new ideas are getting harder to come by. But don't let that put you off trying something new and outlandish. It just might work!

CASE STUDY

Mapmaker locates his online niche

John Moen didn't know a thing about computer graphics when he first started his online business, Graphic Maps, way back in 1995. He didn't know how to write *HyperText Markup Language* (HTML), the set of instructions used to create Web pages. (Even fewer people knew how to use it in 1995 than do today.) But he did know a lot about maps. And he heard that setting up shop on the Web was 'the thing to do'. He scraped together £170 in start-up costs, learned to create simple Web pages without any photos (only maps and other graphics), and went online.

At first, business was slow. 'I remember saying to my wife, "You know what? We had ten page views yesterday."' The Graphic Maps site (www.graphicmaps.com) was averaging about 30 page views per day when Moen decided to do something that many beginners may find counterproductive, even silly: He started giving away his work for free. He

created some free art (called clip art) and made it available for people to copy. And he didn't stop there: He began giving away his knowledge of geography, too. John answered questions submitted to him by school children and teachers.

Soon, his site was getting 1,000 visits a day. Today, he reports, 'We are so busy, we literally can't keep up with the demand for custom maps. Almost 95 per cent of our business leads come from the Web, and that includes many international companies and Web sites. Web page traffic has grown to more than 3 million hits per month, and banner advertising now pays very well.'

John now has six employees, receives many custom orders for more than £5,500, and has done business with numerous Fortune 500 companies. To promote his site, John gives away free maps to not-for-profit organisations, operates a daily geography contest with a £50 prize to the first person with the correct answer, and answers e-mail promptly. 'I feel strongly that the secret on the Web is to provide a solution for a problem, and for the most part, do it free,' he suggests. 'If the service is high quality, and people get what they want . . . they will tell their friends and all will beat a path to your URL, and then, and only then, will you be able to sell your products to the world, in a way you never imagined was possible.'

Moen created a second site called WorldAtlas. com (www.worldatlas.com, as shown here) that is devoted to geography. That site generates revenue from pop-up and banner ads that other companies place there because so many people visit. 'It is not unusual to have 20 million impressions on that site and hundreds of thousands of geography questions a month from teachers and students,' says Moen.

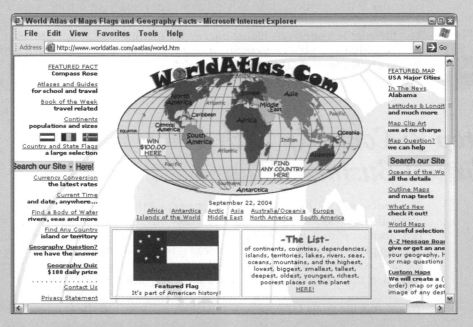

When asked how he can spare the time to answer questions for free when he has so much paying business available, he responds: 'How can you not? I normally work 12-hour, and sometimes 16- or 18-hour days. If a student comes home from school, and says, "Grandpa, I need to find out what's the tallest mountain in North America," and he does a search on Google that directs him to go to WorldAtlas. com, we will try to answer that question.'

His advice for beginning entrepreneurs: 'Find your niche and do it well. Don't try to compete

with larger companies. For instance, I can't compete with Microsoft, but I don't try to. Our map site, GraphicMaps.com, is one of the few custom map sites on the Web. When we started, there was no software yet available to do automatic mapping for a client. If you need a map for a wedding or for your office, we can make you one. I fill some needs that they don't fill, and I learned long ago how to drive business to my site by offering something for free. The fact is that if you have good ideas and you search for clients, you can still do well on the Web.'

Step 2: Know What You're Offering

Business is all about identifying customers' needs and figuring out exactly what goods or services you're going to provide to meet those needs. It's the same both online and off.

To determine what you have to offer, make a list of the items you plan to sell or the services that you plan to provide to your customers. Next, you need to decide where you're going to obtain them. Are you going to create sale items yourself? Are you going to purchase them from a supplier? Jot down your ideas on paper and keep them close at hand as you develop your business plan.

The Internet is a personal, highly interactive medium. Be as specific as possible with what you plan to do online. Don't try to do everything; the medium favours businesses that do one thing well. The more specific your business, the more personal the level of service you can provide to your customers.

Step 3: Come Up with a Virtual Business Plan

The process of setting goals and objectives and then working out how you'll attain them is essential when starting a new business. What you end up with is a *business plan*. A good business plan should be your guide not only in the startup phase, but also as your business grows. It should provide a blueprint for how you run your business on a day-to-day basis and can also be instrumental in helping you obtain a bank loan or any other type of funding.

To set specific goals for your new business, ask yourself these questions:

- ✔ Why do you want to start a business?
- ✔ Why do you want to start it online?
- ✔ What would attract you to a Web site (regardless of what it's selling)?
- ✔ Why do you enjoy using some Web sites and not others?
- ✔ Why are you loyal to some Web sites and not others?

These questions may seem simple, but many businesspeople never take the time to answer them. Make sure that you have a clear game plan for your business so that your venture has a good chance of success over the long haul. (See Chapter 2 for more on setting goals and envisioning your business.)

Working at home?

If you use part of your home as a base for your business (and plenty of fledgling entrepreneurs do), then you should get on top of how that will affect your taxes. For example, the rooms you use may qualify for business rates instead of council tax, and you may also have to pay capital gains tax when you come to sell the property.

Better news is that you should get some tax relief on household bills, and you can claim value added tax (VAT) back on household purchases made in your business's name. For example, office furniture, a lick of paint, and stationery may be a bit cheaper.

You can link your plan to your everyday tasks by taking the following steps:

1. **Write a brief description of your business and what you hope to accomplish with it.**

2. **Draw up a marketing strategy.**

3. **Anticipate financial incomings and outgoings. (See Chapter 15 for specifics.)**

Consider using specialised software to help you prepare your business plan. Programs such as Business Plan Pro by Palo Alto Software (www.paloalto.co.uk) lead you through the process by making you consider every aspect of how your business will work. If you don't want to splash out on software, take a look at one of the many free guides to business plans out there. Business Link (www.businesslink.gov.uk), the government network supporting small businesses, is one of the best places to start.

Step 4: Get Your Act Together and Set Up Shop

One of the great advantages of opening a shop on the Internet rather than on the high street is the savings you should be able to make. Showcasing your products online instead of in a real life shop means that you won't have to pay rent, decorate, or worry about lighting and heating the place. Instead of renting a space and putting up furniture and fixtures, you can buy a domain name, sign up with a hosting service, create some Web pages, and get started with an investment of only a few hundred pounds, or maybe even less.

In addition to your virtual showroom, you also have to find a real place to conduct the operations and logistics of your business. You don't necessarily have to rent a warehouse or other large space. Many online entrepreneurs use a home office or even just a corner in a room where computers, books, and other business-related equipment sit.

Finding a host for your Web site

Although doing business online means that you don't have to rent space in a shopping centre or open a real, physical shop, you do have to set up a virtual space for your online business. You do so by creating a Web site and finding a company to host it. In cyberspace, your landlord is called a Web hosting service. A Web *host* is a company that, for a fee, makes your site available 24 hours a day by maintaining it on a special computer called a Web *server*.

A Web host can be as large and well known as America Online (AOL), which gives all its customers a place to create and publish their own Web pages. Some Web sites, such as Yahoo! GeoCities (`uk.geocities.yahoo.com`) or Tripod (`www.tripod.lycos.co.uk`), act as hosting services and provide easy-to-use Web site creation tools as well.

When Greg's brother decided to create his Web site, he signed up with a company called Webmasters.com, a US-based company, which charged him about $15 per month and offers many features. For example, the form shown in Figure 1-1 enables you to create a simple Web page without typing any HTML. You can opt for this simple template style Web site from a range of British hosts. For more information, see Chapter 3.

Figure 1-1:
Take the time to choose an affordable Web host that makes it easy for you to create and maintain your site.

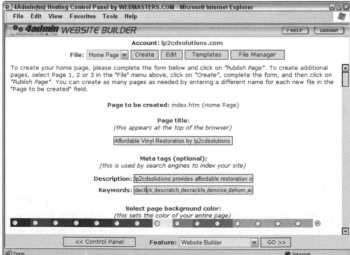

www.Webmasters.com

The company that gives you access to the Internet – your Internet Service Provider (ISP) – may also offer to publish your Web pages. Make sure that your host has a fast connection to the Internet and can handle the large numbers of simultaneous visits, or *page impressions,* that your Web site is sure to get eventually. You can find a detailed description of Web hosting options in Chapter 3.

In Chapter 2, we describe two methods of plying your trade online that don't require a Web site – online classifieds and auctions. But most online businesses find that having a Web site is indispensable for generating and making sales. And hosts like Fasthosts (www.fasthosts.co.uk) and Easyspace (www.easyspace.com) make it easy to create your own site (see Chapter 3).

Assembling the equipment you need

Think of all the equipment you *don't* need when you set up shop online: You don't need shelving, a cash register, a car park, fancy displays, or lighting . . . the list goes on and on. You may need some of those for your home, but you don't need to purchase them especially for your online business itself.

For doing business online, your most important piece of equipment is your computer. Other hardware, such as scanners, printers, cameras, modems, and monitors, are also essential. You need to make sure that your computer equipment is up to scratch because you're going to be spending a lot of time online: answering e-mails, checking orders, revising your Web site, and marketing your product. Expect to spend anywhere between £500 and £5,000 for equipment, if you don't have any to begin with.

It's a good idea to buy second-hand equipment, especially if items are unopened and still come under a guarantee. It saves you money, and as long as you're careful with what you buy and who you buy it from, you can get as much use as from a product bought new. Remember that your business is likely to grow, so choose equipment that can accommodate the extra use you'll get out of it as you move forward. (For more suggestions on buying business hardware and software, see Chapter 2.)

Choosing business software

You can build a Web site by either doing it yourself or paying someone else to do it for you. The first option is cheaper, but nine times out of ten, the latter produces something a lot more sophisticated. Try searching for *Web design,* and you'll be confronted with a long list of businesses that offer design skills. Pick one that is reputable, has good references, and allows you to contact current customers for their views on the service. However, if you're confident about your ability to learn fast and are determined to create your Web site by yourself, then you'll need to buy in some funky software.

Keeping track of your inventory

You can easily overlook inventory and setting up systems for processing orders when you're just starting out. But as Lucky Boyd, an entrepreneur who started MyTexasMusic.com and other Web sites, pointed out to Greg, you need to make sure you have a 'big vision' early in the process of creating your site. In his case, it meant having a site that could handle lots of visitors and make purchasing easy for them. In other cases, it may mean having sufficient inventory to meet demand.

On the whole, having too many items for sale is preferable to not having enough. 'We operated on a low budget in the beginning, and we didn't have the inventory that people wanted,' one entrepreneur commented. 'People online get impatient if they have to wait for things too long. Make sure you have the goods you advertise. Plan to be successful.'

Many online businesses keep track of their inventory by using a database that's connected to their Web site. When someone orders a product from the Web site, that order is automatically recorded in the database, which then produces an order for replacement stock.

In this kind of arrangement, the database serves as a so-called *back end* or *back office* to the Web-based shop front. This sophisticated arrangement is not for beginners. However, if orders and inventory get to be too much for you to handle yourself, consider hiring a Web developer to set up such a system for you. If you're adventurous and technically oriented, you can link a database to a Web site by using a product such as FrontPage or Dreamweaver. For more information about these products and how they work, check out *FrontPage 2003 For Dummies*, by Asha Dornfest, and *Dreamweaver MX For Dummies*, by Janine Warner and Ivonne Berkowitz (both published by Wiley).

For the most part, the programs you need in order to operate an online business are the same as the software you use to surf the Internet. But you may need a wider variety of tools than you would use for simple information gathering.

Because you're going to be in the business of information *providing* now, as well as information gathering, you need programs such as the following:

- ✔ **A Web page editor:** These programs, which you may also hear called *Web page creation tools* or *Web page authoring tools,* make it easy for you to format text, add images, and design Web pages without mastering HTML.

- ✔ **Graphics software:** If you decide to create your business Web site yourself instead of finding someone to do it for you, you need a program that can help you draw or edit images that you want to include on your site, such as Microsoft FrontPage or Adobe Dreamweaver.

> ✔ **Shop-front software:** You can purchase software that leads you through the process of creating a fully fledged online business and getting your pages on the Web.
>
> ✔ **Accounting programs:** You can write your expenses and income on a sheet of paper. But it's far more efficient to use software that acts as a spreadsheet, helps you with billing, and even calculates VAT.

Step 5: Get Help

Conducting online business does involve relatively new technologies, but they aren't impossible to figure out. In fact, the technology is becoming more accessible all the time. Many people who start online businesses find out how to create Web pages and promote their companies by reading books, attending classes, or networking with friends and colleagues. Of course, just because you *can* do it all doesn't mean that you have to. You may be better off hiring help, either to advise you in areas where you aren't as strong or simply to help you tackle the growing workload – and help your business grow at the same time.

Hiring technical bods

Spending money up front to hire professionals who can point you in the right direction can help you maintain an effective Web presence for years to come. Many businesspeople who usually work alone (us included) hire knowledge-able individuals to do design or programming work that they would find impossible to tackle otherwise.

Don't be reluctant to hire professional help in order to get your business off the ground. The Web is full of developers that can provide customers with Web access, help create Web sites, and host sites on their servers. The expense for such services may be relatively high at first – probably several thousand pounds – but it'll pay off in the long term. Choose a designer carefully and check out the sites he's designed by getting in contact with customers and asking whether they're satisfied. Don't just tell a designer your business plan; send them the document (omitting your projected finances), explaining in fine detail exactly what you want each page to do.

If you do find a business partner, make sure that the person's abilities balance your own. If you're great at sales and public relations, for example, find a writer, Web page designer, or someone who is good with the accounts to partner with.

TIP

Who are the people in your neighbourhood?

Try to find an expert or helper right in your own town. Greg works with a graphic designer who lives right around the corner from him, and he uses a consultant who lives across the street from him. Ask around your school, university, or workplace, as well as any social venue you attend. Your neighbours may even be able to help you with various projects, including your online business . . . and your online business just may be able to help them, too.

Don't work in a vacuum. Get involved with mailing lists and discussion groups online. Make contacts through these mediums and strike up relationships with people who can help you. Try UK Business Forums (`www.ukbusinessforums.co.uk`) to start with and go from there.

Gathering your team

Many fast growing businesses are family affairs. For example, a husband-and-wife team started Scaife's Butcher Shop in England, which has a simple Web site (`www.jackscaife.co.uk`). A successful eBay business, Maxwell Street Market is run by a husband-and-wife team, as well as family members and neighbours. The husband does the buying; the wife prepares sales descriptions; and the others help with packing and shipping.

John Moen found some retired teachers to help answer the geography questions that come into his WorldAtlas.com site. The convenience of the Internet means that these geography experts can log on to the site's e-mail inbox from home and answer questions quickly. (For more about John Moen and his Web site, see the 'Mapmaker locates his online niche' sidebar, earlier in this chapter.)

Early on, when you have plenty of time for planning, you probably won't feel a pressing need to hire others to help you. Many people wait to seek help when they have a deadline to meet or are in a financial crunch. Waiting to seek help is okay – as long as you realise that you probably *will* need help, sooner or later.

TIP

Of course, you don't have to hire family and friends, it's just that they'll probably be more sympathetic to your startup worries. They'll probably work harder for you and may even lend a hand for free.

If you feel you have to hire someone from the outside world, you must find people who are reliable and can make a long-term commitment to your project. Keep these things in mind:

- ✔ Because the person you hire will probably work online quite a bit, pick someone who already has experience with computers and the Internet.

- ✔ Online hiring works the same as hiring offline: You should always review a *CV* (or work history) get a couple of references, and ask for samples of the candidate's work.

- ✔ Choose someone who responds promptly and in a friendly manner and who demonstrates the talents you need.

Step 6: Construct a Web Site

Even the most prolific eBay.co.uk sellers (see Chapter 10) usually complement their shop with their own Web site. Luckily, Web sites are becoming easier to create. You don't have to know a line of HTML in order to create an okay-looking Web page yourself. (Chapter 5 walks you through the tasks involved in organising and designing Web pages. Also, see Chapter 6 for tips on making your Web pages content-rich and interactive.)

Make your business easy to find online. Pick an easy-to-remember Web address (otherwise known as a *domain name* or a *URL*). If the ideal .com or .co.uk name isn't available, you can try one of the newer domain suffixes, such as .biz. (See Chapter 3 and Chapter 8 for more information on domain name aliases.)

Making your site content-rich

The words and pictures of a Web site (as well as the products) are what attract visitors and keep them coming back on a regular basis. The more useful information and compelling content you provide, the more visits your site will receive. By compelling content, we're talking about words, headings, or images that make visitors want to continue reading. You can make your content compelling in a number of ways:

- ✔ Provide a call to action, such as 'Click Here!' or 'Buy Now!'

- ✔ Explain how the reader will benefit by clicking a link and exploring your site. ('Visit our News and Offers page to find out how to win double discounts this month.')

✔ Briefly and concisely summarise your business and its mission. Make it sound important.

✔ Use a digital camera to capture images of your sale items (or of the services you provide), as we describe in Chapter 5, and post them on a Web page.

Don't forget the personal touch when it comes to connecting with your customers' needs. People who shop online don't get to meet the shop owner in person, so anything you can tell them about yourself helps make the process more personal and puts your visitors at ease. For example, one of Lucky Boyd's primary goals for his MyTexasMusic.com site is to encourage people to become members so that they're more likely to visit on a regular basis. His photos of music fans (see Figure 1-2) personalise the site and remind visitors that they are members of a community of music lovers. Let your visitors know that they're dealing with real people, not remote machines and computer programs.

Figure 1-2: Personalise your business to connect with customers online.

Sneaking a peek on other businesses' Web sites – to pick up ideas and see how they handle similar issues to your own – is a common and perfectly legitimate practice. In cyberspace, you can visit plenty of businesses that are comparable to yours from the comfort of your home office, and the trip takes mere minutes.

Copying other Web sites will land you in legal trouble, although there's no harm in gaining inspiration from what other people do well.

Establishing a visual identity

When you start your first business on the Web, you have to do a certain amount of convincing. You need to show customers that you're competent and professional. One factor that helps build trust is a visual identity. A site with an identity has a consistent look and feel no matter what part of the Web site you access. For example, take a look at Figure 1-3, as well as Figure 1-4 later in this chapter. Both pages are from the Graphic Maps Web site. Notice how each has the same white background, the same distinctive and simple logo, and similar heading styles. Using these standard elements from page to page creates a brand identity that gives your business credibility and helps users find what they're looking for.

Figure 1-3: Through careful planning and design, the Graphic Maps site maintains a consistent look and feel, or visual identity, on each page.

Step 7: Process Your Sales

Many businesses go online and then are surprised by their own success. They don't have systems in place for completing sales, shipping goods in a timely manner, and tracking finances and stock.

An excellent way to plan for success is to set up ways to track your business finances and to create a secure online purchasing environment for your customers. That way, you can build on your success rather than be surprised by it.

Providing a means for secure transactions

Getting paid is the key to survival, let alone success. When your business exists online only, the payment process is not always straightforward. Make your Web site a safe and easy place for customers to pay you. Provide different payment options and build customers' level of trust any way you can.

Although the level of trust among people who shop online is increasing steadily, a few Web surfers are still squeamish about submitting credit-card numbers online. And fresh-faced businesspeople are understandably intimidated by the requirements of processing credit-card transactions. In the past, many businesses used simple forms that customers had to print and mail along with a cheque. This arrangement is a pretty rare practice nowadays, because it slows down what should be a lightening quick transaction. Handling transactions in this manner today will raise some eyebrows among your customers and many will go elsewhere.

You can use numerous types of transaction software. PayPal and Google both operate their own, for example, and a host of independent businesses have also set up cheap alternatives. These services are often free to use, but do take a small percentage of the money you make every time you complete a sale. Customers expect to see this kind of transaction software when they shop online; gone are the days when the majority of e-shoppers paid over the phone or by post.

You may want to offer these low-tech payment methods as an option to newer ones, however; there are plenty of sticklers for tradition out there!

When you're able to accept credit cards, make your customers feel at ease by explaining what measures you're taking to ensure that their information is secure. Such measures include signing up for an account with a Web host that provides a *secure server,* a computer that uses software to encrypt data and uses digital documents called certificates to ensure its identity. (See Chapters 7 and 11 for more on Internet security and secure shopping systems.)

After much searching, emerging entrepreneur Lucky Boyd signed up with a company called GoEmerchant (`www.goemerchant.com`), which provides him with the payment systems that many online shoppers recognise when they want to make a purchase. First, there's a *shopping trolley* – a set of pages that acts as an electronic 'holding area' for items before they are purchased. Next, there's a secure way for people to make electronic purchases by providing online forms, where people can safely enter credit card and other personal information. The note stating that the payment area is protected by Secure Sockets Layer (SSL) encryption tells people that, even if a criminal intercepts their credit-card data, he won't be able to read it.

Safeguarding your customers' personal information is important, but you also need to safeguard your business. Many online businesses get burned by bad guys who submit fraudulent credit-card information. If you don't verify the information and submit it to your bank for processing, you're liable for the cost. Strongly consider signing up with a service that handles credit-card verification for you in order to cut down on lost revenue. See Chapter 7 for more on these and other security issues.

How not to cook your books

What does *keeping your books* mean, anyway? In the simplest sense, it means recording all your business's financial activities – in other words, your incomings and outgoings, including any expenses you incur, all the income you receive, as well as your equipment and tax deductions. The financial side of running a business also means creating reports, such as profit-and-loss statements, that banks require if you apply for a loan. Such reports also give you good information about how well business is going, and where (if it all) things need to improve.

You can record all this information the old-fashioned way by writing it in ledgers and journals, or you can use a spreadsheet (like Microsoft Excel), or you can use accounting software. (See Chapter 15 for some suggestions of easy-to-use accounting packages that are great for financial novices.). Because you're making a commitment to using computers on a regular basis by starting an online business, it's only natural for you to use computers to keep your books, too. Accounting software can help you keep track of expenses and provide information that may save you a headache when the taxman comes knocking.

After you've saved your financial data on your hard drive, make backups so that you don't lose information you need to do business. See Chapter 7 for ways to back up and protect your files.

Step 8: Provide Personal Service

The Internet, which runs on cables, networks, and computer chips, may not seem like a place for the personal touch. But technology didn't actually create the Internet and all its content; *people* did that. In fact, the Internet is a great place to provide your clients and customers with outstanding, personal customer service.

In many cases, customer service on the Internet is a matter of being available and responding quickly to all enquiries. You check your e-mail regularly; you make sure you respond within a day; you cheerfully solve problems and hand out refunds if needed.

By helping your customers, you help yourself, too. You build loyalty as well as credibility among your clientele. For many small businesses, the key to competing effectively with larger competitors is to provide superior customer service. (See Chapter 12 for more ideas on how you can offer great customer service.)

Sharing your expertise

Your knowledge and experience are among your most valuable commodities. So you may be surprised when we suggest that you give them away for free. Why? It's a *try-before-you-buy* concept. Helping people for free builds your credibility and makes them more likely to pay for your services down the road.

Back when Dan was editor of Startups.co.uk, he regularly saw lawyers and accountants give away free advice on the Web site's forum. One accountant in particular, James Smith, has posted well over a thousand pieces of advice to fledgling entrepreneurs. Why? Because they'll remember his sound advice down the line when they need to pay for financial expertise. You should be thinking along the same lines.

When your business is online, you can easily communicate what you know about your field and make your knowledge readily available. One way is to set up a Web page that presents the basics about your company and your field of interest in the form of Frequently Asked Questions (FAQs). Another technique is to create your own newsletter in which you write about what's new with your company and about topics related to your work. See Chapter 12 for more on communicating your expertise through FAQs, newsletters, and advanced e-mail techniques.

Greg's brother, who runs his own Web business, was sceptical when Greg recommended to him that he include a page full of technical information explaining exactly what equipment he uses and describing the steps involved in audio restoration. He didn't think anyone would be interested; he also didn't want to give away his 'trade secrets'. *Au contraire, mon frère!* By and large, people who surf the Internet gobble up all the technical details they can find. The more you wow them with the names and model numbers of your expensive equipment, not to mention the work you go through to restore their old records, the more they'll trust you. And trust will get them to place an order with you. This approach doesn't necessarily work with any business; it often makes sense to keep things simple, but if your selling a technical service – in other words anything that people are unlikely to understand easily – don't be afraid to let people know just how gifted you have to be to perform the task!

Making your site appealing

Many *ontrepreneurs* (online entrepreneurs) succeed by making their Web sites not only a place for sales and promotion but also an indispensable resource, full of useful hyperlinks and other information, that customers want to visit again and again. For example, the World Atlas Web site, which we profile earlier in this chapter in the section 'Mapmaker locates his online niche', acts as a resource for anyone who has a question about geography. To promote the site, John Moen gives away free maps for not-for-profit organisations, operates a daily geography contest with a £50 prize to the first person with the correct answer (shown in Figure 1-4), and answers e-mail promptly. 'I feel strongly that the secret on the Web is to provide a solution to a problem and, for the most part, to do it for free,' he suggests.

Figure 1-4: This site uses free art, a mailing list, and daily prizes to drum up business.

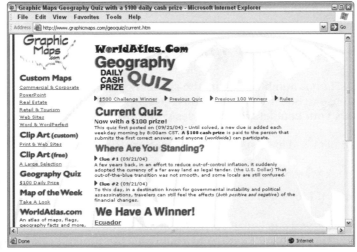

MySpace (www.myspace.com) uses its 'community' ethic to strengthen connections with users and to build its brand – something it has achieved with extraordinary success. The main purpose of the site is to let people interact with each other. You can share photos, music files, blogs, the works. It means someone living in the United States can share all kinds of information with someone in the UK. And best of all, it's completely free. The site makes its money through advertising.

The site ties musicians with music lovers, artists, photographers, and people who just want to chat. Its members provide information about who they are and where they live, and they create their own username and password so that they can access special content and perform special functions on the site.

For any online business, knowing the names and addresses of people who visit and who don't necessarily make purchases is a gold mine of information. The business can use the contact information to send members special offers and news releases; the more frequently contact is maintained, the more likely casual shoppers or members will eventually turn into paying customers.

The concept of membership also builds a feeling of community among customers. By turning the e-commerce site into a meeting place for members who love Texas musicians, MyTexasMusic.com helps those members make new friends and have a reason to visit the site on a regular basis. Community building is one way in which commerce on the Web differs from traditional brick-and-mortar selling, and it's something you should consider, too.

Another way to encourage customers to congregate at your site on a regular basis is to create a dedicated discussion area. In Chapter 12, we show you how to provide a discussion page right on your own Web site.

E-mailing your way to the top

E-mail is, in our humble opinion, the single most important marketing tool that you can use to boost your online business. Becoming an expert e-mail user increases your contacts and provides you with new sources of support, too.

The two best and easiest e-mail strategies are the following:

- ✔ Check your e-mail as often as possible.
- ✔ Respond to e-mail enquiries immediately.

Additionally, you can e-mail enquiries about co-operative marketing opportunities to other Web sites similar to your own. Ask other online business owners if they'll provide links to your site in exchange for you providing links to theirs. And always include a signature file with your message that includes the name of your business and a link to your business site. See Chapter 12 for more information on using e-mail effectively to build and maintain relations with your online customers.

Note: We're encouraging you to use e-mail primarily for one-to-one communication. The Internet excels at bringing individuals together. Mailing lists, desktop alerts, and newsletters can use e-mail effectively for marketing, too. However, we're *not* encouraging you to send out mass quantities of unsolicited commercial e-mail, a practice that turns off almost all consumers and that can get you in trouble with the law, too.

Step 9: Alert the Media and Everyone Else

In order to be successful, small businesses need to get the word out to the people who are likely to purchase what they have to offer. If this group turns out to be a narrow demographic, so much the better; the Internet is great for connecting to niche markets that share a common interest.

The Internet provides many unique and effective ways for small businesses to advertise, including search services, e-mail, blogs, forums, electronic mailing lists, and more.

Listing your site with Internet search services

How, exactly, do you get listed on the search engines such as Yahoo! and Google? Frankly, it's getting more difficult. While you can almost always get listed for free, your chances of getting noticed next to search-dominating mega-brands is pretty slim in many cases. It was this problem that inspired Dan to create InfoZoo.co.uk.

However, you can increase the chances that search services will list your site by including special keywords and site descriptions in the HTML commands for your Web pages. You place these keywords after a special HTML command (the <META> tag), making them invisible to the casual viewer of your site. (Turn to Chapter 13 for details.)

Entrepreneurs John Moen and Lucky Boyd have both created multiple Web sites for different purposes. One purpose is to reach different markets. Another is to improve rankings on search engines such as Google: By linking one site to several other sites, the site is considered more 'popular' and its ranking rises. (See Chapter 13 for more on this and other tips on getting listed by Internet search engines.)

Reaching the whole Internet

Your Web site may be the cornerstone of your business, but if nobody knows it's out there, it can't help you generate sales. Perhaps the most familiar form of online advertising are *banner ads* (which run across the top of Web sites) and *skyscrapers* (which run vertically down the side of pages), those little electronic billboards that appear at the top and down the side (respectively) of high traffic Web sites.

But banner advertising can be expensive and may not be the best way for a small business to advertise online. In fact, the most effective marketing for some businesses hasn't been traditional banner advertising or newspaper/ magazine placements. Rather, the e-marketers target electronic bulletin boards and mailing lists where people already discuss the products being sold. You can post notices on the bulletin boards where your potential customers congregate, notifying them that your services are now available. (Make sure that the board in question permits such solicitation before you do so, or you'll chase away the very customers you want.)

This sort of direct, one-to-one marketing may seem tedious, but it's often the best way to develop a business on the Internet. Reach out to your potential customers and strike up an individual, personal relationship with each one.

Chapter 12 contains everything you need to know about advertising with mailing lists and newsgroups.

Step 10: Review, Revise, and Improve

For any long-term endeavour, you need to establish standards by which you can judge its success or failure. You must decide for yourself what you consider success to be. After a period of time, take stock of where your business is and then take steps to do even better.

Taking stock

After 12 months online, Web entrepreneur Lucky Boyd took stock. His site was online, but he wasn't getting many page views. He redid the site, increased the number of giveaways, and traffic rose. Now, he wants to make music downloads available on his site; he's preparing to redo all his Web pages with the Hypertext Preprocessor programming language (PHP).

HTML is a mark-up language: It identifies parts of a Web page that need to be formatted as headings, text, images, and so on. It can be used to include scripts, such as those written in the JavaScript language. But by creating his pages from scratch using PHP (a common scripting language), Lucky Boyd can make his site more dynamic and easier to update. He can rotate random images, process forms, and compile statistics that track his visitors by using PHP scripts, for example. He can design Web pages in a modular way so that they can be redesigned and revised more quickly than with HTML, too.

When all is said and done, your business may do so well that you can reinvest in it by buying new equipment or increasing your services. You may even be in a position to give something back to not-for-profits and those in need. The young founders of The Chocolate Farm (www.thechocolatefarm.com) set up a scholarship fund designed to bring young people from other countries to the United States to help them find out about free enterprise. Perhaps you'll have enough money left over to reward yourself, too – as if being able to tell everyone 'I own my own online business' isn't reward enough!

The truth is, plenty of entrepreneurs are online for reasons other than making money. That said, it *is* important from time to time to evaluate how well you're doing financially. Accounting software, such as the programs that we describe in Chapter 15, makes it easy to check your revenues on a daily or weekly basis. The key is to establish the goals you want to reach and develop measurements so that you know when and if you reach those goals.

Updating your data

Getting your business online and then updating your site regularly is better than waiting to unveil the perfect Web site all at once. In fact, seeing your site improve and grow is one of the best things about going online. Over time, you can create contests, strike up relationships with other businesses, and add more background information about your products and services.

Consider The Chocolate Farm, which is still owned and operated by siblings Evan and Elise MacMillan of Denver, Colorado. The business was started when Elise was just 10 years old and Evan was 13. They began by selling chocolates with a farm theme, such as candy cows; these days, they focus more on creating custom chocolates – sweets made to order for businesses, many of which bear the company's logo. Evan, who manages the company's Web site, now updates it from his college dorm room in California. He and his sister oversee the work of 50 full- and part-time employees.

Businesses on the Web need to evaluate and revise their practices on a regular basis. Lucky Boyd studies reports of where visitors come from before they reach his site, and what pages they visit on the site, so that he can attract new customers. Online business is a process of trial and error. Some promotions work better than others. The point is that it needs to be an ongoing process and a long-term commitment. Taking a chance and profiting from your mistakes is better than not trying in the first place.

Chapter 2

Choosing and Equipping Your New E-Business

In This Chapter

▶ Picturing your successful online business

▶ Understanding your options: sales, services, and auctions

▶ Making your e-shop stand out from the crowd

▶ Buying or upgrading your computer hardware

▶ Assembling a business software suite

. . . .

Starting your online business is like refurbishing an old house – something Greg is constantly doing. Both projects involve a series of recognisable phases:

✔ **The idea phase:** First, you tell people about your great idea. They hear the enthusiasm in your voice, nod their heads, and say something like, 'Good luck.' They've seen you in this condition before and know how it usually turns out.

✔ **The decision phase:** Undaunted, you begin honing your plan. You read books (like this one), ask questions, and shop around until you find just the right tools and materials to get you on your way. Of course, when you're up to your neck in work, you may start to panic, asking yourself whether you're really up for the task.

✔ **The assembly phase:** Undeterred, you forge ahead. You plug in your tools and go to work. Drills spin, and sparks fly, as your idea becomes reality.

✔ **The test-drive phase:** One fine day, out of the dust and fumes, your masterpiece emerges. You invite everyone over to enjoy the fruits of your labour. All those who were sceptical before are now awe-struck and full of admiration. Satisfied with the result, you enjoy your project for years to come.

If refurbishing a house doesn't work for you, think about restoring an antique car, planning an anniversary party, or devising a mountain-climbing excursion in Tibet. The point is that starting an online business is a project like any other – one that you can construct and accomplish in stages. Right now, you're at the first stage of launching your new business. Your creativity is working overtime. You may even have some rough sketches that only a mother could love.

This chapter helps you get from concept to reality. Your first step is to imagine how you want your business to look and feel. Then you can begin to develop and implement strategies for achieving your dream. You've got a big advantage over those who started new businesses a few years ago: You've got thousands of predecessors to show you what works and what doesn't.

Starting Off on the Right Foot

As you travel along the path from idea to reality, you must also consider equipping your online business properly – just like you would have to equip a traditional, bricks-and-mortar business. One of the many exciting aspects of launching a business online, however, is the absence of many *overheads* (that is, operating expenses). Many real world businesses resort to taking out loans to pay the rent and design their shop fronts, pay fees, and purchase shop furniture. In contrast, the primary overhead for an online business is computer gadgetry. It's great if you can afford top-of-the-line equipment, but you'll be happy to know that the latest bells and whistles aren't absolutely necessary in order to build a business online and maintain it effectively. But in order to streamline the technical aspects of connecting to the Internet and creating a business Web site, some investment is always necessary.

Don't rush into a contract with a Web designer or hosting company without researching the market and finding out exactly what you're getting for your money. Dan once made the mistake of paying upfront for a hosting and design package; he now believes that once they've got your money, they sit back and don't work hard for your business. You should demand an invoice for work done and make them tell you what they will actually do for your business in the real world. If they include a *search engine optimisation package,* for example, find out what that means from a practical point of view and how it's going to help you. Most importantly, make them spell out a timeline of progress so that you have a rough idea of when you'll be ready to launch.

Mapping Out Your Online Business

How do you get off square one? Start by imagining the kind of business that is your ultimate goal. This step is the time to indulge in some brainstorming. Envisioning your business is a creative way of asking yourself the all-important questions: Why do I want to go into business online? What are my goals? Table 2-1 illustrates possible objectives and suggests how to achieve them. By envisioning the final result you want to achieve, you can determine the steps you need to take to get there.

Table 2-1	Online Business Models	
Goal	*Type of Web Site*	*What to Do*
Make big bucks advertisers	Sales	Sell items or get lots of paying
Gain credibility and attention	Marketing	Put your CV and samples of your work online
Turn an interest into a source of income	Hobby/special interest	Invite like-minded people to share your passion, participate in your site, and generate traffic so that you can gain advertisers or customers.

Looking around

You don't need to feel like you have to reinvent the wheel. A great idea doesn't necessarily mean something completely fresh that has never been done before (although if you have a great, new idea, then good for you!). Sometimes, spending just half an hour surfing the Net can stimulate your mental network. Find sites with qualities you want to emulate. Throughout this book, we suggest good business sites you can visit to find good models to follow.

Many people start up online selling to people just like themselves. For example, a motorbike enthusiast may start up a parts business or an informative site about the best bikes and where to buy them. If you're a hobby geek, then your own likes and dislikes have a lot of value. As you search the Web for inspiration, make a list as you go of what you find appealing and jot down notes on logos, designs, text, and *functionality* (how the site lets you access its features). That way, you'll have plenty of data to draw upon as you begin to refine what you yourself want to do.

Making your mark

The online world has undergone a population explosion. According to Internet Systems Consortium's Domain Survey (www.isc.org), in 2006, 439.2 million computers that hosted Web sites were connected to the Internet, compared with 171.6 million in 2002. As an *ontrepreneur* (online entrepreneur), your goal is to stand out from the crowd – or to 'position yourself in the marketplace', as business consultants like to say. Consider the following tried-and-tested suggestions if you want your Web site to be a popular corner of the Internet:

- **Do something you know all about.** Experience adds value to the information you provide. Doing something that you have experience of also keeps you interested throughout the roller-coaster ride that is starting a business. Most importantly, in the online world, expertise sells.

- **Make a statement.** On your Web site, include a mission statement that clearly identifies what you do, the customers you hope to reach, and how you're different from your competitors. Depending on what you plan to set up, this statement may be on the home page (in the form of a concise About Us statement) or in an FAQ section of the site.

- **Include contact details.** We may be in a digital age, but people still crave the personal touch. You must prove that you're not a machine by keeping the language you use friendly, and by including a phone number. People are also very suspicious of Web sites that don't declare their address.

- **Give something away for free.** This tip really can't be said enough. Giveaways and promotions are proven ways to gain attention and develop a loyal customer base. In fact, entire Web sites are devoted to providing free stuff online, such as www.freestuffjunction.co.uk or www.thefreesite.com. You don't have to give away an actual product; it can be words of wisdom based on your training and experience.

- **Be obvious.** The domain names listed in the preceding bullet all do free stuff. What do they have in common? The word 'free'. It helps if your Web site tells people what is does before they even get to the home page. Dan's Web site, InfoZoo.co.uk, is called such because it lets users access a *zoo* (in other words, a diverse selection) of different types of information.

- **Find your niche.** Web space is a great place to pursue *niche marketing*. In fact, it often seems that the quirkier the item, the better it sells. Don't be afraid to target a narrow audience and direct all your sales efforts to a small group of devoted followers.

✔ **Do something you love.** The more you love your business, the more time and effort you're apt to put into it and, therefore, the more likely it is to be successful. Such businesses take advantage of the Internet's worldwide reach, which makes it easy for people with the same interests to gather at the same virtual location.

Scan through the list of *Real Business* magazine's (www.realbusiness.co.uk) top new economy millionaires, and you find many examples of businesses that follow all the aforementioned strategies. Take Rightmove.co.uk. It made £8.9 million profit in 2005, because its founders saw a trend toward people looking for property online. The founders built a simple and functional Web site and gradually cornered the burgeoning market. With more and more home-hunters piling online, the firm expects (quite realistically) to make £40 million profit in 2008.

Nick Robertson's ASOS.com (formally known as As Seen On Screen) jumped on people's insatiable appetite for the lifestyles of the rich and famous. The premise was simple: Dress like the stars you worship. The Web site's meteoric success has allowed it to expand beyond its TV-based roots, and now it boasts a huge array of celebrity-inspired fashion. Oh, and the company is rumoured to be worth more than £60 million.

Evaluating commercial Web sites

Is your Web site similar to others? How does it differ? (Or to put it another way: How is it better?) Your customers will be asking these questions, so you may as well start out by asking them as well.

Commercial Web sites – those whose Internet addresses usually end with .co.uk, .com, or .biz – are the fastest-growing segment of the Net and is the area you'll be entering. The trick is to be comfortable with the size and level of complexity of a business that's right for you. In general, your options are

✔ **A big commercial Web site:** The Web means big business, and plenty of big companies create Web sites with the primary goal of supplementing a product or service that's already well known and well established. Just a few examples are the Ribena Web site (www.ribena.co.uk), the Pepsi World Web site (www.pepsiworld.com), and the Toyota Web site (www.toyota.com). True, these commercial Web sites were created by corporations with many millions of pounds to throw around, but you can still look at them to get ideas for your own site.

✔ **A mid-size site:** You can look at mid-sized companies, too, who use the Web as an extension of their brand. Brilliant examples of mid-sized companies are Ben & Jerry's ice cream (www.benjerry.co.uk) and

Innocent Smoothies (www.innocentsmoothies.co.uk). John Cleese has a simply awesome Web site (www.thejohncleese.com – note that www.johncleese.com was pinched by a look-alike before the real one could get in there, which businesses can learn a lot from). Sites such as CD Wow (www.cdwow.co.uk) and Play.com (www.play.com) are mid-sized companies, but their Web sites are as good as any blue chip you're likely to come across.

✔ **A site that's just right:** No prerequisites for prior business experience guarantee success on the Web. It's also fine to start out as a single person, couple, or family. In fact, the rest of this book is devoted to helping you produce a top-notch, home-grown entrepreneurial business with the minimum of assistance. This chapter gets you off to a good start by examining the different kinds of business you can launch online and some business goals you should be setting yourself.

Flavours of Online Businesses You Can Taste Test

If you're an excitable character, you may have to curb your enthusiasm as you comb the Internet for ideas. Use the following examples to create a picture of your business and then zero in on the kind of sites that can help you formulate its look and feel.

Selling consumer products

The Web has always attracted those looking for unique items or something customised just for them. Consider taking your wares online if one or both of the following applies to you:

✔ You're a creative person who creates as a hobby the type of stuff people may want to buy (think artists, designers, model makers, and so on). For example, Dan's mum is great at calligraphy, and he thinks she'd make a packet by selling her writing online.

✔ You have access to the sort of products or services that big companies simply can't replicate. Those items may mean regional foods, hand-made souvenirs, or items for car enthusiasts; the list is truly endless – you just have to find your niche.

Sorry to bang on about Ben & Jerry's (we're both big fans), but we sometimes go to their Web site (`www.benjerry.com` or `www.benjerrys.co.uk`) just to drool. These guys should be your role models. The motivation for starting their business was that they just couldn't get enough of ice cream and loved creating bizarre flavours. They're entrepreneurs just like you, and we think their Web site is nearly as tasty as their products. It focuses on the unique flavours and high quality of their ice cream, as well as their personalities and business standards.

Innocent Smoothies (`www.innocentdrinks.co.uk`) are the same. They build on that 'community' feel by offering you fun things to do when you're bored. They even suggest popping over to Fruit Towers (their headquarters) for a visit. Their branding is brilliant and rare – try to match it (without copying), but remember that you must reflect your own business-style and the people you want to sell to.

Punting what you're good at

Either through a Web site or through listings in indexes and directories, offering your professional services online can expand your client base dramatically. It also gives existing clients a new way to contact you or just see what's new with your business. Here are just a few examples of professionals who are offering their services online:

- ✔ **Solicitors:** John Pickering and Partners are personal injury solicitors (aren't they all nowadays) who specialise in severe diseases and critical injuries sustained at work. The firm is based in Manchester, but its Web site gives it a national and even global reach (`www.johnpickering.co.uk`). To give it a professional feel, something which is vital in this profession, the Web site features relevant news updates, information about claims, and even information on how to choose a solicitor.

- ✔ **Psychotherapists:** Dr. Thomas Kraft, a Harley Street practitioner, has a nice, easy-to-understand Web site at `www.londonpsychotherapy.co.uk` see Figure 2-1). The format is simple, yet a good amount of important information appears on the home page. Without clicking, we know his name, fields of expertise, and phone number. On top of this easy navigation there are chunky buttons providing a visible route to other facts you may need to know.

- ✔ **Architects:** At the time of writing, the Web site of Robertson Francis Partnership, a chartered architect based in Cardiff, was under construction (`www.rfparchitects.co.uk`). Plenty of professional Web sites take an age to get up and running because people are too busy running their businesses. If this sounds like you, do what these guys did and at least get something up there – even if it's just your name and contact details.

- ✔ **Music teachers:** Do a search on Gumtree (www.gumtree.com) or Google local (local.google.co.uk) and you'll see just how many music teachers are plying their wares online. Many don't have a Web site themselves, but are savvy enough to know that people will be searching for their services online.

We're busy people who don't always have the time to pore over the small print. Short and snappy nuggets of information draw customers to your site and make them feel as though they're getting 'something for free'. One way you can put forth this professional expertise is by starting your own online newsletter. You get to be editor, writer, and mailing-list manager. Plus, you get to talk as much as you want, network with tons of people who subscribe to your publication, and put your name and your business before lots of people. Judy Vorfeld (profiled in Chapter 6) puts out a regular newsletter called Communication Expressway that supplements her site (www.ossweb.com), as do many of the other online businesspeople we mention in this chapter.

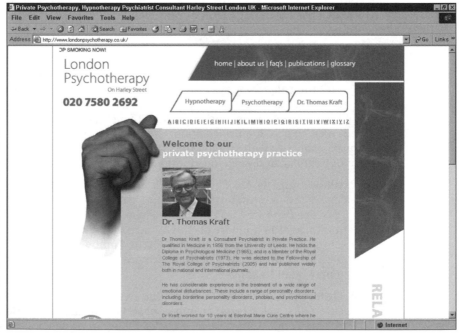

Figure 2-1:
A London psycho-therapist provides his contact information and fields of expertise on this simple, yet informative, Web page.

www.londonpsychotherapy.co.uk

Making money from your expertise

The original purpose of the Internet was to share knowledge via computers, and information is the commodity that has fuelled cyberspace's rapid growth. As the Internet and commercial online networks continue to expand, information remains key.

Collecting and disseminating data can be a profitable pastime. Think of all the Web sites where information is the chief commodity rather than clothes or music. The fact is, people love to get knowledge they trust from the comfort of their own homes.

Here are just a few examples of the types of business that feed on our love of knowledge:

- **Search engines:** Some businesses succeed by connecting Web surfers with companies, organisations, and individuals that specialise in a given area. Yahoo! (www.yahoo.co.uk) is the most obvious example. Originally started by two college students, Yahoo! has become an Internet behemoth by gathering information in one index so that people can easily find things online.

- **Links pages:** On her 'Grandma Jam's I Love to Win' sweepstakes site (www.grandmajam.com), Janet Marchbanks-Aulenta gathers links to current contests along with short descriptions of each one. Janet says her site receives as many as 22,000 visits per month and generates income through advertising and affiliate links to other contest Web sites. She says she loves running her own business despite the hard work involved with keeping it updated. 'The key to succeeding at this type of site is to build up a regular base of users that return each day to find new contests – the daily upkeep is very important,' she says.

- **Personal recommendations:** The personal touch sells. Just look at Web 2.0 site Digg.com (more about Web 2.0 appears in Chapter 4). This guide to the online world provides Web surfers with a central location where they can track down popular news stories. It works because real people submit the stories, and only the most popular stories make it to the top of page one. The users themselves are who 'digg' stories – the most popular ones rise up the rankings. Just listen to Digg's description of itself:

  'Digg is all about user powered content. Every article on digg is submitted and voted on by the digg community. Share, discover, bookmark, and promote the news that's important to you!'

  Note that the emphasis is on *the user* and that it's written for *you*. Describing your services in this way makes people feel at home.

Resource sites can transform information into money in several ways. In some cases, individuals pay to become members. Sometimes, businesses pay to be listed on a site. Other times, a site attracts so many visitors on a regular basis that other companies pay to post advertising on the site. Big successes – such as MySpace (www.myspace.com) and Digg (www.digg.com) – carry a healthy share of ads and strike lucrative partnerships with big companies as well.

Creating opportunities with technology

What could be more natural than using the Web to sell what you need to get and stay online? The online world itself, by the very fact that it exists, has spawned all kinds of business opportunities for entrepreneurs:

- **Computers:** Some discount computer houses have made a killing by going online and offering equipment for less than conventional high street shops. Being on the Internet means that they save on overheads and then pass on those savings to their customers.

- **Internet Service Providers:** These businesses connect you to the Internet. Many ISPs, such as AOL or BT Retail, are big concerns. But smaller companies, such as Eclipse Internet, offer home-based broadband, similar levels of service, and sometimes discounts, too.

- **Software:** Matt Wright is well known on the Web for providing free computer scripts that add important functionality to Web sites, such as processing information that visitors submit via online forms. Matt's Script Archive site (www.worldwidemart.com/scripts) now includes an ad for a book on scripting that he co-authored, as well as an invitation to businesses to take out advertisements on his site.

Being a starving artist without starving

Being creative no longer means you have to live out of your flower-covered VW van, driving from art fairs to craft shows (unless you want to, of course). If you're simply looking for exposure and feedback on your creations, you can put samples of your work online. Consider the following suggestions for virtual creative venues (and revenues):

- **Host art galleries.** Thanks to online galleries, artists whose sales were previously limited to one region can get enquiries from all over the world. Artists Online (www.artistsonline.org.uk) is a new Web site dedicated to promoting artists who are not yet well known. It showcases and sells artwork and lets users know about upcoming events and exhibitions.

The personal Web site (see Figure 2-2) created by artist Marques Vickers (www.marquesv.com) has received worldwide attention. (The upcoming sidebar, 'Painting a new business scenario', profiles Vickers's site.)

✔ **Publish your writing.** *Blogs* (Web logs, or online diaries) are all the rage these days. The problem is that absolutely millions exist, and most aren't worth your time. However, the most successful are generating ad revenue. To find out how to create one yourself, check out Blogger (www.blogger.com). For inspiration, check out a successful independent blog, such as Seth Godin's (sethgodin.typepad.com) or a blog attached to an online newspaper. *The Times*'s Web site has a whole host of them.

✔ **Sell your music.** Singer-songwriter Sam Roberts sells his own CDs, videos, and posters through his online shop (www.samrobertsband.com).

You can, of course, also sell all that junk that's been accumulating in your loft, as well as anything else you no longer want, on eBay.co.uk; see Chapter 10 for more information on this exciting business opportunity.

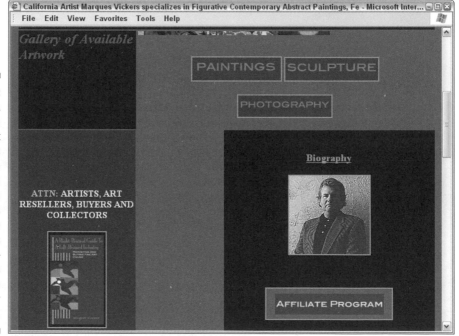

Figure 2-2: A Californian artist created this Web site to gain recognition and sell his creative work. It's very basic — but seems all the more artistic for that fact.

Marketing One-to-One with Your Customers

After you've reviewed Web sites that conduct the sorts of business ventures that interest you, you can put your goals into action. First you develop a marketing strategy that expresses your unique talents and services. People need encouragement if they're going to flock to your Web site, so try to come up with a cunning plan. One marketing ploy may be enough; we suggest coming up with five individual means to bring the customers in. For example, you can blog about your Web site, answer questions in forums, do a competition, go to networking events, and so on.

The fact is that online communities are often close-knit, long-standing groups of people who are good friends. The Web, newsgroups, and e-mail allow you to communicate with these communities in ways that other media can't match.

Focus on a customer segment

Old-fashioned business practices, such as getting to know your customers as individuals and providing personal service, are alive and well in cyberspace. Your No. 1 business strategy when it comes to starting your business online sounds simple: Know your market.

What's not so simple about this little maxim is that, in cyberspace, it takes some work to get to know exactly who your customers are. Web surfers don't leave their names, addresses, or even e-mail addresses when they visit your site. Instead, when you check the raw, unformatted records (or *logs*) of the visitors who have connected to you, you see pages and pages of what appears to be computer gobbledygook. You need special software, such as the program WebTrends, to interpret the information.

How do you develop relationships with your customers?

- **Get your visitors to identify themselves.** Encourage them to send you e-mail messages, place orders, enter contests, or provide you with feedback. (For more specific suggestions, see Chapter 6.)

- **Become an online researcher.** Find existing users who already purchase goods and services online that are similar to what you offer. Visit newsgroups that are relevant to what you sell, search for mailing lists, and participate in discussions so that people can find out more about you.

✔ **Keep track of your visitors.** Count the visitors who come to your site and, more importantly, the ones who make purchases or seek out your services. Manage your customer profiles so that you can sell your existing clientele the items they're likely to buy.

✔ **Help your visitors get to know you.** Web space is virtually unlimited. Feel free to tell people about aspects of your life that don't relate directly to your business or to how you plan to make money. Consider Judy Vorfeld, who does Internet research, Web design, and office support. Her Web site (`www.ossweb.com`), shown in Figure 2-3, includes the usual lists of clients and services; however, it also includes a link to her personal home page and a page that describes her community service work.

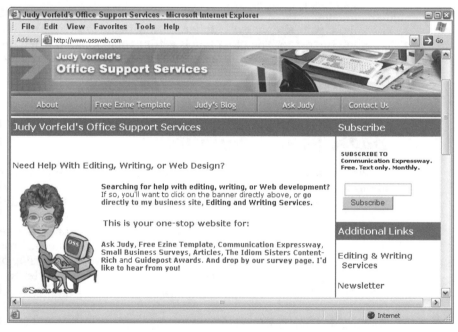

Figure 2-3:
Telling potential customers about yourself makes them more comfortable telling you about themselves.

After you get to know your audience, job No. 2 in your marketing strategy is to catch their attention. You have two ways to do this:

✔ **Make yourself visible.** In Web-space, your primary task is simply making people aware that your site exists at all. You do so by getting yourself included in as many indexes, search sites, and business listings as possible. Chapter 13 outlines some strategies for listing yourself with search engines. You can also do a bit of self-promotion in your own online communications: Seth Godin, the marketing whiz whose blog people flock to in search of ways to promote themselves better, posted this recently:

'Thirty Galleys

Free and first.

[UPDATE . . . twenty minutes later, sold out, sorry]

First 30 people to drop a note to <u>Allison Sweet</u> get a free copy of my new book, <u>Small is the New Big</u>. It's out in August, but you get it in July.'

Did you spot the statement here? By updating his post a mere 20 minutes later with his Sold Out sign instead of just removing the post completely, Seth is indicating just how popular his Web site is and how well his book is likely to sell.

✔ **Make your site an eye-catcher.** Getting people to come to you is only half the battle. The other half is getting them to shop when they get there. Combine striking images with promotions, offering useful information, and providing ways for customers to interact with you. (See Chapters 5 and 6 for details.)

Boost your credibility

Marketing task No. 3 is to transfer your confidence and sense of authority about what you do to anyone who visits you online. Convince people that you're an expert and a trustworthy person with whom they can do business.

Customers may have fewer reasons to be wary about using the Internet nowadays. But remember that the Web as we know it has been around only a short time, and a large minority of people are still wary of surfing online, let alone shopping. Here, too, you can do a quick two-step in order to market your expertise.

Document your credentials

Feature any honours, awards, or professional affiliations you have that relate to your online work. If you're providing professional or consulting services online, you may even make a link to your online CV. If you feel it's relevant, give details about how long you've been in your field and how you got to know what you know about your business.

If these forms of verification don't apply to you, all is not lost. Just move to the all-important technique that we describe in the next section.

CASE STUDY

Painting a new business scenario

Marques Vickers is an artist based in Vallejo, California. Through his self-named Web site (www.marquesv.com), as well as 15 to 20 'mini-sites', he markets his own painting, sculpture, and photography, as well as his books on marketing and buying fine art online. He first went online in November 1999 and spends about 20 hours a week working on his various Web sites. His sites receive anywhere from 25,000 to 40,000 visits per month.

Q. What are the costs of running all your Web sites and doing the associated marketing?

A. It costs approximately £18 a month for a Web site hosting and Internet access package. New domain name registrations and renewals probably add another £140 as I own more than 20 domain names.

Q. What would you describe as the primary goals of your online business?

A. My initial objective was to develop a personalised round-the-clock global presence in order to recruit sales outlets, sell directly to the public, and create a reference point for people to access and view my work. A Web presence will be a marketing necessity for any future visual artist and a lifelong outlet for their work. Having an online presence builds my credibility as a fine artist and helps me to take advantage of the evolution of the fine arts industry, too.

Q. Has your online business been profitable financially?

A. Absolutely – but make no mistake, achieving sales volume and revenue is a trial-and-error process and involves a significant time commitment. I'm still perfecting the business model, and it may require years to achieve the optimum marketing plan.

Q. How do you promote your site?

A. With the Internet, you can take advantage of multiple promotional sources. Experimenting is

essential because you never know who's going to pick up your Web site. Postings in cyberspace are often stumbled across by sources that you never knew existed, let alone planned for. I try multiple marketing outlets, including paid ad-positioning services such as Yahoo! Search Marketing (formerly called Overture) and Google, bartered advertising space, and reciprocal links. Some have had moderate success, some unforeseen and remarkable exposure. Unlike traditional advertising media that have immediate response times, the Internet may lag in its response. It is a long-term commitment and one that cannot be developed by short-term tactics or media blitzes.

Q. Do you create your Web pages yourself, or do you work with someone to do that?

A. I'm too particular about the quality of content to subcontract the work out. Besides, I know what I want to say, how, and am capable of fashioning the design concepts I want. The rectangular limitations of HTML design make colour a very important component, and the very minimal attention span of most Web viewers means that you'd better get to the point quickly and concisely. The more personalised, timely, and focused your content, the more reason an individual has to return to your Web site.

Q. What advice would you give to someone starting an online business?

A. Don't hesitate one minute longer than necessary. Read a diverse selection of sources on the subject. Subscribe to ezines on related subject matter and query the webmasters of sites that impress you with their content. Go to informational seminars; ask questions. Experiment with marketing ideas and by all means, consider it a lifelong project. The Internet is continuing to evolve and the opportunities have never been more prevalent.

Convince with must-have information

Providing useful, practical information about a topic is one of the best ways to market yourself online. One of the great things about starting an online business is that you don't have to incur the design and printing charges to get a brochure or flyer printed. You have plenty of space on your online business site to talk about your sales items or services in as much detail as you want. Try not to bore people though, will you!

Most Internet Service Providers (ISPs) give you 20MB (megabytes, that is) or more of space for your Web pages and associated files. Because the average Web page occupies only 5 to 10K (that's kilobytes) of space not counting the space taken up by images and multimedia files, it'll take a long time before you begin to run out of room.

What, exactly, can you talk about on your site? Here are some ideas:

- Provide detailed descriptions and photos of your sale items.
- Include a full list of clients you have worked for previously.
- Publish a page of testimonials from satisfied customers.
- Give your visitors a list of links to Web pages and other sites where people can find out more about your area of business.
- Toot your own horn: Explain why you love what you do and why you're so good at it.

Ask satisfied customers to give you a good testimonial. All you need is a sentence or two that you can use on your Web site.

A site that contains compelling, entertaining content will become a resource that online visitors bookmark and return to on a regular basis. Be sure to update it regularly, and you'll have fulfilled the dream of any online business owner.

Create customer-to-customer contact: Everybody wins

A 16-year-old cartoonist named Gabe Martin put his cartoons on his Web site, called The Borderline. Virtually nothing happened. But when his dad put up some money for a contest, young Gabe started getting hundreds of visits and enquiries. He went on to create 11 mirror sites around the world, develop a base of devoted fans, and sell his own cartoon book.

People regularly take advantage of freebies online by, for example, downloading *shareware* or *freeware* programs (programs that are developed and distributed for free). They get free advice from newsgroups, and they find free companionship from chat rooms and online forums. Having already paid for network access and computer equipment, they actually *expect* to get something for free.

Your customers will keep coming back if you devise as many promotions, giveaways, or sales as possible. You can also get people to interact through online forums or other tools, as we describe in Chapter 6.

In online business terms, anything that gets your visitors to click links and enter your site is good. Provide as many links to the rest of your site as you can on your home page. Many interactions that don't seem like sales do lead to sales, and it's always your goal to keep people on your site as long as possible.

See Chapters 5 and 6 for instructions on how to create hyperlinks and add interactivity to your Web site. For more about creating Web sites, check out *Creating Web Pages For Dummies,* 7th Edition, by Bud E. Smith and Arthur Bebak (Wiley).

Be a player in online communities

You may wait until the kids go off to school to tap away at your keyboard in your home office, but that doesn't mean that you're alone. Thousands of home-office workers and entrepreneurs just like you connect to the Net every day and share many of the same concerns, challenges, and ups and downs as you.

Starting an online business isn't only a matter of creating Web pages, scanning photos, and taking orders. Marketing and networking are essential to making sure that you meet your goals. Participate in groups that are related either to your particular business or to online business in general. Here are some ways that you can make the right connections and get support and encouragement at the same time.

Be a newsgroupie

Businesspeople tend to overlook newsgroups or forums because of admonitions about *spam* (pesky e-mails sent without permission by people trying to make money dishonestly) and other violations of *Netiquette* (the set of rules that govern newsgroup communications). However, when you approach newsgroup participants on their own terms (not by spamming them but by answering questions and participating in discussions), newsgroups can be a wonderful resource for businesspeople. They attract knowledgeable consumers who are strongly interested in a topic – just the sort of people who make great customers.

A few newsgroups (in particular, the ones with `biz` at the beginning of their names) are especially intended to discuss small business issues and sales. Here are a few suggestions:

- ✔ `www.realbusiness.co.uk/Forums.aspx`
- ✔ `www.startups.co.uk/Forums/ShowForum.aspx?ForumID=223`
- ✔ `www.ukbusinessforums.co.uk/forums`

The easiest way to access newsgroups is to use Google's Web-based directory (`www.google.co.uk/grphp?hl=en`). You can also use the newsgroup software that comes built into the most popular Web browser packages. Each browser or newsgroup program has its own set of steps for enabling you to access Usenet. *Usenet* is an Internet discussion system that has existed since the earliest days of the Web; users post messages to distributed newsgroups in a kind of bulletin board system. Use your browser's online help system to find out how you can access newsgroups in this way.

Be sure to read the group's FAQ (frequently asked questions) page before you start posting. It's a good idea to *lurk before you post* – that is, simply read messages being posted to the group in order to find out about members' concerns. Stay away from groups that seem to consist only of get-rich-quick schemes or other scams. When you do post a message, be sure to keep your comments relevant to the conversation and give as much helpful advice as you can.

The most important business technique in communicating by either e-mail or newsgroup postings is to include a signature file at the end of your message. A *signature file* is a simple message that newsgroup and mail software programs automatically add to your messages (just like corporate e-mails). A typical one includes your name, title, and the name of your company. You can also include a link to your business's home page. A good example is Judy Vorfeld's signature file, shown in Figure 2-4.

Be a mailing list-ener

A *mailing list* is a discussion group that communicates by exchanging e-mail messages between members who share a common interest. Each e-mail message sent to the list is distributed to all the list's members. Any of those members can, in turn, respond by sending e-mail replies. The series of back-and-forth messages develops into discussions.

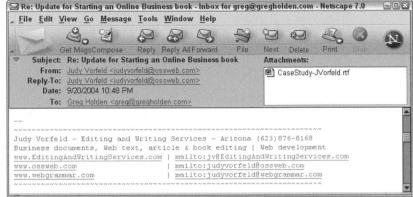

Figure 2-4:
A descriptive signature file on your messages serves as an instant business advertisement.

The nice thing about a mailing list is that it consists only of people who have subscribed to the list, which means that they really want to be involved and participate.

An excellent mailing list to check out is the Small and Home-Based Business Discussion List (`www.talkbiz.com/bizlist/index.html`). This list is *moderated,* meaning that someone reads through all postings before they go online and filters out any comments that are inappropriate or off-topic. Also, try searching the Topica directory of discussion groups (`lists.topica.com`). Click Small Business (under Choose From Thousands Of Newsletters And Discussions) to view a page full of discussion groups and other resources for entrepreneurs.

The number of groups you join and how often you participate in them is up to you. The important thing is to regard every one-to-one-personal contact as a seed that may sprout into a sale, a referral, an order, a contract, a bit of useful advice, or another profitable business blossom.

It's not a newsgroup or a mailing list, but a Web site called iVillage.com (`www.ivillage.com`) brings women together by providing chat rooms where they can type messages to one another in real time, as well as message boards where they can post messages. (Men, of course, can participate, too.) Experts (and some who just claim to be experts) often participate in these forums.

Add ways to sell and multiply your profits

Many successful online businesses combine more than one concept of what constitutes electronic commerce. Chapter 8 discusses ways to sell your goods and services on your Web site, but the Internet offers other venues for promoting and selling your wares.

Selling through online classifieds

If you're looking for a quick and simple way to sell products or promote your services online without having to pay high overhead costs, consider taking out a classified ad in an online publication or a popular site like Craigslist (www.craigslist.org) or InfoZoo (www.infozoo.co.uk).

The classifieds work the same way online as they do in print publications: You pay a fee and write a short description along with contact information, and the publisher makes the ad available to potential customers. However, online classifieds have a number of big advantages over their print equivalents:

- ✔ **Audience:** Rather than hundreds or thousands who may view your ad in print, tens of thousands, or perhaps even millions, can see it online.

- ✔ **Searchability:** Online classifieds are often indexed so that customers can search for particular items with their Web browser. This index makes it easier for shoppers to find exactly what they want, whether it's a Precious Moment figurine or a Martin guitar.

- ✔ **Time:** On the Net, ads are often online for a month or more.

- ✔ **Cost:** Some sites, such as Commerce Corner (www.comcorner.com), let you post classified ads for free.

On the downside, classifieds are often buried at the back of online magazines or Web sites, just as they are in print, so they're hardly well-travelled areas. Also, most classifieds don't make use of the graphics that help sell and promote goods and services so effectively throughout the Web.

Dan's site InfoZoo.co.uk gets around this obstacle by letting customers upload their own logo and by including a search mechanism that prevents adverts from becoming buried. It's aimed at small UK-based businesses, too – so you're in good company.

Classifieds are an option if you're short on time or money. But don't forget that on your own online business site you can provide more details and not have to spend a penny.

Selling via online auctions

Many small businesses, such as antique dealerships or jewellery shops, sell individual merchandise through online auctions. eBay.co.uk and other popular auction sites provide effective ways to target sales items at collectors who are likely to pay top dollar for desirable goodies. If you come up with a system for finding things to sell and for turning around a large number of transactions on a regular basis, you can even turn selling on eBay into a full-time source of income. See Chapter 10 for more information about starting a business on eBay.co.uk.

Easyware (Not Hardware) for Your Business

Becoming an information provider on the Internet places an additional burden on your computer and peripheral equipment, such as your phone, printer, scanner, and so on. When you're 'in it for the money', you may very well start to go online every day, perhaps for hours at a time, especially if you buy and sell on eBay.co.uk. The better your computer setup, the more e-mail messages you can download, the more catalogue items you can store, and so on. In this section, we introduce you to many upgrades you may need to make to your existing technology.

Some general principles apply when assembling equipment (discussed in this section) and programs (discussed in a subsequent section, 'Software Solutions for Online Business') for an online business:

- ✔ **Look on the Internet for what you need.** You can find just about everything you want to get you started.

- ✔ **Be sure to pry before you buy!** Don't pull out that credit card until you get the facts on what warranty and technical support your hardware or software vendor provides. Make sure that your vendor provides phone support 24 hours a day, 7 days a week. Also ask how long the typical turnaround time is in case your equipment needs to be serviced.

If you purchase lots of new hardware and software, remember to update your insurance by sending your insurer a list of your new equipment. Also consider purchasing insurance specifically for your computer-related items from a company such as Insure and Go (`www.insureandgo.com`) or Hiscox (`business.hiscox.co.uk`).

The right computer for your online business

You very well may already have an existing computer setup that's adequate to get your business online and start the ball rolling. Or you may be starting from scratch and looking to purchase a computer for personal and/or business use. In either case, it pays to know what all the technical terms and specifications mean. Here are some general terms you need to understand:

- **Gigahertz (GHz) and megahertz (MHz):** This unit of measure indicates how quickly a computer's processor can perform functions. The central processing unit (CPU) of a computer is where the computing work gets done. In general, the higher the processor's internal clock rate, the faster the computer.

- **Random access memory (RAM):** This is the memory that your computer uses to temporarily store information needed to operate programs. RAM is usually expressed in millions of bytes, or megabytes (MB). The more RAM you have, the more programs you can run simultaneously.

- **Synchronous dynamic RAM (SDRAM):** Many ultra-fast computers use some form of SDRAM synchronised with a particular clock rate of a CPU so that a processor can perform more instructions in a given time.

- **Double data rate SDRAM (DDR SDRAM):** This type of SDRAM can dramatically improve the clock rate of a CPU.

- **Auxiliary storage:** This term refers to physical data-storage space on a hard drive, tape, CD-RW, or other device.

- **Virtual memory:** This is a type of memory on your hard drive that your computer can 'borrow' to serve as extra RAM.

- **Network interface card (NIC):** You need this hardware add-on if you have a cable or DSL modem or if you expect to connect your computer to others on a network. Having a NIC usually provides you with Ethernet data transfer to the other computers. (*Ethernet* is a network technology that permits you to send and receive data at very fast speeds.)

The Internet is teeming with places where you can find good deals on hardware. A great place to start is a review site, such as Ciao (`www.ciao.co.uk`) or Review Centre (`www.reviewcentre.com`), which allows customers to express their views about the equipment they have bought. Visit a few of these sites and select the most popular items.

Processor speed

Computer processors are getting faster all the time. Don't be overly impressed by a computer's clock speed (measured in megahertz or even gigahertz). By the time you get your computer home, another, faster chip will already have hit the streets. Just make sure that you have enough memory to run the types of applications shown in Table 2-2. (Note that these numbers are only estimates, based on the Windows versions of these products that were available at the time of writing.)

Building an online presence: An ongoing process

Judy Vorfeld, founder of Office Support Services (www.ossweb.com) and profiled in Chapter 6, needs to update her computer hardware regularly even though she works in the editorial field rather than a 'techie' profession. As far as equipment goes, Judy estimates that each year she spends about £550 on computer hardware and £200 on software related to her business. She has two networked desktop computers, which she upgrades as needed. She has a CD/DVD burner on her main computer, and backs up her files on DVDs. Her 6-lb laptop, which she uses whenever she travels, has a CD-RW/DVD-ROM drive, and 256MB of RAM. For software, she uses the Web page editor Macromedia HomeSite to create Web pages, Paint Shop Pro to work with graphics, and Microsoft Word for most of her book editing.

Table 2-2	Memory Requirements	
Type of Application Recommended	*Example*	*Amount of RAM*
Web browser	Internet Explorer	32MB
Web page editor	Macromedia Dreamweaver	128MB
Word processor	Microsoft Word	136MB (on Windows XP)
Graphics program	Paint Shop Pro	256MB
Accounting software	Microsoft Excel	8MB (if you are already running an Office application)
Animation/Presentation	Macromedia Flash	128MB

The RAM recommended for the sample applications in Table 2-2 adds up to a whopping 688MB. If you plan to work, be sure to get at least 512MB of RAM – more if you can swing it. Memory is cheap nowadays, and the newer PCs allow you to install several GB (that's gigabytes) of RAM.

Hard drive storage

Random access memory is only one type of memory your computer uses; the other kind, *hard drive*, stores information, such as text files, audio files, programs, and the many essential files that your computer's operating system needs. Most of the new computers on the market come with hard drives that store many gigabytes of data. Any hard drive with a few gigabytes of storage space should be adequate for your business needs if you don't do a lot of graphics work. But most new computers come with hard drives that are 60GB or larger in size.

CD-RW/DVD±RW drive

Although a DVD and/or CD recordable drive may not be the most important part of your computer for business use, it can perform essential installation, storage, and data communications functions, such as installing software and saving and sharing data. A large number of machines are now available with a *digital versatile disc* (DVD) drive. You can fit 4.7GB or more of data on a DVD±RW, compared with the 700MB or so that a conventional CD-RW can handle.

Be sure to protect your equipment against electrical problems that can result in loss of data or substantial repair bills. You can limit the damage caused by power outages or surges, or just by glitches in your computer programs, simply by saving your data. You can buy separate hard drives, as well as disks and data sticks on which you can store your most precious data. Keep this away from your workstation so that in the event of a fire or flood you'll still have a surviving copy.

Monitor

In terms of your online business, the quality or thinness of your monitor doesn't affect the quality of your Web site directly. Even if you have a poor-quality monitor, you can create a Web site that looks great to those who visit you. The problem is that you won't know how good your site really looks to customers who have high-quality monitors.

Flat-panel LCD (liquid crystal display) monitors continue to be a hot item, and they're becoming more affordable, too. You've got a real choice between a traditional CRT (cathode-ray tube) monitor and a flat LCD. Whether you choose flat or traditional, the quality of a monitor depends on a few factors:

✔ **Resolution:** The resolution of a computer monitor refers to the number of pixels it can display horizontally and vertically. A resolution of 640 x 480 means that the monitor can display 640 pixels across the screen and 480 pixels down the screen. Higher resolutions, such as 800 x 600 or 1,024 x 768, make images look sharper but require more RAM in your computer. Anything less than 640 x 480 is unusable these days.

- ✓ **Size:** Monitor size is measured diagonally, as with TVs. Sizes such as 14 inches, 15 inches, and up to 21 inches are available. (Look for a 17-inch CRT monitor, which can display most Web pages fully, and which is now available for less than £100.)

- ✓ **Refresh rate:** This is the number of times per second that a video card redraws an image on-screen (at least 60 Hz [hertz] is preferable).

Keep in mind that lots of Web pages seem to have been designed with 17-inch or 21-inch monitors in mind. The problem isn't just that some users (especially those with laptops) have 15-inch monitors, but you can never control how wide the viewer's browser window will be. The problem is illustrated in the page from the Yale Style Manual (www.webstyleguide.com), one of the classic references of Web site design.

Computer monitors display graphic information that consists of little units called *pixels*. Each pixel appears on-screen as a small dot – so small that it's hard to perceive with the naked eye, unless you magnify an image to look at details close up. Together, the patterns of pixels create different intensities of light in an image, as well as ranges of colour. A pixel can contain one or more bytes of binary information. The more pixels per inch (ppi), the higher a monitor's potential resolution. The higher the resolution, the closer the image appears to a continuous-tone image such as a photo. When you see a monitor's resolution described as 1,280 x 1,024, for example, that refers to the number of pixels that the monitor can display. *Dot pitch* refers to the distance between any two of the three pixels (one red, one green, and one blue) that a monitor uses to display colour. The lower the dot pitch, the better the image resolution that you obtain. A dot pitch of 0.27 mm is a good measurement for a 17-inch monitor.

Fax equipment

A fax machine is no longer an essential item for a small business. E-mail and scanners have made faxes nearly obsolete, but if you simply can't do without one, you can install software that helps your computer send and receive faxes. You have three options:

- ✓ You can install a fax modem, a hardware device that usually works with fax software. The fax modem can be an internal or external device.

- ✓ You can use your regular modem but install software that enables your computer to exchange faxes with another computer or fax machine.

- ✓ You can sign up for a service that receives your faxes and sends them to your computer in the body of an e-mail message.

We also recommend that you look into WinFax PRO by Symantec, Inc. (www.symantec.co.uk). Your Windows computer needs to be equipped with a modem in order to send or receive faxes with WinFax.

If you plan to fax and access the Internet from your home office, you should get a second phone line or a direct connection, such as DSL or cable modem. The last thing a potential customer wants to hear is a busy signal.

Image capture devices

When you're ready to move beyond the basic hardware and on to some jazzy value-adding add-ons, think about obtaining a tool for capturing photographic images. (By *capturing,* we mean *digitising* an image or, in other words, saving it in digital format.) Photos are often essential elements of business Web pages: They attract a customer's attention, they illustrate items for sale in a catalogue, and they can provide before-and-after samples of your work. If you're an artist or designer, having photographic representations of your work is vital.

Including a clear, sharp image on your Web site greatly increases your chances of selling your product or service. You have two choices for digitising: a scanner or digital camera.

Digital camera

Not so long ago, digital cameras cost thousands of pounds. These days, you can find a good digital camera made by a reputable manufacturer, such as Nikon, Fuji, Canon, Olympus, or Kodak, for £150 to £300. You have to make an investment up front, but this particular tool can pay off for you in the long run. With the addition of a photo printer, you can even print your own photos, which can save you a pile in photo lab costs.

Don't hesitate to fork over the extra dough to get a camera that gives you good resolution. Cutting corners doesn't pay when you end up with images that look fuzzy, but you can find many low-cost devices with good features. For example, the Fujifilm FinePix S 5600, which Dan spotted online for £180, has a resolution of more than 5 megapixels – fine enough to print on a colour printer and to enlarge. *Megapixels* are calculated by multiplying the number of pixels in an image – for example, when actually multiplied, 1,984 x 1,488 = 2,952,192 pixels or 2.9 megapixels. The higher the resolution, the fewer photos your camera can store at any one time because each image file requires more memory. Getting a bigger memory card with more storage potential (Dan's has a 1GB card) solves this problem.

Online material is primarily intended to be displayed on computer monitors (which have limited resolution), so having super-high resolution images isn't critical for Web pages. Before being displayed by Web browsers, images must be compressed by using the GIF or JPEG formats. (See Chapter 5 for more scintillating technical details on GIF and JPEG.) Also, smaller and simpler images (as opposed to large, high-resolution graphics) generally appear more quickly on the viewer's screen. If you make your customers wait too long to see an image, they're well within their rights to go to someone else's online shop.

When shopping for a digital camera, look for the following features:

- ✔ The ability to download images to your computer via a FireWire or USB connection
- ✔ Bundled image-processing software
- ✔ The ability to download image files directly to a memory card that you can easily transport to a computer's memory card reader
- ✔ An included LCD screen that lets you see your images immediately

On the downside, because of optical filtering that's intended to reduce *colour artefacts* – distortions of an image caused by limitations in hardware – photos taken with digital cameras tend to be less sharp than conventional 35mm photos. Correcting this problem in a graphics program can be time consuming. For high-quality close-ups on the cheap, try a scanner instead.

Digital photography is a fascinating and technical process, and you'll do well to read more about it in other books, such as *Digital Photography All-in-One Desk Reference For Dummies*, 2nd Edition, by David Busch or *Digital Photography For Dummies,* 4th Edition, by Julie Adair King (both by Wiley).

Scanners

Scanning is the process of turning the colours and shapes contained in a photographic print or slide into digital information (that is, bytes of data) that a computer can understand. You place the image in a position where the scanner's camera can pass over it, and the scanner turns the image into a computer document that consists of tiny bits of information called *pixels*. The type that we find easiest to use is a flatbed scanner. You place the photo or other image on a flat glass bed, just like what you find on a photocopier. An optical device moves under the glass and scans the photo.

The best news about scanners is that they've been around for a while, which, in the world of computing, means that prices are going down at the same time that quality is on the rise. The bargain models are well under £50, and you can pick one up for around £30 if you use cost comparison Web sites, such as Pricerunner (www.pricerunner.co.uk) or Kelkoo (www.kelkoo.co.uk).

A low-budget alternative

If you only want to get a photo on your Web site without investing in any of the hardware that we mention here, not to worry. Just call your local photo shop or copy centre. Many high street photographic shops, like Jessops and Snappy Snaps, for example, provide computer services that include scanning photos. You can also have the images placed online or on a CD when you develop your snaps.

Wherever you go, be sure to tell the technician that you want the image to appear on the Web, so it should be saved in GIF or JPEG format.

Also, if you have an idea of how big you want the final image to be when it appears online, tell that to the technician, too. They can save the image in the size that you want so you don't have to resize it later in a graphics program.

If you don't even want to buy a camera, you can always try Flickr (`www.flickr.com`), the online photo album that anyone can add to. People who post their pics can choose to allow others to use them for free. Always make sure that you have the photographer's permission if you take this route.

A type of scanner that has lots of benefits for small or home-based businesses is a multifunction device. You can find these units, along with conventional printers and scanners, at computer outlets or at the online search engines mentioned in the preceding paragraph. Greg has a multifunction device, in his home office. It sends and receives faxes, scans images, acts as a laser printer, and makes copies – plus it includes a telephone and answering machine. Now, if it could just make a good cup of espresso. . . .

Getting Online: Connection Options

In the past, the monthly cost of Internet access would be up there among your biggest online business expense. Thankfully, *metered Internet access,* where you pay for the amount of time you spend on line, is practically extinct. Now you can get a broadband connection from a reputable company for £15 a month. You can also bundle Internet access up with your phone connection and even digital TV to save a bit more cash.

No one uses dialup any more; there's simply no point. It's only marginally cheaper than broadband, and the frustration caused by painfully slow surfing will leave you wishing you'd spent the extra cash. This frustration is especially true for a small business, because being able to upload Web pages quickly can help you improve your productivity. A broadband connection can save you an hour a day, which you can spend on planning, on stock checks, or taking well-earned rests.

Broadband, also known as a Digital Subscriber Line (DSL), is a generic term describing the bandwidth of your Internet connection. It's broad, so more information can pass through it in a shorter space of time. DSL comes in different varieties. *Asymmetrical Digital Subscriber Line* (ADSL) transmits information at different speeds depending on whether you're sending or receiving data. *Symmetrical Digital Subscriber Line* (SDSL) transmits information at the same speed in both directions. As DSL gets more popular, it becomes more widely available, and the pricing drops. In no time at all, we should be seeing light-speed Internet access for less than ten quid a month.

Software Solutions for Online Business

One of the great things about starting an Internet business is that you get to use Internet software. As you probably know, the programs you use online are inexpensive (sometimes free), easy to use and install, and continually updated.

Although you probably already have a basic selection of software to help you find information and communicate with others in cyberspace, the following sections describe some programs you may not have as yet and that will come in handy when you create your online business.

Don't forget to update your insurance by sending your insurer a list of new software (and hardware) or even by purchasing insurance specifically for your computer-related items.

Anyone who uses firewall or antivirus software will tell you how essential these pieces of software are, for home or business use. Find out more about such software in Chapter 7 or in Greg's book *Norton Internet Security For Dummies* (Wiley). See Chapter 15 for suggestions of accounting software – other important software you'll need.

Web browser

A *Web browser* is software that serves as a visual interface to the images, colours, links, and other content contained on the Web. The most popular such program is Microsoft Internet Explorer, which powers 90 per cent of UK Web browsers (that's why Bill Gates has so much dosh). However, new and increasingly popular browsers such as Mozilla Firefox and Opera are gaining new fans every day. See which one you like the best.

Your Web browser is your primary tool for conducting business online, just as it is for everyday personal use. When it comes to running a virtual shop or consulting business, though, you have to run your software through a few more paces than usual. You need your browser to

- Preview the Web pages you create
- Display frames, animations, movie clips, and other goodies you plan to add online
- Support some level of Internet security, such as Secure Sockets Layer (SSL), if you plan to conduct secure transactions on your site

In addition to having an up-to-date browser with the latest features, installing more than one kind of browser on your computer is a good idea. For example, if you use Microsoft Internet Explorer because that's what came with your operating system, be sure to download the latest copy of Firefox as well. That way, you can test your site to make sure that it looks good to all your visitors. Remember, too, that people use Apple Macs as well as PCs, laptops, palmtops, and, increasingly, 4G mobile phones. Your Web site has to look good on all of them.

Web page editor

HyperText Markup Language (HTML) is a set of instructions used to format text, images, and other Web page elements so that Web browsers can correctly display them. But you don't have to master HTML in order to create your own Web pages. Plenty of programs, called *Web page editors,* are available to help you format text, add images, make hyperlinks, and do all the fun assembly steps necessary to make your Web site a winner.

In many cases, Web page editors come with electronic shop-front packages. QuickSite comes with Microsoft FrontPage Express. Sometimes, programs that you use for one purpose can also help you create Web documents: Microsoft Word has an add-on called Internet Assistant that enables you to save text documents as HTML Web pages, and Microsoft Office 98 and later (for the Mac) or Office 2000 or later (for Windows) enable you to export files in Web page format automatically.

Taking e-mail a step higher

You're probably very familiar with sending and receiving e-mail messages. But when you start an online business, you should make sure that e-mail software has some advanced features:

✔ **Autoresponders:** Some programs automatically respond to e-mail requests with a form letter or document of your choice.

✔ **Mailing lists:** With a well-organised address book (a feature that comes with some e-mail programs), you can collect the e-mail addresses of visitors or subscribers and send them a regular update of your business activities or, better yet, an e-mail newsletter.

✔ **Quoting:** Almost all e-mail programs let you quote from a message to which you're replying, so you can respond easily to a series of questions.

✔ **Attaching:** Attaching a file to an e-mail message is a quick and convenient way to transmit information from one person to another.

✔ **Signature files:** Make sure that your e-mail software automatically includes a simple electronic signature at the end. Use this space to list your company name, your title, and your Web site URL.

Both Outlook Express, the e-mail component of Microsoft Internet Explorer, and Netscape Messenger, which is part of the Netscape Communicator suite of programs, include most or all these features. Because these functions are all essential aspects of providing good customer service, we discuss them in more detail in Chapter 12.

Discussion group software

When your business site is up and running, consider taking it a step farther by creating your own discussion area right on your Web site. This sort of discussion area isn't a newsgroup as such; it doesn't exist in Usenet, and you don't need newsgroup software to read and post messages. Rather, it's a Web-based discussion area where your visitors can compare notes and share their passion for the products you sell or the area of service you provide.

Programs such as Microsoft FrontPage enable you to set up a discussion area on your Web site. See Chapter 12 for more information.

FTP software

FTP (File Transfer Protocol) is one of those acronyms you see time and time again as you move around the Internet. You may even have an FTP program that your ISP gave you when you obtained your Internet account. But chances are you don't use it that often.

In case you haven't used FTP yet, start dusting it off. When you create your own Web pages, a simple, no-nonsense FTP program is the easiest way to transfer them from your computer at home to your Web host. If you need to correct and update your Web pages quickly (and you will), you'll benefit by having your FTP software ready and set up with your Web site address, user-name, and password so that you can transfer files right away. See Chapter 3 for more about using File Transfer Protocol.

Image editors

You need a graphics-editing program either to create original artwork for your Web pages or to crop and adjust your scanned images and digital pho-tographs. In the case of adjusting or cropping photographic image files, the software you need almost always comes bundled with the scanner or digital camera, so you don't need to buy separate software for that.

In the case of graphic images, the first question to ask yourself is, 'Am I really qualified to draw and make my own graphics?' If the answer is yes, think shareware first. Two programs we like are Adobe Photoshop Elements (www.adobe.co.uk) and Paint Shop Pro by Jasc, Inc. You can download both these programs from the Web to use on a trial basis. After the trial period is over, you'll need to pay a small fee to the developer in order to reg-ister and keep the program.

The ability to download and use free (and almost free) software from share-ware archives and many other sites is one of the nicest things about the Internet. Keep the system working by remembering to pay the shareware fees to the nice folks who make their software available to individuals like you and me.

Instant messaging

You may think that MSN Messenger, AOL Instant Messenger, Google Talk, and Yahoo Messenger are just for chatting online, but instant messaging has its business applications, too. Here are a few suggestions:

  ✔ If individuals you work with all the time are hard to reach, you can use a messaging program to tell you whether those people are logged on to their computers. The program allows you to contact them the moment they sit down to work (provided they don't mind your greeting them so quickly, of course).

✔ You can cut down on long-distance phone charges by exchanging instant messages with far-flung colleagues.

✔ With a microphone, sound card, and speakers, you can carry on voice conversations through your messaging software.

MSN Messenger enables users to do file transfers without having to use FTP software or attaching files to e-mail messages.

Backup software

Losing copies of your personal documents is one thing, but losing files related to your business can hit you hard in the pocket. That makes it even more important to make backups of your online business computer files. Iomega Zip or Jaz drives (www.iomega.com) come with software that lets you automatically make backups of your files. If you don't own one of these programs, we recommend you get really familiar with the backup program included with Windows XP, or you can check out backup software on the Review Centre Web site (www.reviewcentre.co.uk).

Chapter 3

Selecting the Right Web Host and Design Tools

*Y*ou *can* sell items online without having a Web site. But do you really want to? Doing real online business without some sort of online 'home base' is simply inefficient. The vast majority of online commercial concerns use their Web sites as the primary way to attract customers, convey their message, and make sales. A huge number of micro-entrepreneurs use online auction sites such as eBay (www.ebay.co.uk) to make money, but the auctioneers who depend on eBay for a regular income often have their own Web pages, too.

The success of a commercial Web site depends in large measure on two important factors: where it's hosted and how it's designed. These factors affect how easily you can create and update your Web pages, what special features such as multimedia or interactive forms you can have on your site, and how your site appears to your users. Some hosting services provide Web page creation tools that are easy to use but that limit the level of sophistication you can apply to the page's design. Other services leave the creation and design up to you. In this chapter, we provide an overview of your Web hosting options as well as different design approaches that you can implement.

Plenty of Web sites and CD-ROMs claim that they can have your Web site up and running online 'in a matter of minutes' using a 'seamless' process. The actual construction may indeed be quick and smooth – as long as you've done all your preparation work. This preparation work includes identifying your goals for going online, deciding what market you want to reach, deciding what products you want to sell, writing descriptions and capturing images of those products, and so on. Before you jump over to Yahoo! Small Business or Microsoft Small Business Centre and start assembling your site, be sure that you've done all the groundwork that we discuss in Chapter 2, such as identifying your audience and setting up your hardware.

Getting the Most from Your Web Host

An Internet connection and a Web browser are all you need if you're just interested in surfing through the Web, consuming information, and shopping for online goodies. But when you're starting an online business, you're no longer just a consumer; you're becoming a provider of information and consumable goods. In addition to a means to connect to the Internet, you need to find a hosting service that will make your online business available to your prospective customers.

A *Web hosting service* is the online world's equivalent of a landlord. Just as the owner of a building gives you office space or room for a shop front where you can hang your shingle, a hosting service provides you with space online where you can set up shop.

You can operate an online business without a Web site if you sell regularly on eBay. But even on eBay, you can create an About Me page or an eBay shop; eBay itself is your host in both cases. (You pay a monthly fee to eBay in order to host your shop. See Chapter 10 for more information.)

A Web host provides space on special computers called *Web servers* that are connected to the Internet all the time. Web servers are equipped with software that makes your Web pages visible to people who connect to them by using a Web browser. The process of using a Web hosting service for your online business works roughly like this:

1. **You decide where you want your site to appear on the Internet.**

   Do you want it to be part of a virtual shopping centre that includes many other businesses? Or do you want a standalone site that has its own Web address and doesn't appear to be affiliated with any other organisation?

2. **You sign up with a Web host.**

   Sometimes you pay a fee. In some cases, no fee is required. In all cases, you're assigned space on a server. Your Web site gets an address – or *URL* – that people can enter in their browsers to view your pages.

3. **You create your Web pages.**

   Usually, you use a Web page editor to do this.

4. **After creating content, adding images, and making your site look just right, you transfer your Web page files (HTML documents, images, and so on) from your computer to the host's Web server.**

   You generally need special File Transfer Protocol (FTP) software to do the transferring. But many Web hosts help you through the process by providing their own user-friendly software. (The most popular Web editors, such as Macromedia Dreamweaver, let you transfer, too.)

5. **You access your own site with your Web browser and check the contents to make sure that all the images appear and that any hypertext links you created go to the intended destinations.**

   At this point, you're open for business – visitors can view your Web pages by entering your Web address in their Web browser's Go To or Address box.

6. **You market and promote your site to attract potential clients or customers.**

Carefully choose a Web host because the host will affect which software you'll use to create your Web pages and get them online. The Web host also affects the way your site looks, and it may determine the complexity of your Web address. (See the 'What's in a name?' sidebar, later in this chapter, for details.)

What's in a name?

Most hosts assign you a URL that leads to your directory (or folder) on the Web server. For example, Greg's account with his ISP includes space on a Web server where he can store his Web pages, and the address looks like this:

`http://homepage.xo.com/~gholden`

This is a common form of URL that many Web hosts use. It means that Greg's Web pages reside in a directory called `~gholden` on a computer named `homepage`. The computer, in turn, resides in his provider's domain on the Internet: `xo.com`.

However, for an extra fee, some Web hosts allow you to choose a shorter domain name, provided that the one you want to use isn't already taken by another site. For example, if Greg had paid extra for a fully-fledged business site, his provider would have let him have a catchier, more memorable address, like this: `www.gregholden.com`.

Finding a Web Server to Call Home

Hi! We're your friendly World Wide Web real estate agents. You say you're not sure exactly what kind of Web site is right for you, and you want to see all the options, from a tiny shop front in a shopping centre to your own landscaped corporate complex? Your wish is our command. Just hop into our 2007-model Internet Explorer, buckle your seat belt, and we'll show you around the many different business properties available in cyberspace.

Here's a road map of our tour:

- **Online Web-host-and-design-kit combos:** Fasthosts, Yahoo!, GeoCities, and Blogger, among others.
- **eBay:** A site that lets its users create their own About Me Web pages and their own shops. (Chapter 10 is devoted to this topic.)
- **An online shopping centre:** You can rent a space in these virtual malls.
- **Your current Internet Service Provider (ISP):** Many ISPs are only too happy to host your e-commerce site – for an extra monthly fee in addition to your access fee.
- **Companies devoted to hosting Web sites full time:** Businesses whose primary function is hosting e-commerce Web sites and providing their clients with associated software, such as Web page building tools, shopping trolleys, catalogue builders, and the like.

Adding music, photos, and artwork

Suppose that you've built a basic Web site, and you want to have music CDs, photos, or artwork that can be printed and sold on clothing. You've created the art or saved the photos as GIF or JPEG image files, and you want to place them on products you can sell to friends, family, or anyone who's interested. A popular service called PrintShop (www.printshop.co.uk) makes it easy for you to create and sell such products online for free. The hard part is deciding what you want to sell, how best to describe your sales items, and how to promote your site. Getting your words and images online is remarkably straightforward:

1. Connect to the Internet, start up your Web browser, and go to the PrintShop signup page (www.printshop.co.uk/signup.asp), shown in the figure.

2. Enter your details, including your business name and Web address.

3. Add details of the type of products you want to sell, such as t-shirts, hoodies, mugs, mouse mats, and so on.

4. After submitting approval your application, PrintShop asks for any logos, pictures, and text you'd like to be included in your shop.

Once all the information is in, PrintShop designs a shop for you within two working days (see figure). You can start selling straight away – PrintShop does all the logistical, stock, and admin bit – for a slice of your profits, of course.

PrintShop's services are essentially free, and you only 'pay' them when you make a sale. This system gives you modest profits (you get £2 for the sale of a t-shirt, £1 for a mug), but they hold all the stock and take on the job of delivering your items. That vastly reduces the pressure on you and may be a great way to start your journey as an online entrepreneur. Maintaining stock levels and judging your cash flow are tricky things to master.

For no charge, PrintShop gives you:

- A branded shop front that looks like your Web site
- Free customer service for your buyers
- A range of products to feature your designs
- Plenty of colours to choose from
- No minimum stock levels
- The ability to sell in pounds, dollars, and euros

Some of these options combine Web hosting with Web page creation kits. Whether you buy these services or use them on the Web for free, you simply follow the manufacturer's instructions. Most of these hosting services enable you to create your Web pages by filling in forms; you never have to see a line of HTML code if you don't want to. Depending on which service you choose, you have varying degrees of control over how your site ultimately looks.

Others tend to be do-it-yourself projects. You sign up with the host, you choose the software, and you create your own site. However, the distinction between this category and the others is blurring. As competition between Web hosts grows keener, more and more companies are providing ready-made solutions that streamline the process of Web site creation for their customers. For you, the end user, this streamlining is a good thing: You have plenty of control over how your site comes into being and how it grows over time.

If you simply need a basic Web site and don't want a lot of choices, go with one of the kits. Your site may seem a little generic and basic, but setup is easy, and you can concentrate on marketing and running your business.

However, if you're the independent type who wants to control your site and have lots of room to grow, consider taking on a do-it-yourself project. The sky's the limit as far as the degree of creativity you can exercise and the amount of blood, sweat, and tears you can put in (as long as you don't make your site so large and complex that customers have a hard time finding anything, of course). The more work you do, the greater your chances of seeing your business prosper.

Housing your Web site for free

Free Web hosting is still possible for small businesses. If you're on a tight budget and looking for space on a Web server for free, turn first to your ISP, which probably gives you server space to set up a Web site. You can also check out one of a handful of sites that provide customers with hosting space for no money down and no monthly payments, either. They may make you advertise their products or use their Internet connection to design your site, but if you're happy with this tradeoff, then you can get a basic Web site up and running fairly easily.

  ✔ **Freeola (www.freeola.co.uk):** For no charge, Freeola gives you unlimited (or unmetered) Web space and free use of a big stock of Freeola domain names, as well as optional database software. Freeola rewards the best sites built using its design tools by promoting them on its Web site. Customer reviews of Freeola say that it's easy to use and you can achieve decent results.

- ✔ **Lycos Tripod (www.tripod.lycos.co.uk):** Like Freeola, Lycos doesn't make you share its ads and allows to create a simply Web site without too much fuss. In fact, you can publish a site with your CV, contact details, and pictures in a matter of moments. Lycos also lets you create more sophisticated Web sites using Microsoft's Frontpage, or you can transfer an existing Web site to its hosting platform in seconds.

- ✔ **Yahoo! GeoCities (geocities.yahoo.com):** Yahoo! GeoCities is a popular spot for individuals who want to create home pages and fully fledged personal and business Web sites at a low cost. The site provides a free hosting option that requires users to display ads on the sites they create.

Most importantly, be sure that the site you choose lets you set up for-profit business sites for free.

Investigating electronic shop-front software

Another option for creating a business site and publishing it online is to buy an application that carries you through the entire process of creating an electronic shop front. The advantage is control: You own and operate the software and are in charge of the entire process (at least until the files get to the remote Web servers). The speed with which you develop a site depends on how quickly you master the process, not on the speed of your Internet connection.

Like hosting services such as Yahoo! Store, Tripod, and Freeola, electronic shop-front software lets you create Web pages while shielding you from having to master HTML. Most shop-front software provides you with pre-designed Web pages, called *templates,* which you customise for your particular business. Some types of electronic shop-front options go a step or two beyond the other options by providing you with shopping trolley systems that enable customers to select items and tally the cost at the checkout. They should also provide some sort of electronic payment option, such as credit-card purchases.

Usually, you sign up to transaction software online and tie it to your Web site in a few simple steps. Plenty of options are out there, so do some research and weigh up the pros and cons of each. Try these sites for a start: ekmPowershop (www.ekmpowershop.com), Storefront.net (www.storefront.net), or Lynx Internet (www.lynxinternet.co.uk).

ekmPowershop

ekmPowershop (www.ekmpowershop.com) bills itself as 'easy to use' and promises 'instant results'. It's meant for people with little or no experience of payment software, and for a monthly fee of £20, you can set up a fully operational e-commerce shop. Put simply, when you sign up to ekmPowershop, you get a blank space on their servers where you can add your logos, text, product categories, and pictures of the products themselves. You have the choice of integrating the software onto an existing Web site or using it on its own as a place to sell your goods.

The service is good because the site is updated regularly, and the technologies that your site relies on aren't allowed to go out of date. There is real customer support (not just a robot), and because you don't have to install any software, you're less likely to need help anyway. You also get a complimentary search engine submission and a secure server as standard.

A minor problem with the Web site is that you can't update your shop in beta mode. In other words, all the updates you make are live and viewable by your customers, so you have to get changes right first time and tinkering with your design isn't much of an option. Another small glitch is that you can't build a single, multilanguage site. If you want to sell to people that don't speak English, you must build a new Web site for each additional language. That'll cost more, especially if, like the BBC, you want to get published in 42 languages!

The standard service costs £19.99 a month plus an initial setup charge of £49.95. Again, the results aren't as good as if you'd employed a professional Web design company and hosting service, but then the cost is tiny by comparison.

You should consider the following features when selecting your checkout software:

- **The shop front:** The shop front contains the Web pages that you create. Some packages include predesigned Web pages that you can copy and customise with your own content.

- **The inventory:** You can stock your virtual shop-front shelves by presenting your wares in the form of an online catalogue or product list.

- **The delivery van:** Some shop-front packages streamline the process of transferring your files from your computer to the server. Instead of using FTP software, you publish information simply by clicking a button in your Web editor or Web browser.

- **The checkout counter:** Most electronic shop-front packages give you the option to accept orders online with a credit card, but you may want to consider taking them by phone or fax, too.

Besides providing you with all the software that you need to create Web pages and get them online, electronic shop fronts instruct you on how to market your site and present your goods and services in a positive way. In addition, some programs provide you with a back room for your business, where you can record customer information, orders, and fulfilment.

The problem with many electronic shop-front packages is that they can be very expensive – some cost thousands of pounds. Watch out for the ones that aren't intended for individuals starting a small businesses, but for large corporations that want to branch out to the Web. A few packages provide a Ford-type alternative to the Rolls-Royce shop fronts.

Moving into an online shopping centre

In addition to Web site kits, Internet service providers, and businesses that specialise in Web hosting, online 'shopping centres' – or directories – provide another way to show off your Web site. After you've set up your site, possibly using one of the methods listed in the preceding sections, you should sign up to one of the many directories out there. eDirectory.co.uk (www.edirectory. co.uk), Yahoo! Business Finder (uk.search.yahoo.com/yp), Google Local (www.google.co.uk/lochp?hl=en), and InfoZoo (www.infozoo.co.uk) all offer a home for your business.

Some are free, and some are paid for. Some are the Web site's core business, and some are mere offshoots of the Web site's main business. But the good news is that you don't have to restrict yourself to just one directory. Each has its own audience of potential customers and can offer you increased exposure, so sign up to as many as you can.

The directory may be a simple list of shops on a single Web page. For larger centres with a thousand shops or more, the online businesses are arranged by category and can be found in a searchable index.

In theory, an online shopping centre gives small businesses additional exposure in more than one way. A customer who shops at one of the directory's outlets may notice other businesses on the same site and visit them, too. A few function as Web hosts that enable their customers to transfer Web page files and present their shops online, using one of their Web servers. Most, however, let people list their business in the shopping centre with a hyperlink.

Amazon.co.uk doesn't look like an online shopping centre, but it has instituted some opportunities for entrepreneurs to sell items on its site. Unlike eBay.co.uk, you can't create your own shop front, but you have the option of selling items individually on the Amazon.co.uk site. You pay fees to list items for sale and for completed sales as well. Find out more by going to the

Amazon.co.uk home page (www.amazon.co.uk) and clicking the Sell Your Stuff link near the top of the page.

Turning to your ISP for Web hosting

People sometimes talk about Internet Service Providers (ISPs) and Web hosts as two separate types of Internet businesses, but that's not necessarily the case. Providing users with access to the Internet and hosting Web sites are two different functions, to be sure, but they may well be performed by the same organisation.

In fact, it's only natural to turn to your own ISP first to ask about its Web hosting policies for its customers. If you already go online with Pipex, using sister business 123-Reg (www.123-reg.co.uk) for your hosting makes sense. Likewise, if you have a broadband Internet account with the ISP Fasthosts (www.fasthosts.co.uk), by all means, consider Fasthosts as a Web host for your business site.

Fasthosts is run by a guy who's still in his mid-20s, but don't let that put you off. It comes highly recommended by individuals and small businesses alike. In fact, Andrew Michael started the company while still in his teens because he couldn't find anyone who'd host a small business Web site cost-effectively. That was back in the dotcom boom, when Web sites commanded silly money. Now, companies like Fasthosts encourage small and micro-sized businesses, too.

Fasthosts offers three types of hosting packages (home, developer, and business), each with increasingly sophisticated tools to create and run a Web site. The main differences are to do with the amount of Web space available to you, the number of subdomains you can use, and how many e-mail accounts you can have. Prices range from £3.99 for the starter package to £15.99 for the most sophisticated one. However, all the packages have certain things in common:

- **Visitor statistics:** Shows you who's looking where on your Web site.
- **Search engine optimisation:** Fasthosts' own TrafficDriver helps to boost your search engine rankings.
- **SSL secure Web space:** Gives you secure ecommerce capabilities and data transactions.
- **Password protected Web site folders:** Are available to restrict access to specific areas of your site.
- **MS SQL and MySQL databases plus open database connectivity:** Are all available.

What should you look for in an ISP Web hosting account, and what constitutes a good deal? For one thing, price: Expect to pay no more than £5 a month for a small amount of Web space, say 500 to 750MB. Look for a host that doesn't limit the number of Web pages that you can create. Also find one that gives you at least a couple of e-mail addresses with your account and that lets you add extra addresses for a nominal fee. Finally, look for a host that gives you the ability to include Web page forms on your site so that visitors can send you feedback.

What to expect from an ISP Web hosting service

The process of setting up a Web site varies from ISP to ISP. Here are some general features that you should look for, based on Greg's experience with his own ISP:

- ✓ **Web page editor:** You don't necessarily need to choose a provider that gives you a free Web page editor. You can easily download and install the editor of your choice. Greg tends to use one of two programs, either Microsoft FrontPage or Macromedia Dreamweaver, to create Web pages. (We describe both programs later in this chapter – see 'Fun with Tools: Choosing a Web Site Editor'.)

- ✓ **Password and username:** When Greg's Web pages are ready to go online, he can use the same username and password to access his Web site space that he uses when he dials up to connect to the Internet. Although you don't need to enter a password to view a Web site through a browser (well, at least at most sites), you do need a password to protect your site from being accessed with an FTP program. Otherwise, anyone can enter your Web space and tamper with your files.

- ✓ **FTP software:** When Greg signed up for a hosting account, he received a CD-ROM containing a basic set of software programs, including a Web browser and an FTP program. FTP is the simplest and easiest-to-use software to transfer files from one location to another on the Internet. When he accesses his Web site space from his Macintosh, he uses an FTP program called Fetch. (Check out this link to find out how to use it: `www.elated.com/tutorials/management/ftp/fetch`). From his PC, he uses a program called WS-FTP. Cute FTP (`www.cuteftp.com`) is another program that many Web site owners use, which costs $39.95 (around £20). Many FTP programs are available for free on the Internet or can be purchased cheaply.

  Check out some other programs on the market:
  - Coffee Cup FTP (`www.coffeecup.com`)
  - FTP Client (`www.ftpclient.com`)
  - Smart FTP (`www.smartftp.com`)

✔ **URL:** When you set up a Web site using your ISP, you're assigned a directory on a Web server. The convention for naming this directory is *~username*. The *~username* designation goes at the end of your URL for your Web site's home page. However, you can (and should) register a shorter URL with a domain name registrar, such as Nominet. You can then 'point' the domain name to your ISP's server so that it can serve as an 'alias' URL for your site.

After you have your software tools together and have a user directory on your ISP's Web server, it's time to put your Web site together. Basically, when Greg wants to create or revise content for his Web site, he opens the page in his Web page editor, makes the changes, saves the changes, and then transfers the files to his ISP's directory with his FTP program. Finally, he reviews the changes in his browser.

CASE STUDY

Finding a host that makes your business dynamic

Whether you choose Yahoo!, Freeola, Pipex, or another ISP, the Web host you choose can have a big impact on how easy it is to get online and run your business successfully. Just ask Doug Laughter. He and his wife Kristy own The Silver Connection, a business based in the United States, which sells sterling silver jewellery imported from India, Asia, and Mexico. They began their business when Kristy brought back some silver jewellery from Mexico. The Silver Connection went online in April 1998 at www. silverconnection.com and is hosted by CrystalTech Web Hosting (www.crystal tech.com).

CrystalTech don't operate in the UK, but the following case study is a good reflection of what you should consider when you choose an ISP.

Q. Why did you choose CrystalTech as your Web host?

A. CrystalTech is my second Web host. I didn't have any problems with my previous host, but the issue of changing Web hosts came down to the Web development technology I wanted to

choose for my site. I settled on CrystalTech because it supported the Web Application Server that I chose, which was a Windows platform running Internet Information Server. I also wanted to use Microsoft Access or Microsoft SQL Server for my database solution to support the development of Active Server Pages (ASP).

Q. What makes CrystalTech such a good Web host?

A. It gives its clients access to a Control Centre that allows complete administrative control for the domain. Included in this are mail, FTP, and Domain Name Systems with automatic ODBC (Open Database Connectivity) for databases. A client also gets access to several utilities that analyse traffic to your Web site. I also use the comprehensive knowledge base and online forums that carry on discussions about programming, Web site design, databases, networking, and other topics.

Q. What kinds of customer service features do you use that other business owners should look for?

A. One feature that CrystalTech is very good with is notification. If Web hosting or mail services will be offline for a certain amount of time, I receive an e-mail in advance specifying exactly what is going to happen and when. I have always been treated very well by tech support when I have needed to call.

Q. What kinds of questions should small business owners and managers ask when they're shopping around for a hosting service? What kinds of features should they be looking for initially?

A. I would first suggest considering how you want to develop your Web site. Today's e-commerce site needs to be dynamic in nature, so the business needs to research and determine what Web server application it will use. A Web server application consists of the following:

- ✔ **Server Side Technology:** Active Server Pages, ColdFusion, Java Server Pages, PHP

- ✔ **Database Solution:** Microsoft SQL Server, MS Access, MySQL, Oracle

- ✔ **Server Application:** IIS, Apache, iPlanet, Netscape Enterprise

- ✔ **Operating Platform:** Windows, UNIX

So the decision on how the e-commerce Web site will be developed and in what technology is a very key decision to make from the onset. Once this is decided, choose a Web host that supports your Web server application of choice.

Q. After the development platform is determined, what features should you look for?

A. Look for dedicated disk space for database applications. From 250MB to 500MB of disk space may be fine for your Web site files, but throw in a highly developed Microsoft SQL Server relational database management system, and you'll be paying for some additional space.

Also ask about how much data transfer you can do in a given period, how many e-mail addresses are given with the domain, and whether there's an application that lets you control and administer your entire Web site. If you don't have your own shopping trolley application, ask your host what it offers in this area. Specifically, find out what application it offers, how transactions are completed, and how credit card purchases are processed. Finally, make sure there's an application that can analyse traffic, such as WebTrends, or SmarterStats, or Media House Services.

What's the ISP difference?

What's the big difference between using a kit, such as Lycos Tripod, to create your site, and using your own inexpensive or free software to create a site from scratch and post it on your ISP's server? It's the difference between putting together a model airplane from a kit and designing the airplane yourself. If you use a kit, you save time and trouble; your plane ends up looking pretty much like everyone else's, but you get the job done faster. If you design it yourself, you have absolute control. Your plane can look just the way you want. It takes longer to get to the end product, but you can be sure you get what you wanted.

On the other hand, three differences lie between an ISP-hosted site and a site that resides with a company that does *only* Web hosting, rather than providing Internet dialup access and other services:

- ✔ A business that does only Web hosting charges you for hosting services, whereas your ISP may not.

- ✔ A Web hosting service lets you have your own domain name (www. company.co.uk), whereas an ISP may not. (Some ISPs require that you upgrade to a business hosting account in order to obtain the vanity address. See the 'What's in a name?' sidebar, earlier in this chapter, for more about how Web hosting services offer an advantage in the domain-name game.)

- ✔ A Web hosting service often provides lots of frills, such as super-fast connections, one-button file transfers with Web editors such as Microsoft FrontPage, and tons of site statistics, as well as automatic backups of your Web page files.

To find out more about using a real, full-time Web hosting service, see the section, 'Going for the works with a Web hosting service', later in this chapter.

Where to find an ISP

What if you don't already have an Internet service provider, or you're not happy with the one you have? On today's Internet, you can't swing a mouse without hitting an ISP. How do you find the one that's right for you? In general, you want to look for the provider that offers you the least expensive service with the fastest connection and the best options available for your Web site.

Bigger doesn't necessarily mean cheaper or better; many smaller ISPs provide good service at rates that are comparable to the giants such as Tiscali, Pipex, or NTL. When you're shopping around for an ISP, be sure to ask the following types of questions:

- ✔ What types of connections do you offer?

- ✔ What type of tech support do you offer? Do you accept phone calls or e-mail enquiries around the clock or only during certain hours?

- ✔ Are real human beings always available on call, or are clients sent to a phone message system?

- ✔ Are there any hidden costs?

- ✔ What other services do you offer?

- ✔ Can I speak to existing customers?

Some Web sites are well known for listing ISPs by the services they offer. Here are a few good starting points in your search for the ideal ISP:

- ✔ **ADSL Guide:** This great Web site (`www.adslguide.org.uk`) gives you the low-down on a big range of ISPs in an accessible format. You can search for specific services or by price. It's well worth a look.

- ✔ **ISP Review:** This site (`www.ispreview.co.uk`) provides authoritative articles, news, and reviews dedicated to ISPs in the UK. It's a very useful site if you really want to know your ISP inside-out.

Going for the works with a Web hosting service

After you've had your site online for a while with a free Web host, such as Freeola (`www.freeola.co.uk`) or Heart Internet (`www.heartinternet.co.uk`), you may well decide that you need more room, more services (such as Web site statistics), and a faster connection that can handle many visitors at one time. In that case, you want to locate your online business with a full-time Web hosting service.

As the preceding sections attest, many kinds of businesses now host Web sites. But in this case, I'm defining *Web hosting service* as a company whose primary mission is to provide space on Web servers for individual, nonprofit, and commercial Web sites.

What to look for in a Web host

Along with providing lots of space for your HTML, image, and other files (typically, you get anywhere from 100MBs to a few GBs of space), Web hosting services offer a variety of related services, including some or all the following:

- ✔ **E-mail addresses:** You're likely to be able to get several e-mail addresses for your own or your family members' personal use. Besides that, many Web hosts give you special e-mail addresses called *auto-responders*. These are e-mail addresses, such as `info@yourcompany.com`, that you can set up to automatically return a text message or a file to anyone looking for information.

- ✔ **Domain names:** Virtually all the hosting options that we mention in this chapter give customers the option of obtaining a short domain name, such as `www.infozoo.co.uk` (in Dan's case). But some Web hosts simplify the process by providing domain-name registration in their flat monthly rates.

✔ **Web page software:** Some hosting services include Web page authoring/editing software, such as Microsoft FrontPage. Some Web hosting services even offer Web page forms that you can fill out online in order to create your own online shopping catalogue. All you have to provide is a scanned image of the item you want to sell, along with a price and a description. You submit the information to the Web host, who then adds the item to an online catalogue that's part of your site.

✔ **Multimedia/CGI scripts:** One big thing that sets Web hosting services apart from part-time hosts is the ability to serve complex and memory-intensive content, such as RealAudio sound files or RealVideo video clips. They also let you process Web page forms that you include on your site by executing computer programs called *CGI scripts*. These programs receive the data that someone sends you (such as a customer service request or an order form) and present the data in readable form, such as a text file, e-mail message, or an entry in a database. See Chapter 6 for more about how to set up and use forms and other interactive Web site features.

✔ **Shopping trolley software:** If part of your reason for going online is to sell items, look for a Web host that can streamline the process for you. Most organisations provide you with Web page forms that you can fill out to create sale items and offer them in an online shopping trolley, for example.

✔ **Automatic data backups:** Some hosting services automatically back up your Web site data to protect you against data loss – an especially useful feature because, in extreme cases, major data losses have been known to sink businesses. The automatic nature of the backups frees you from the worry and trouble of doing it manually.

✔ **Site statistics:** Virtually all Web hosting services also provide you with site statistics that give you an idea (perhaps not a precisely accurate count, but a good estimate) of how many visitors you've received. Even better is access to software reports that analyse and graphically report where your visitors are from, how they found you, which pages on your site are the most frequently viewed, and so on.

✔ **Shopping and electronic commerce features:** If you plan to give your customers the ability to order and purchase your goods or services online by using their credit cards, be sure to look for a Web host that provides you with secure commerce options. A *secure server* is a computer that can encrypt sensitive data (such as credit-card numbers) that the customer sends to your site. For a more detailed discussion of secure electronic commerce, see Chapter 7.

Having so many hosting options available is the proverbial blessing and curse. It's good that you have so many possibilities and that the competition is so fierce because that can keep prices down. On the other hand, deciding which host is best for you can be difficult. In addition to asking about the preceding list of features, here are a few more questions to ask prospective Web hosts to help narrow the field:

- ✔ **Do you limit file transfers?** Many services charge a monthly rate for a specific amount of electronic data that is transferred to and from your site. Each time a visitor views a page, that user is actually downloading a few kilobytes of data in order to view it. If your Web pages contain, say, 1MB of text and images and you get 1,000 visitors per month, your site accounts for 1GB of data transfer per month. If your host allocates you less than 1GB per month, it will probably charge you extra for the amount you go over the limit.

- ✔ **What kind of connection do you have?** Your site's Web page content appears more quickly in Web browser windows if your server has a super-fast T1 or T3 connection. Ask your ISP what kind of connection *it* has to the Internet. If you have a DSL line, speeds differ depending on the ISP: You may get a fast 1.5MBps connection or a more common 684Kbps connection. Make sure that you're getting the fastest connection you can afford.

- ✔ **Will you promote my site?** Some hosting services (particularly online shopping centres) help publicise your site by listing you with Internet search indexes and search services so that visitors are more likely to find you.

Besides these questions, the other obvious ones to ask any contractor apply to Web hosting services as well. These include questions like 'How long have you been in business?' and 'Can you suggest customers who will give me a reference?'

The fact that we include a screen shot of a particular Web hosting service's site in this chapter or elsewhere in this book doesn't mean that we're endorsing or recommending that particular organisation alone. A number of companies can offer your business a good deal, so shop around carefully and find the one that's best for you. Check out the hosts with the best rates and most reliable service. Visit some other sites that they host and e-mail the owners of those sites for their opinion of their hosting service.

Competition is tough among hosting services, which means that prices are going down. But it also means that hosting services may seem to promise the moon in order to get your business. Be sure to read the small print and talk to the host before you sign a contract, and always get statements about technical support and backups in writing.

What's it gonna cost?

Because of the ongoing competition in the industry, prices for Web hosting services vary widely. If you look in the classified sections in the back of magazines that cover the Web or search on the Internet itself, you'll see ads for hosting services costing next to nothing. Chances are, these prices are for a basic level of service – Web space, e-mail addresses, domain name, and software – which may be all you need.

The second level of service provides CGI script processing, the ability to serve audio and video files on your site, regular backups, and extensive site statistics, as well as consultants who can help you design and configure your site. This more sophisticated range of features costs more and may set you back £20 to £50 a month, depending on the service level you require. At Easyspace.com, for example, you can conduct secure electronic commerce on your site as part of hosting packages that cost between £70 and £160 a year. MySQL database support starts at £70 a year.

Fun with Tools: Choosing a Web Page Editor

A carpenter has his or her favourite hammer and saw. A chef has an array of utensils and pots and pans. Likewise, a Web site creator has software programs that facilitate the presentation of words, colours, images, and multimedia in Web browsers.

Knowing HTML comes in handy when you need to add elements that Web page editors don't handle. Some programs, for example, don't provide you with easy buttons or menu options for adding <META> tags, which enable you to add keywords or descriptions to a site so that search engines can find them and describe your site correctly.

If you really want to get into HTML or find out more about creating Web pages, read *HTML 4 For Dummies,* 4th Edition, by Ed Tittel and Natanya Pitts, or *Creating Web Pages For Dummies,* 6th Edition, by Bud Smith and Arthur Bebak (both by Wiley).

It pays to spend time choosing a Web page editor that has the right qualities. What qualities should you look for in a Web page tool, and how do you know which tool is right for you? To help narrow the field, we've divided this class of software into different levels of sophistication. Pick the type of program that best fits your technical skills.

For the novice: Use your existing programs

A growing number of word-processing, graphics, and business programs are adding HTML to their list of capabilities. You may already have one of these programs at your disposal. By using a program with which you're already comfortable, you can avoid installing a Web page editor.

Here are some programs that enable you to generate one type of content and then give you the option of outputting that content in HTML, which means that your words or figures can appear on a Web page:

- **Microsoft Word:** The most recent versions of the venerable word processing standby work pretty much seamlessly with Web page content. You can open Web pages from within Word and save Word files in Web page format.

- **Adobe PageMaker/Quark Xpress:** The most recent versions of these two popular page layout programs let you save the contents of a document as HTML – only the words and images are transferred to the Web, however; any special typefaces become generic Web standard headings.

- **Microsoft Office XP, 2003, or 2007:** Word, Excel, and PowerPoint all give users the option of exporting content to Web pages.

- **WordPerfect and Presentations 12:** These two component programs within Corel's suite of tools let you save files as an HTML page or a PDF file that you can present on the Web. If you have chosen to present one slide per Web page, the program adds clickable arrows to each slide in your presentation so that viewers can skip from one slide to another.

Although these solutions are convenient, they probably won't completely eliminate the need to use a Web page editor. Odds are, you'll still need to make corrections and do special formatting after you convert your text to HTML.

For intermediate needs: User-friendly Web editors

If you're an experienced Web surfer and eager to try out a simple Web editor, try a program that lets you focus on your site's HTML and textual content, provides you with plenty of functionality, and is still easy to use. Here are some user-friendly programs that are inexpensive (or, better yet, free), yet allow you to create a functional Web site.

Editors that'll flip your whizzy-wig

Web browsers are multilingual; they understand exotic-sounding languages such as FTP, HTTP, and GIF, among others. But one language browsers don't speak is English. Browsers don't understand instructions such as 'Put that image there' or 'Make that text italic'. HyperText Markup Language, or HTML, is a translator, if you will, between human languages and Web languages.

If the thought of HTML strikes fear into your heart, relax. Thanks to modern Web page creation tools, you don't have to master HTML in order to create Web pages. Although knowing a little HTML does come in handy at times, you can depend on these special user-friendly tools to do almost all your English-to-HTML translations for you.

The secret of these Web page creation tools is their WYSIWYG (pronounced whizzy-wig)

display. WYSIWYG stands for 'What You See Is What You Get'. A WYSIWYG editor lets you see on-screen how your page will look when it's on the Web, rather than forcing you to type (or even see) HTML commands like this:

```
<H1> This is a Level 1
    Heading </H1>
<IMG SRC = "lucy.gif"> <BR>
<P>This is an image of
    Lucy.</P>
```

A WYSIWYG editor, such as CoffeeCup HTML Editor for Windows (www.coffeecup.com), shows you how the page appears even as you assemble it. Besides that, it lets you format text and add images by means of familiar software shortcuts such as menus and buttons.

The following programs don't include some of the bells and whistles you need to create complex, interactive forms, format a page using frames, or access a database of information from one of your Web pages. These goodies are served up by Web page editors that have a higher level of functionality, which we describe in the upcoming section for advanced commerce sites.

BBEdit

If you work on a Macintosh and you're primarily concerned with textual content, BBEdit is one of the best choices you can make for a Web page tool. It lives up to its motto: 'It doesn't suck.' BBEdit is tailored to use the Mac's highly visual interface, and Version 8 will run on the Mac OS 10.3.5 or later. You can use Macintosh drag-and-drop to add an image file to a Web page in progress by dragging the image's icon into the main BBEdit window, for example. Find out more about BBEdit at the Bare Bones Software, Inc. Web site (www.barebones.com/products/bbedit/index.html).

Other good choices of Web editors for the Macintosh are Taco HTML Edit by Taco Software (www.tacosw.com) or PageSpinner by Optima System (www.optima-system.com).

Macromedia HomeSite

HomeSite is an affordable tool for Web site designers who feel at ease working with HTML code. However, HomeSite isn't just an HTML code editor. It provides a visual interface so that you can work with graphics and preview your page layout. HomeSite also provides you with step-by-step utilities called *wizards* to quickly create pages, tables, frames, and JavaScript elements. A version of HomeSite is bundled with Macromedia Dreamweaver MX 2004, the latest version of the Dreamweaver Web site editor. HomeSite is also available as a standalone program that works with Windows 98 or later; find out more about it at www.macromedia.com/uk/software/homesite.

Microsoft FrontPage Express

Microsoft doesn't support FrontPage Express any more, but if you still use Windows 98 and you're on a tight budget, give it a try. The software comes bundled with Windows 98, and you don't have to do a thing to install it. Just choose Start➪Programs➪Internet Explorer➪FrontPage Express to open FrontPage Express.

CoffeeCup HTML Editor

CoffeeCup HTML Editor, by CoffeeCup Software (www.coffeecup.com), is a popular Windows Web site editor that contains a lot of features for a low price of about £26). You can begin typing and formatting text by using the CoffeeCup HTML Editor menu options. You can add an image by clicking the Insert Image toolbar button, or use the Forms toolbar to create the text boxes and radio buttons that make up an interactive Web page form. You can even add JavaScript effects and choose from a selection of clip art images that come with the software.

CoffeeCup HTML Editor doesn't let you explore database connectivity, add Web components, or other bonuses that come with a program like FrontPage or Dreamweaver. But it does have everything you need to create a basic Web page.

Netscape Composer

When we read reviews of Web page software, we don't often see Netscape Composer included in the list. But to us, it's an ideal program for an entrepreneur on a budget. Why? Let us spell it out for you: F-R-E-E.

Netscape Composer is the Web page editing and authoring tool that comes with Netscape 7.2 as well as earlier versions. It's not available through the UK Web site, but all you have to do is download one of these packages from the US Netscape Browser Central page (channels.netscape.com/ns/browsers/default.jsp) and Composer is automatically installed on your computer along with Navigator (the Netscape Web browser) and several other Internet programs.

With Composer, you can create sophisticated layout elements, such as tables (which we discuss further in Chapter 5), with an easy-to-use graphical interface. After you edit a page, you can preview it in Navigator with the click of a button. Plus, you can publish all your files by choosing a single menu item.

For advanced commerce sites: Programs that do it all

If you plan to do a great deal of business online, or even want to add the title of Web designer to your list of talents (as some of the entrepreneurs profiled in this book have done), it makes sense to spend some money up front and use a Web page tool that can do everything you want – today and for years to come.

The advanced programs that we describe here go beyond the simple designation of Web page editors. They not only let you edit Web pages but also help you add interactivity to your site, link dynamically updated databases to your site, and keep track of how your site is organised and updated. Some programs (notably, FrontPage) can even transfer your Web documents to your Web host with a single menu option. This way, you get to concentrate on the fun part of running an online business – meeting people, taking orders, processing payments, and the like.

Macromedia Dreamweaver

What's that you say? You can never have enough bells and whistles? The cutting edge is where you love to walk? Then Dreamweaver, a Web authoring tool by Adobe (formerly Macromedia), is for you. Dreamweaver is a feature-rich, professional piece of software.

Dreamweaver's strengths aren't so much in the basic features such as making selected text bold, italic, or a different size; rather, Dreamweaver excels in producing *Dynamic HTML* (which makes Web pages more interactive through scripts) and HTML style sheets. Dreamweaver has ample FTP settings, and it gives you the option of seeing the HTML codes you're working within one window and the formatting of your Web page within a second, WYSIWYG window. The latest version, Dreamweaver 8, is a complex and powerful piece of software. It lets you create Active Server pages, connect to the ColdFusion database, and contains lots of templates and wizards. Dreamweaver is available for both Windows and Macintosh computers; find out more at the Adobe Web site (www.adobe.com/uk/products/dreamweaver).

Microsoft FrontPage

FrontPage (www.microsoft.com/uk/frontpage) is a powerful Web authoring tool that has some unique e-commerce capabilities. For one thing, it provides you with a way to organise a Web site visually. The main FrontPage
window is divided into two sections. On the left, you see the Web page on
which you're currently working. On the right, you see a treelike map of all the
pages on your site, arranged visually to show which pages are connected to
each other by hyperlinks.

Another nice thing about FrontPage – something that you're sure to find helpful if you haven't been surfing the Web or working with Web pages for very
long – is the addition of wizards and templates. The FrontPage wizards enable
you to create a discussion area on your site where your visitors can post
messages to one another. The wizards also help you connect to a database or
design a page with frames. (See Chapter 5 for more about creating frames.)

Chapter 4

Profiting from New Business Tools

. . . .

In This Chapter

▶ Taking advantage of round-the-clock availability and new communications

▶ Identifying new products and services

▶ Marketing your views, opinions, and commentary through your Web site

▶ Creating your own business blog

▶ Making sure that your online business promotes community spirit

. . . .

*W*hen you open shop on the Internet, you don't just begin to operate in isolation. The whole point of the Web is the fact that it's a community. It's the same for businesses as it is for individuals. Whether you like it or not, you're not alone. You have access to thousands, even millions, of other businesses that are in the same situation you are – or that went through the same kinds of uncertainties you're encountering before they achieved success.

Advantages of Doing Business Online

The fact that you're online means that you enjoy advantages over businesses operating solely in the bricks-and-mortar marketplace. E-mail, blogging, and the Internet in general give you much better access to your customers – and there's no equivalent in the offline world. You also have access to services such as search engines that can help you find suppliers and do business research and marketing. This chapter provides you with a user friendly overview of the many new opportunities available to you when you start an online business, including tools, services, and opportunities for partnering so that you can advertise your new business in ways that help you succeed without breaking your budget.

Sometimes, a big step toward success is simply being aware of all the opportunities available to you. The worst reason you can have for going online is simply that 'everybody's doing it'. Instead of focusing on one way of advertising or selling, take stock of all the aspects of online business that you can exploit. Then when you create your Web site, select a payment option, or set up security measures, you'll do things right the first time around. The next few sections describe some advantages you need to make part of your business plan.

Operating 24/7

One of the first reasons why entrepreneurs flock to the Web is the ability to do business around the clock with customers all over the world. It still applies today: It may be 2 a.m. in the UK, but someone can still be making a purchase in Rome, Los Angeles, or Sydney from your Web site or eBay shop.

If you're just starting out and you're trying to reach the widest possible audience of consumers for your goods or services, be sure they're

- ✔ **Small:** That means they're easy to pack and easy to ship.
- ✔ **Something that people need and can use worldwide:** DVDs, CDs, computer products, action figures, and sports memorabilia appeal to many.
- ✔ **Something that people can't find in their local area:** Many sites resell gourmet foodstuffs that can't easily be found overseas, for example.

Make sure that you appeal to a small, niche segment of individuals around the world. It's better to do one thing extremely well than lots of things badly. That applies to all businesses, from the smallest start-ups to the biggest multinationals. Keeping your business lean and mean improves your chances of success.

If you do sell DVDs online, be aware that DVD players are required to include codes that prevent the playback of DVDs in geographical regions where movies haven't been released to video as yet. A disc purchased in one country may not play on a player purchased in another country. You need to pay attention to the codes assigned to the DVDs you sell so that your customers will actually be able to play them.

Communicating with etools

Nothing beats e-mail, in our opinion, for reaching customers in a timely and friendly way. We know all about the immediacy of talking to people over the phone, the sophistication of desktop alerts, and the benefits of print advertising. But phone calls can be intrusive, alerts are expensive, and mag ads only work for certain types of business. As you can probably testify as a consumer, most people are wary of anyone who wants to market to them with an out-of-the-blue phone call that interrupts their day. E-mail messages can come in at any time of the day or night, but they don't interrupt what customers are doing. And if customers have already made a purchase from your company, they may welcome a follow-up contact by e-mail, especially because they can respond to you at their own convenience. Not only that, but you can include links to products and services in e-mails that could tempt customers into further purchases. You can announce new product ranges, special offers, even an entirely new business.

One of the most popular online communications systems, instant messaging (IM), is useful for keeping in touch with business partners and colleagues. But be very wary of using it to approach current or potential customers. Consumers are used to dropping everything to answer instant messages from friends. When they discover that it's a marketing message, they're not going to be happy – it's the online equivalent of taking a telesales call when you're enjoying a nice bath.

Besides e-mail newsletters, what kinds of communications strategies work with online shoppers? The following sections give a few suggestions.

Giving away a free sample

Greg was in the grocery shop the other day, looking at a hunk of luxury cheese that costs a pretty penny, wishing he could open up the package and taste-test it before handing over big bucks. The concept of the 'free sample' is one that everyone loves – especially Web surfers. Newspapers like the *Financial Times* and *The Independent* do it by making the first few paragraphs of archived articles available online; if you want to read the rest, you're asked to pay a pound, or a similar nominal fee. Amazon.co.uk makes brief excerpts of selected CD tracks available on its Web site so that shoppers can listen to the music before deciding whether or not to buy the CD.

On the Internet, software producers have been giving away free samples for many years in the form of computer *shareware:* software program that users can download and use for a specified period of time. After the time period expires, the consumers are asked (or required, if the program ceases to function) to pay a shareware fee if they want to keep the program. A tiny Texas company called id Software started giving away a stripped-down computer game on the Internet back in 1993, in the hope of getting users hooked on it so that they would pay for the full-featured version. The plan worked, and since then, more than 100,000 customers have paid as much as $40 (£22) for a full copy of the game, which is called Doom. id Software has gone on to create and sell many other popular games since.

Giving out discounts

One reason shoppers turn to the Internet is to save money. Thanks to sites such as PriceRunner (www.pricerunner.co.uk), Kelkoo (www.kelkoo.co.uk), and Moneysupermarket.com (www.moneysupermarket.com), which allow you to compare prices on various Web sites for books, holidays, electrical equipment, or whatever you like, shoppers expect some sort of discount from the Internet. They love it if you offer special Internet-only prices on your Web site or give them money off or 'promotional' offers like the one offered by Sky in Figure 4-1.

Giving customers the chance to talk back

Another great thing about the Internet is that it gives customers the chance to get involved in the design and manufacturer of products. They can create their own clothing ranges, sportswear, or even artwork and have it sent to them by post. Adidas is a famous example of a brand that people like to customise to their own tastes, and Sweat Shop (www.sweatshop.co.uk), shown in Figure 4-2, lets you do just that. Through the Web site, you can book an appointment at their Harrods-based shop, where you're measured up, given a choice of colour and design combinations, and even have your feet tested to see what combination of cushioning and support you need.

Figure 4-1: Use vouchers, discounts, and Internet-only specials to entice more customers or drive them to a bricks-and-mortar shop.

mysky.sky.com/portla/site/skycom/offers

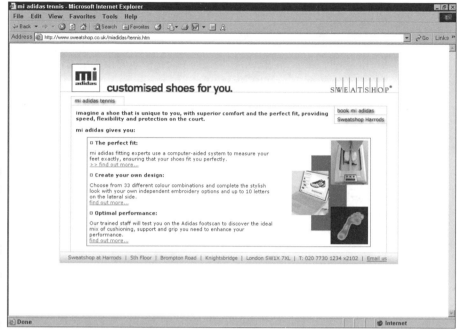

Figure 4-2:
The Web
enables
manufac-
turers to put
customers
in charge of
the design
process.

A number of forward-looking companies are building their reputations by letting customers voice opinions and make suggestions online. The shoe and sporting apparel manufacturer Nike isn't exactly a small business, but it's taken a leading position in building community among its customers. Every week, a live chat session is held for Nike customers. Discussion boards are also available; the site (www.nikechat.com) boasts more than 33,000 registered members and a total of 3.5 million messages posted.

Chat doesn't make sense unless you have a solid user base of at least several hundred regular users who feel passionately about your goods and services and are dedicated enough to want to type real-time messages to one another and to you. However, discussion groups are practical, even for small businesses; you can set them up with a discussion area through Microsoft FrontPage or on Yahoo! (uk.groups.yahoo.com). Find out more about making your Web site interactive in Chapter 6.

Taking advantage of micropayments' rebirth

Credit-card payments make the Web a viable place for e-commerce. But the cost of the typical credit-card transaction makes payments of less than £1 pointless. The popular payment service PayPal (www.paypal.co.uk)

charges 3.4 per cent plus a 20p fee for each sale, which makes it impractical for content providers to sell something for, say, 30p. Such small transactions are known as *micropayments*.

In the early dotcom days, the term micropayment was thrown around quite a bit, both by writers and by companies hoping that they could induce Web surfers to pay small amounts of money for bits of online content. Many of those companies failed to find success and disappeared, in part because the process of setting up micropayments was cumbersome and highly technical.

Today, micropayment systems are attempting a comeback. A large percentage of Web surfers have high-speed broadband connections and are used to paying for content online. A system called BitPass brings small payments to more than 100 Web sites. There's much more content online, including articles, music clips, and cartoons, that could only be sold for small amounts of money. If your business involves text, music, art, or other kinds of content, you may be able to make a few pence for your work by using one of the following payment services:

- ✔ **BT Click&Buy:** Thousands of businesses around the world use BT's micropayments service (www.clickandbuy.com). It allows payments from as little as 50p to hundreds of pounds, whilst giving customers the option of being charged through their phone bill. Your customers get a 24/7 helpline and the reassurance that they're using a reputable company. But charges are fairly steep at just under 10 per cent commission plus a one-off set up fee and a small monthly charge.

- ✔ **mENABLE:** This Mobile Enable solution (www.m-enable.com/content) is a pretty natty bit of kit. It allows Web sites to charge for access, using micropayments over SMS, WAP, phone, credit card, or bank debit. The company has won awards for its secure service and has a big range of payment options, which you can tailor to your business's needs.

- ✔ **SpaceCoin:** This company (www.spacecoin.com) is based in Sweden but operates all over the world. It offers plenty of payment options, including its quick set-up Plug and Play Shop and shopping trolley software.

- ✔ **TechnaPay:** These guys (www.tecknapay.com) are WorldPay-accredited resellers who specialise in products complementing WorldPay's payment platform. On top of the usual stuff, they offer payment page design for £149, shopping trolley functionality, and even £50 cashback when you sign up to their service.

If you can link your Web site, eBay shop, or other venues to your offerings on these micropayment sites, you begin to achieve synergy: Your various sales sites point to one another and build attention for your overall sales efforts.

Auctioning off your professional services

There's nothing new about making a living selling your design, consultation, or other professional services. But the Internet provides you with new and innovative ways to get the word out about what you do. Along with having your own Web site in which you describe your experience, provide samples of your work, and make references to clients you've helped, you can find new clients by auctioning off your services in what's known as a *reverse auction*. In a reverse auction, the provider of goods or services doesn't initiate a transaction – rather, the customer does.

The UK government is a big fan of reverse auctions as a way of getting the best price for contracts. For example, say the Department for Culture, Media and Sport needs a new stationery supplier. It advertises the contract in the form of a tender and invites bids; the lowest bid (from a reputable supplier) wins the deal. Even the Ministry of Defence is involved. Check out www. contracts.mod.uk if you don't believe us!

Elance Online, a reverse auction site based in the United States, enables professional contractors to offer their services and bid on jobs. (Go to www. elance.com and click Elance Online.) The site is ideal if you don't offer bits of content, such as stories or articles, but usually charge by the hour or by the job for your services. In this case, the customer is typically a company that needs design, writing, construction, or technical work. The company posts a description of the job on the Elance site. Essentially, it's a Request for Bids or Request for Proposals: Freelancers who have already registered with the site then make bids on the job. The company can then choose the lowest bid or choose another company based on its qualifications.

Exploring New Products and Services You Can Sell

The choices you make when you first get started in e-commerce have an impact on the success with which you target your customers. One of the main choices is determining what you plan to sell online. Because you've made the decision to sell on the Internet, chances are good that you're a technology-savvy businessperson. You're open to new technologies and new ways of selling. The 21st century has seen an explosion in products and services that were unheard of just a decade or so ago. If you can take advantages of one of these opportunities, you increase your potential customer base.

Music files and other creative work

Today's online customers are quite sophisticated about shopping online. You can make your music or audio clips available online from your Web site. The easiest option is to use your computer or a digital recorder to make the recording and save the file in .wav (Waveform Audio Format), MP3, .ram (RealAudio), or .wma (Windows Media Audio). Chances are excellent that your visitors have one or more media players that can process and play at least one of these types of files.

The Arctic Monkeys are one of the biggest bands in the UK at the moment, but they owe their success, at least in part, to devoted fans sharing their music online. In interviews with the band, journalists regularly refer to their massively popular page on MySpace (www.myspace.com), which features photos, gig reviews, and samples of the band's music. It was this popularity online that made the band an overnight success when they released their first single. A huge fan base was ready and waiting to hit the shops when the single came out. The band's first two singles stormed to No. 1 in the charts, as did the album a couple of months later. All this success, yet the band admits that the MySpace page was constructed by fans; they claim that at the time they had no idea what MySpace was.

One of the biggest online music stories of the last few years is, of course, the music marketplace Napster (www.napster.co.uk). It started as an illegal site for sharing music cheaply, by bypassing licensing laws. After a clamp-down a few years back, Napster went legit and is no less successful for that move. Groups routinely provide links to their albums on the Napster music site, where you can download each track separately for less than a pound each, and albums for around eight quid. Even if you're just starting out in the biz, you can digitise your audio files and post them online so that others can download them in the same way.

Groceries and other household services

Small, easily shipped merchandise like golf balls or tools are undeniably well suited to online sales. But your online business doesn't need to be restricted to such items. Even perishable items like foodstuffs can be, and frequently are, purchased online. Initially, the field attracted *pure plays* – companies that devoted their sales activities solely to the Internet. They failed to compete with bricks-and-mortar shops.

The good news is that traditional bricks-and-mortar grocery shops are finding success by selling their products on the Web as a way of supplementing their traditional in-store offering. The Web site for Wiltshire Farm Foods (www.wiltshirefarmfoods.com), shown in Figure 4-3, gives its customers the convenience of 'meals on wheels' delivered to their door – but with an emphasis on quality. Elderly customers who aren't able to visit one of its outlets around the UK can buy tasty meals online and have them delivered.

Big supermarkets such as Sainsbury's (www.sainsburys.co.uk) and Waitrose (www.ocado.co.uk), who spend millions of pounds promoting, maintaining, and selling through their Web sites, have conducted numerous studies into what makes people buy food online. Generally, people buy groceries this way for three main reasons:

- ✔ Cost savings
- ✔ Convenience
- ✔ Greater product variety

If you're able to offer food items that consumers can't find elsewhere, and at a competitive price, you should consider selling food online. People hate navigating multi-storey car parks and waiting in long queues at the checkout. People who live alone and who have difficulty getting out (such as the elderly or sick) naturally turn to buying their groceries online.

Figure 4-3:
Regional grocers and food producers are widening their customer bases thanks to the Web.

Are you interested in reaching online grocery shoppers online? The Food Standards Agency has a useful Web site (www.eatwell.gov.uk/ keepingfoodsafe/shoppingforfood/onlinemailorder) detailing the standards of quality, packaging, and delivery you have to achieve.

Customers have plenty of rights in this area; for example you have to make descriptions of your products full and accurate, and you must send a confirmation e-mail once your customer has ordered food. Non-food sellers also have to provide a 'cooling off period' of seven days, during which customers are allowed to change their minds and cancel orders. Also check out Food First (www.foodfirst.co.uk) for details and inspiration about the food industry.

M-commerce

The needs and habits of consumers drive what sells best online. These days, consumers are going online in many more ways than just sitting at a computer – that is, they're branching out from e-commerce to *m-commerce* (mobile commerce). Consumers are using their mobile phones, PDAs, and pocket computers to connect to cyberspace. Retailers are hungry to reach these new mediums any way they can; here are just three examples:

- ✔ Receiving an unsolicited text trying to sell you something is just as annoying as e-mail spam. So, what kinds of selling *do* work online? Here's an example: When Greg first got his spiffy new Web-enabled mobile phone, he thought it would be fun to get some gimmicks for the kids (at least, he told them the gimmicks were for them; they were for him, too). He went online and downloaded a ring tone that was available on his phone, and he later purchased a game that could be played on his phone as well. Companies like Jamster (www.jamster.co.uk) have made millions selling ringtones, mobile wallpaper, and games. Unforgivably, however, they also brought you the crazy frog.

- ✔ With new and more powerful phones available, retailers have adapted and expanded what they sell through mobile technologies. On Dan's PDA, he surfs the Internet almost as easily as on his laptop. He can check out bargains at eBay.co.uk and shop online at Amazon.co.uk.

- ✔ M-commerce group Reporo (www.reporo.co.uk) has been going for a few years now. It lets you download Java-based software, which you can use to shop via your e-mail. Reporo has teamed up with a host of retailers, including Boots, Dominos Pizza, CD Wow, Firebox.com, and Game.

Companies selling software so that you can sell to mobile users are cropping up all over the place. One of the bigger ones, Bango (www.bango.com), has partnered with big mobile companies such as Vodafone, Orange, Telefonica, and O2 and can process micropayments through phone bills, premium SMS (text messages), and PayPal.

Adding Online Content and Commentary

Plenty of traditional publications have discovered that they can supplement home delivery and newsstand sales by providing some parts of their content online on a subscription-only basis. Typically, some content is available for free, while other stories are designated as *premium content*, made available only to subscribers who have paid to subscribe to the site and who can enter a valid username and password.

The online versions of the *Economist* (www.economist.com) and *The Spectator* (www.spectator.co.uk) both have premium content that is available only to paying subscribers. However, more and more magazines are starting to offer extra content for free, reasoning that they'll make more money through advertising on a free Web site than through subscriptions on a paid-for model. For example, as we were writing this book, *The Guardian* had just announced that more of its content would be accessible for no charge.

Technically, it's not as difficult as you may think to make some content on your Web site publicly available and some content restricted only to those who have a username and password. Most Web server software enables Webmasters to designate certain directories as password protected and others as freely available. If you're technically savvy and decide to operate your own Web server, you can use the open-source application Apache to password-protect some parts of your Web site. The tricky part is not in restricting the content but in creating the system that enables buyers to assign themselves usernames and passwords and pay for their subscriptions in the first place. It's best to hire a Web designer or sign up with an e-commerce hosting service with support staff that can lead you through the process of setting up such systems.

Blogging to build your brand

People have been speaking their minds for fun and profit for as long as there have been media to broadcast their words. Think about famous orators like Socrates, Lenin, and Martin Luther King. What would they have done in the age of the Internet? They would have started their own blogs, that's what!

A *weblog* (*blog* for short) is a type of online journal or diary that can be frequently updated. Blogs can be about anything in particular or nothing at all: You can blog about your daily activities or travels and let your family and friends know what you've been up to lately, or you can get your views and opinions out in the world and develop a community of like-minded readers. Many blogs consist of commentary by individuals who gather news items or cool Web pages and make them available to their friends (or strangers who happen upon their blogs). This vision, in fact, was the original idea behind blogs, and the concept followed by many of the most popular ones: highlighting little-known Web sites or articles or shops in the media that readers are too busy to visit, and providing alternative views and commentary about those Web sites, news stories, or other current events.

Is it really possible to make a living by blogging? It's certainly possible to supplement one's income this way. Andrew Sullivan, who writes Daily Dish (`www.andrewsullivan.com`) in the United States, one of the most popular blogs around, reported on his site that he was getting as many as 300,000 visitors each day in the days leading up to the presidential election of 2004, when dedicated readers like Greg were flocking to politically oriented blogs to get opinion and analysis. After the election, visits went down, but they still hit 100,000 a day. And Sullivan could proclaim in his blog that ad revenue from an advertising service that specialises in blogs, Blogads (`www.blogads.com`), was making it possible for him to continue.

Of course, the best bloggers are good writers and have special knowledge that is in demand. If you plan to make money through blogging, it's absolutely essential that you have something to say. People aren't going to flock to a site that talks about daily life in a boring way.

One of the most popular blogs around is by former Microsoft whiz kid Robert Scoble (`scobleizer.wordpress.com`). For many years, 'the Scobleizer' was as much a public face of Microsoft as Bill Gates, and his insights into technological developments fascinated many. The same could be said for Seth Goden (`sethgodin.typepad.com`) who talks about marketing strategies in an inventive and engaging way. His blog is read by most people in marketing who want to sharpen up their skills.

Finding your niche

Blogging, like anything on the Web, works when you identify a niche group and target that group by providing those people with content that they're likely to want. The challenge is finding something to say and putting time and energy into saying it on a regular basis. Although Greg has set up his own blog at `www.gregholden.com`, he finds it difficult to devote the time and commitment for daily contributions.

Yet, the most successful blogs seem to be ones that are created by people who are used to writing something every day, such as journalists. Dan writes a news blog on his Web site (www.realbusiness.co.uk); it's easy to find time when you're paid to do it! Academic faculty members who are published and well regarded in their fields also run popular blogs. Even CEOs are getting into it, although their position of responsibility makes their writing uncontroversial and therefore usually pretty boring.

What do you feel strongly about? What do you know well? Is there something you would love to communicate and discuss every day? If so, that's what you should use to organise your blog. A blog can be about anything you like – and we mean anything. A prime example: the Appliance Blog, in which an appliance repairman in Springfield, Oregon, provides a daily diary of his service calls and repairs. Along the way, he provides links to the Web sites of major appliance manufacturers as well as a forum where you can ask questions about your own appliance problems. The repairman's blog isn't a place where you can find out what he had for breakfast or what he thinks about world peace; it's focused solely on what he knows, and it's a useful resource for anyone who is having a problem with an appliance.

One of the best-known blogs was the one created by an Iraqi citizen who went by the pseudonym Salam Pax. His blog – Where is Rael? – provided a compelling account of daily life in Iraq in 2002 and 2003, during the US military's campaign to topple the regime of Saddam Hussein.

Starting a blog

How, exactly, do you start a blog? Most people sign up for an account with an online service that streamlines the process. Some of the best known are

- ✔ Blogger (www.blogger.com)
- ✔ Brit Journal (www.brit-journal.com)
- ✔ WordPress (wordpress.org)
- ✔ Typepad (www.typepad.com)

Before the year 2000, you had to be a programmer to figure out how to create a blog on your Web page. But a number of online services are available online to streamline the process for nonprogrammers. Blogger (www.blogger.com) lets you create your own blog for free, so it's a good place to start. Google owns Blogger, so the site enables you to participate in Google's AdWords program (see Chapter 13) as well, so you may gain some revenue from your blog. As with any Web-based content, you should do some planning and write down notes, such as

✔ A name for your blog

✔ What you want to talk about

✔ Some ideas for your first few blog entries

Then follow these steps:

1. **Start up your Web browser, go to the Blogger home page (www. blogger.com), and click Create Your Blog Now.**

   The Create Blogger Account page appears.

2. **Fill out the form with a username, password, and e-mail address; read the terms of service; select the Acceptance of Terms check box; and click Continue.**

   The Name Your Blog page appears.

3. **Come up with a short name for your blog; add that blog to the URL supplied and click Continue.**

   For example, if your blog is called ToolTime, your URL should be tooltime.blogspot.com.

   The Choose A Template page appears.

4. **Click the button beneath the graphic design (or template) you want to use and then click Continue.**

   A page appears with a light bulb icon and the notice Creating Your Blog. After a few seconds, a page appears with the notice Your Blog Has Been Created!

5. **Click Start Posting.**

   A page appears in which you type a title for your first posting and then type the posting itself (see Figure 4-4).

6. **Click the Publish Post button at the bottom of the page.**

   Your blog post is published online. That's all there is to it!

Building an audience

Blogs that are odd, quirky, based on dramatic human-interest situations such as wartime journals, or that are politically oriented tend to be the most successful. That said, here are some ways to build up an audience for your blog:

✔ **Writing for other bloggers:** Your first audience will probably consist of family or friends, or other bloggers who live in the same geographic area or write about the same subjects you do. Contact those bloggers and ask them to exchange links with your blog; ask your other readers to spread the word about your blog, too.

✔ **Sprinkling keywords and categories:** Blogs are like other Web pages: Although their contents change frequently, search engines index them. The more keywords you include in your postings and the greater the range of subjects you cover, the more likely you are to have your blog turn up in a set of search results.

✔ **Posting consistently:** When readers latch on to a blog they like, they visit it frequently. You need to post something – anything – on a daily basis, or at least several times a week.

✔ **Syndicating your blog:** One way of spreading the word about your blog is providing a 'feed' of its latest contents, such as the headings of posts and the dates of the latest posts. This summary is automatically prepared in XML (eXtensible Markup Language) by most blogging tools. You make the feed of your blog available on its home page; sites that aggregate (in other words, collect) the feeds from many of their favorite blogs can collect them and quickly know when the blogs have been updated.

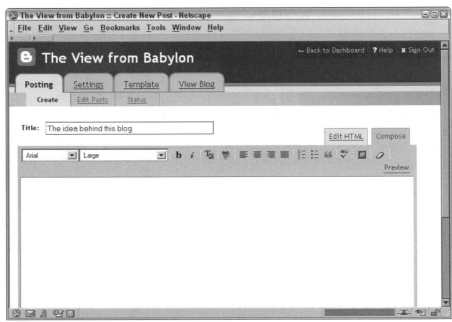

Figure 4-4:
Blogger makes it easy to create a blog for free and give it a graphic design.

If you can make a living at blogging or at least end up with some fun money at the end of each month, more power to you. But don't go into blogging with that attitude, or you'll lose interest right away. Look at a blog as another tool in your online business arsenal – another way of getting your message before the public, another place where you can steer visitors to your Web site or your shop on eBay or Yahoo!. It makes sense to treat your blog as a venue where you talk about what you like to buy and sell online and to strike up ongoing conversations among your customers and clients. In other words, you don't generate income with a blog by selling directly to the public. You try to build up a number of loyal readers and attract advertising revenue – or simply attract more customers to your Web site.

Building a Community

Studies consistently show that people who spend large amounts of time in community venues such as discussion forums end up spending money on the same Web site. (eBay is the perfect example.) It's a *value proposition,* but you can't attach a specific dollar value to it.

Community building on commercial Web sites doesn't necessarily involve discussion boards or chat rooms. Anything you can do to get your customers communicating with one another will do it. On Amazon.com, a kind of community feel is created by the book reviews written by individual readers, and Top 10 book lists let visitors share their views.

Partnerships

The notion of online community cuts both ways: It's not only for consumers who visit Web sites and join communities, but for businesspeople like you, too. Some of the liveliest and most popular online communities are eBay groups – discussion forums started by eBay members themselves. And among those, some of the most popular are the ones in which sellers share tips and advice about boosting their online incomes, finding merchandise to sell, identifying mystery items, and so on.

Don't forget that even though you may run a business by yourself from your home, you're not really alone. If you need some encouragement, join a discussion group, or consult the tips and resources in the Small Business Associations section of this book's Online Directory.

CASE STUDY

No bells, no whistles, all trust: The beauty of Craigslist

When it comes to online communities, you'd be hard pressed to find one stronger than the devoted users who regularly post ads and respond to ads on one of the Craigslist sites around the world. Craigslist (www.craigslist.org) is a true Internet phenomenon. It was started by Craig Newmark back in 1995 as a simple e-mail newsletter announcing upcoming cultural events in Craig's hometown, San Francisco. Over time, the recipients began to use the newsletter to post notices and sell items. Then job notices were posted.

Before long, participants came to depend on Craigslist to find out what was going on in their communities, to find items for sale, or to find jobs. Newmark steadfastly refused to add flashy graphics, high-tech programming, or other features to his site. He also refused many offers to purchase his newsletter. He spent seven days a week keeping his newsletter's content reliable and free of e-mail spams and scams. His grateful visitors have since come to rely on Craigslist's content as 'for real' rather than a come-on, and they faithfully trust it and use it.

The work has generated a substantial income for Craigslist. Reportedly, its annual income approaches $10 million (£5.5 million) (as reported by Newmark's assistant in an article at www.signonsandiego.com/uniontrib/20040913/news_mz1b13craig.html). That income apparently comes not from flashy banner ads or pop-up windows, but from users who pay to post classified ads: Employers pay from $25 to $75 to post job listings, depending on

the city in which they're located. eBay purchased a 25 per cent interest in Craigslist, but has pledged not to change the design. Newmark reportedly wants eBay to help him deflect constant approaches from spammers and scammers.

The same goes for Popbitch, the wildly popular gossip newsletter based in the UK. The style is as basic as it gets, and even the logo is composed of hyphens and forward and backslashes – hardly what you'd call hi-tech. Yet with this simple formula, Web site creator Camilla Wright has attracted 360,000 subscribers to her weekly newsletter (that's more than *The Independent* newspaper). It's just a mix of plain text and links, yet it makes more than £100,000 a year in revenues.

Of course, the best example of a plain Web site making it big is Google (www.google.co.uk), which has merely a search box and a couple of links on its home page, yet is worth billions.

What's the lesson for you? When you're just starting out, it pays to:

✔ Focus on the quality of your content.

✔ Make your site useful for individuals.

✔ Develop a loyal customer or user base.

✔ Knock yourself out to keep your site up to date.

If you can turn your Web site into a resource, income will follow.

Market research

Given the sheer number of consumers who are on the Web, it stands to reason that you can find out a lot about those individuals by going online. If you don't have any awareness of who your potential customers are and what they want, you may never get them to pull out their credit cards. You can do your own market research by going online to find your customers, listen to their views in chat rooms and on discussion forums, and do some market research. Approach consumers who already buy the types of products or services that you want to sell.

Consult the Guerrilla Marketing books (`gmarketing.com`) for insights into different ways to reach your target consumers.

The other aspect of market research that is perfectly executed with a Web browser is research into your own online competitors – businesses that already do what you hope to do. It can be discouraging, at first, to discover companies that have already cleared the trail that you hoped to blaze. The chances of doing something absolutely unique on the Web are small, but use the discovery as an educational opportunity to find out whether a market exists for your product and a way to sell it that differs from existing competitors. Take note of features displayed by your competitors' Web sites, such as the following:

- ✔ **Selling:** How does the Web site do its selling? Does it sell only in one location, or does its Web site supplement eBay.co.uk or Amazon.co.uk sales or a brick-and-mortar business? Does the site make suggestions about related items that a consumer may want (a practice known as up-selling)?

- ✔ **Design:** How does the site look? Is it well put together? What makes it attractive and does it draw you in? It's not the same to ask, Is it pretty? Many ugly Web sites are also virtual gold mines. (See the sidebar 'No bells, no whistles, all trust: The beauty of Craigslist', earlier in this chapter).

- ✔ **Organisation:** How is the Web site organised? Is it easy to find specific products or information about them? How many navigational aids (navigation bars, drop-down menu lists, site maps, and the like) are provided?

- ✔ **Depth:** How many levels of information are included on the Web site? The more information is offered on the site, the *stickier* (more able to hold a visitor's attention) the site becomes. Try to imagine how your customers will react to the content on your Web site; are they encouraged to plough on, uncovering new content, or better yet click through to buy some of your stuff?

In your review of the competition's Web presentation, make a list of features that you can emulate as well as features you can improve on. Your goal should not be to copy the site, but to discover your own unique niche and identify customers whose needs may not be addressed by the other venue.

 Don't you wish you could install a hidden microphone to eavesdrop on your customers as they surf the Web? You can do some eavesdropping, but on a different part of the Internet – namely, Usenet. *Usenet,* the part of the Internet that consists of thousands of newsgroups, is separate from the Web but can be accessed from the Web through sites such as www.usenet.org.uk. You can 'listen in' on newsgroup discussions by finding groups that fit your type of commerce and then *lurking* – that is, reading the messages without responding to them. After acquainting yourself with the group's concerns, you can post your own newsgroup messages and begin to determine your customers' concerns more directly. Keep in mind, though, that it's important to avoid overt advertising for your business in a newsgroup, which can provoke an angry response from the group's membership.

Web 2.0 – What on Earth Does That Mean?

The phrase *Web 2.0* doesn't just mean the second generation of the Internet, although faster connections and greater bandwidth underpins it. In essence, Web 2.0 refers to the ability to collaborate and share information online, in a way that we weren't capable of doing just a few years ago.

Web 1.0 was all one-way traffic. A webmaster would stick something on a site, and you'd either read it or buy it. Now, users are demanding greater involvement in their Web experiences. They don't just want to look at Web sites, they want to help build them! Web sites like MySpace (www.myspace.com), Bebo (www.bebo.co.uk), Digger (www.digger.com), YouTube (www.youtube.com), and hundreds of others all rely on contributions from people like you and us to survive.

It all derives from people's desire to talk about themselves, or to put it another way, to be famous and respected. If you can offer this service to them in an innovative way, then you're bound to build traffic quickly. The great thing about Web 2.0 is that other people populate the site, so you need fewer resources to get the thing going. Bebo, for example, is rumoured to be worth more than £100 million, yet it employs just 12 staff members.

Web sites like Friends Reunited (www.friendsreunited.com) started the craze, by allowing people to write about themselves and seek out old pals. Other sites, such as Startups (www.startups.co.uk), set up forums so that users (in this case, startup businesses) could ask questions and chat about their experiences.

Wikis (Web sites that allow anyone to add their content), *social bookmarking* (the act of bookmarking your favourite Web sites for other like-minded people to share), *podcasting* (downloading audio files), and *vodcasting* (the same but for visual files) have developed from this trend. Now sites from the BBC to Google and Amazon use these cool tools.

The most famous example of a Wiki is Wikipedia.com, which has 5 million pages of content contributed by the public. The Web site is an encyclopaedia of people's knowledge, and despite the fact that anyone can edit it, it's almost totally accurate.

Pod and vodcasting are expensive and certainly don't suit all businesses. A few companies offer to film or tape things for you and convert the information into a downloadable file for your Web site, but it can cost hundreds of pounds a time.

If you want to learn more about what Web 2.0 really means, check out this short essay by Internet expert Tim O'Reilly. It's a nice comprehensive overview of what you need to know:

www.oreillynet.com/pub/a/oreilly/tim/news/2005/09/30/what-is-web-20.html

Part II
Establishing Your Online Presence

'My friends on the dock helped me
with the slogan.'

In this part . . .

Just as business owners in the real world have to rent or buy a facility and fix it up to conduct their businesses, you have to develop an online storefront to conduct your online business. In this part, we explain how to put a virtual roof over your store and light a cyberfire to welcome your customers. You also find out about security strategies to protect your customers' privacy. In other words, this part focuses on the nuts and bolts of your Web site itself.

The World Wide Web is the most exciting and popular place to open an online store. But merely creating a set of Web pages isn't enough to succeed online. Your site needs to be compelling – even irresistible. This part shows you how to organize your site and fill it with useful content that attracts customers in the first place and encourages them to stay to browse. We also show you how to get your pages up and running quickly, to equip your site (and yourself) to handle many different kinds of electronic purchases, and to keep improving your site so that it runs more efficiently.

Chapter 5

Giving Your E-Business Site Structure and Style

In This Chapter

▶ Creating a simple and well-organised business site

▶ Establishing a graphic identity through colour and type

▶ Scanning, cropping, and retouching photos

▶ Using Web page frames and tables effectively

*N*ot so long ago, a business that was on the World Wide Web was distinctive by definition. Nowadays, it seems that every business – from your local newsagent to international conglomerates – is on the Web. As cyberspace fills up with small businesses trying to find their niches, standing out from the crowd and attracting attention on the Internet becomes increasingly difficult.

But the same tried and tested principles apply, even though Web surfers are increasingly mobile and increasingly accustomed to sophisticated content. You don't have to load your site with scripts, animations, and flashy gimmicks. Often, the trick is to have no trick: Keep your site simple, well organised, and content rich.

In this chapter, we present one of the best ways for a new business to attract attention online: through a clearly organised and eye-catching Web site. (Another strategy for attracting visitors – developing promotions and content that encourages interaction – is the subject of Chapter 6.)

Feng Shui Your Web Site

According to the Web site The Geomancer (`thegeomancer.netfirms.com/ fengshui.htm`), *Feng Shui* is the art of arranging objects in an environment to achieve (among other things) success in your career, wealth, and happiness. If that's true, you should try to practise some Feng Shui with your online business environment, too.

You may be tempted to rush into the process of designing and building your Web site, but while enthusiasm is always a good thing, you should try to think with a clear head and take time to plan what you're going to do. Whether you're setting off on a road trip across the country or building a new extension on your house, you'll progress more smoothly by drawing a blueprint of how you want to progress. Do you remember when you were a tiny little nipper and did your homework with a pencil and paper? Dig 'em out again and make a list of the elements you want to have on your site.

Look over the items on your list and break them into two or three main categories. These main categories will branch off your *home page,* which functions as the grand entrance for your online business site. You can then draw a map of your site that assumes the shape of a triangle, as shown in Figure 5-1.

Figure 5-1: A home page is the point from which your site branches into more specific levels of information.

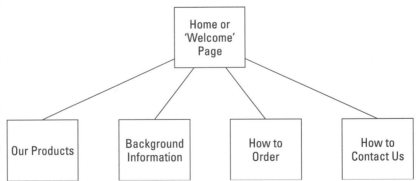

Note: The page heading 'Background Information' is a placeholder for detailed information about some aspect of your online business. For Greg's brother's audio restoration business, he suggested including a page of technical information listing the equipment he uses and describing the steps he takes to process audio. You can write about your experience with and love for what you buy and sell, or anything else that will personalise your site and build trust.

The preceding example results in a very simple Web site. But there's nothing wrong with starting out simple. For Greg's brother, who is creating his first Web site and is intimidated by getting started, this simple model is working well. Many other businesses start with a three-layered organisation for their Web sites. This arrangement divides the site into two sections, one about the company and one about the products or services for sale (see Figure 5-2).

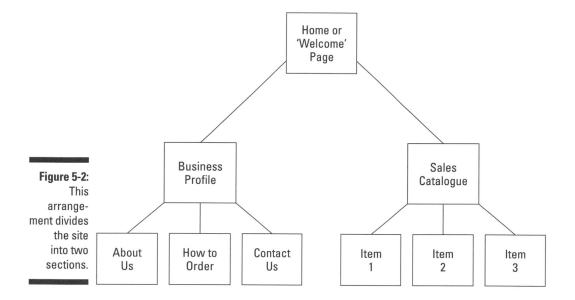

Figure 5-2:
This arrange-
ment divides
the site
into two
sections.

Think of your home page as the lobby of a museum where you get the help of the friendly person at the information desk who hands you a list of the special exhibits you can visit that day and shows you a map so that you can begin to figure out how you're going to get from here to there. Remember to include the following items on your home page:

- ✔ The name of the shop or business
- ✔ Your logo, if you have one
- ✔ Links to the main areas of your site or, if your site isn't overly extensive, to every page
- ✔ Contact information, such as your e-mail address, phone/fax numbers, and (optionally) your business address so that people know where to find you in the Land Beyond Cyberspace

Making them fall in love at first site

First impressions are critical on the Web, where shoppers have the ability to jump from site to site with a click of the mouse button. A few extra seconds of downtime waiting for complex images or mini-computer programs called *Java applets* to download can cause your prospective buyer to lose patience and you to lose a sale.

How do you make visitors to your welcome page feel like they are being greeted with open arms? Here are some suggestions:

✔ **Keep it simple.** Don't overload any one page with more than three or four images. Keep all images 20K or less in size.

✔ **Find a fast host.** Some Web servers have super-fast connections to the Internet and others use slower lines. Test your site; if your pages take more than a couple of seconds to appear, ask your host company why and find out whether they can move you to a faster machine.

✔ **Offer a bargain.** Nothing attracts attention as much as a contest, a giveaway, or a special sales promotion. If you have anything that you can give away, either through a contest or a deep discount, do it. See Chapter 6 for more ideas.

✔ **Provide instant gratification.** Make sure that your most important information appears at or near the top of your page. Readers on the Web don't like having to scroll through several screens worth of material in order to get to the information they want.

Nip and Tuck: Establishing a Visual Identity

The prospect of designing a Web site may be intimidating if you haven't tried it before. But just remember that it really boils down to a simple principle: *effective visual communication that conveys a particular message.* The first step in creating graphics is not to open a painting program and start drawing, but rather to plan your page's message. Next, determine the audience you want to reach with that message and think about how your graphics can best communicate what you want to say. Some ways to do this follow:

✔ Gather ideas from Web sites that use graphics well – both award-winning sites and sites created by designers who are using graphics in new or unusual ways. To find some award winners, check out The Webby Awards (www.webbyawards.com), The International Web Page Awards (www.websiteawards.com), and the Interactive Media Awards (www.interactivemediaawards.com).

> ✔ Use graphics consistently from page to page to create an identity and convey a consistent message.
>
> ✔ Create graphics that meet visitors' needs and expectations. If you're selling fashions to teenagers, go for out-there graphics. If you're selling financial advice to OAPs, choose a distinguished and sophisticated typeface.

How do you become acquainted with your customers when it is likely that you will never meet them face to face? Find newsgroups and mailing lists in which potential visitors to your site are discussing subjects related to what you plan to publish on the Web. You'd be amazing what people are blogging about these days. Don't believe us? Go to www.blogger.com and type *sandwich* or some other obscure subject matter into the search bar. We guarantee you'll be met with a string of blog posts. Now try again with a term relevant to your business. Read the posted messages to get a sense of the concerns and vocabulary of your intended audience.

Wallpaper that will wow

The proper term for the wallpaper behind the contents of a Web page is its *background*. Most Web browsers display the background of a page as light grey or blue unless you specify something different. In this case, leaving it alone isn't good enough. If you don't choose a different colour, viewers are likely to get the impression that the page is poorly designed or that the author of the page hasn't put a great deal of thought into the project. So even a neutral colour, such as white, is better than grey.

You can change the background of your Web page by tinkering with the HTML source code, but why would you want to? Most Web page creation programs offer a simple way to specify a colour or an image file to serve as the background of a Web page. For example, in an HTML editor called Netscape Composer, a free and easily overlooked Web page design tool that comes with the Netscape Communicator Web browser package, you use the Page Colours and Background dialog box (see Figure 5-3) to set your Web page wallpaper.

Colour your Web site effective

You can use colours to elicit a particular mood or emotion and also to convey your organisation's identity on the Web. The right choice of colour can create impressions ranging from elegant to funky.

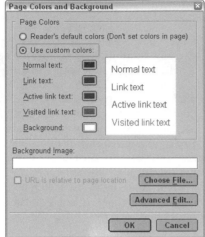

Figure 5-3:
Most Web page editors let you specify background image/ colour options in a dialog box like this.

The basic colour scheme chosen by the phone group T-Mobile (www. t-mobile.co.uk) conveys to customers its professionalism, yet also gives an impression of being with it – cool if you will. Compare that to Dan's favourite Web site, brought to you by John Cleese (www.thejohncleese.com), which is a riot of colour and movement. Remember that while it's a personal Web site, a huge business operation is behind it. Note how many items on the Web site are for sale, as well as the fact that you can pay to become a member.

When selecting colours for your own Web pages, consider the demographics of your target audience. Do some research on what emotions or impressions are conveyed by different colours and which colours best match the remit or identity of your business. Refer to resources such as the online essay by Noble Image Web Design (www.nobleimage.com/no_flash/articles/ color_choices.htm), which examines in some detail the subject of how colour choices make Web surfers react differently.

Even if you have the taste of a professional designer, you need to be aware of what happens to colour on the Web. The best colour choices for Web backgrounds are ones that don't shift dramatically from browser to browser or platform to platform. The best palette for use on the Web is a set of 216 colours that is common to all browsers. These are called *browser-safe colours* because they appear pretty much the same from browser to browser and on different monitors. The palette itself appears on Victor Engel's Web site (the-light.com/netcol.html).

Keep in mind that the colours you use must have contrast so that they don't blend into one another. For example, you don't want to put purple type on a brown or blue background, or yellow type on a white background. Remember to use light type against a dark background, and dark type against a light background. That way, all your page's contents will show up.

Sometimes your own instincts are the best way to decide what colours to use. Do you need to attract kids with wild designs? Or would that put off your older, more discerning customers? Pay attention to your gut reactions, then get feedback from your colleagues, and test your choice on a few sample members of your audience before you make your final decision.

Tiling images in the background

You can use an image rather than a solid colour to serve as the background of a page. You specify an image in the HTML code of your Web page (or in your Web page editor), and browsers automatically *tile* the image, reproducing it over and over to fill up the current width and height of the browser window.

Background images only work when they're subtle and don't interfere with the page contents. Be careful to choose an image that doesn't have any obvious lines that will create a distracting pattern when tiled. The effect you're trying to create should literally resemble wallpaper.

What you absolutely don't want to have happen is that the background image makes the page unreadable. Visit the Maine Solar House home page (www. solarhouse.com), shown later in Figure 5-8, for a rare example of a background image that is faint enough to not interfere with foreground images and that actually adds something to the page's design.

Using Web typefaces like a pro

If you create a Web page and don't specify that the text be displayed in a particular font, the browser that displays the page will use its default font – which is usually Times or Helvetica (although individual users can customise their browsers by picking a different default font).

However, you don't have to limit yourself to the same-old, same-old. As a Web page designer, you can exercise a degree of control over the appearance of your Web page by specifying that the body type and headings be displayed in a particular nonstandard font. A few of the choices available to you have names such as Arial, Courier, Century Schoolbook, and so on.

But just because you fall in love with a particular typeface doesn't mean your audience will be able to admire it in all its beauty. The problem is that you don't have ultimate control over whether a given browser will display the specified typeface because you don't know for sure whether the individual user's system has access to your preferred typefaces. If the particular font you specified is not available, the browser will fall back on its default font (which, again, is probably Helvetica or Times).

That's why, generally speaking, when you design Web pages, you're better off picking a generic typeface that is built into virtually every computer's operating system. This convention ensures that your Web pages look more or less the same no matter what Web browser or what type of computer displays them.

Where, exactly, do you specify type fonts, colours, and sizes for the text on a Web page? Again, special HTML tags tell Web browsers what fonts to display, but you don't need to mess with these tags yourself if you're using a Web page creation tool. The specific steps you take depend on what Web design tool you're using. In Dreamweaver, you have the option of specifying a group of preferred typefaces rather than a single font in the Property Inspector (see Figure 5-4). If the viewer doesn't have one font in the group, another font is displayed. Check the Help files with your own program to find out exactly how to format text and what typeface options you have.

Figure 5-4: Most Web page design tools let you specify a preferred font or fonts for your Web page in a dialog box like this.

Not all typefaces are equal in the eye of the user. Serif typefaces, such as Times Roman, are considered to be more readable (at least, for printed materials) than sans-serif fonts, such as Helvetica. However, an article on the Web Marketing Today Web site (www.wilsonweb.com/wmt6/html-email-fonts.htm) found that by a whopping two-to-one margin, the sans-serif font Arial is considered more readable on a Web page than Times Roman.

If you want to make sure that a heading or block of type appears in a specific typeface (especially a nonstandard one that isn't displayed as body text by Web browsers), scan it or create the heading in an image-editing program and insert it into the page as a graphic image. But make sure that it doesn't clash with the generic typefaces that appear on the rest of your page.

Clip art is free and fun

Not everyone has the time or resources to scan or download photos, or create their own original graphics. But that doesn't mean you can't add graphic interest to your Web page. Many Web page designers use clip-art bullets, diamonds, or other small images next to list items or major Web page headings to which they want to call special attention. Clip art can also provide a background pattern for a Web page or highlight sales headings such as Free!, New!, or Special!

When Greg first started out in the print publications business, he bought catalogues of illustrations, literally clipped out the art, and pasted it down. It's still called clip art, but now the process is different. In keeping with the spirit of exchange that has been a part of the Internet since its inception, some talented and generous artists have created icons, buttons, and other illustrations in electronic form and offered them free for downloading.

Here are some suggestions for sources of clip art on the Web:

- Clip Art Warehouse (www.clipart.co.uk)
- Cool Clips (www.coolclips.com)
- ZeroWeb (www.zeroweb.org)

If you use Microsoft Office, you have access to plenty of clip art images that come with the software. If you're using Word, just choose Insert➪Picture➪ Clip Art to view clip art images as displayed in the Insert Picture dialog box. If these built-in images aren't sufficient, you can also connect to a special Microsoft Office online by clicking the Clip Art On Office Online toolbar button in the Insert Clip Art dialog box. Web page editors – such as Microsoft FrontPage and CoffeeCup HTML Editor – come with their own clip art libraries, too.

Be sure to read the copyright fine print *before* you copy graphics. All artists own the copyright to their work. It's up to them to determine how they want to give someone else the right to copy their work. Sometimes, the authors require you to pay a small fee if you want to copy their work, or they may restrict use of their work to not-for-profit organisations.

A picture is worth a thousand words

Some customers know exactly what they want from the get-go and don't need any help from you. But most customers love to shop around or could use some encouragement to move from one item or catalogue page to another. This is where images can play an important role.

Even if you use only basic clip art, such as placing spheres or arrows next to sale items, your customer is likely to thank you by buying more. A much better approach, though, is to scan or take digital images of your sale items and provide compact, clear images of them on your site. Here's a quick step-by-step guide to get you started:

1. **Choose the right image to scan.**

   After you purchase a scanner or digital camera (see the suggestions in Chapter 2), the next step is to select images (if you're going to scan) or take images (if you're using a camera) that are well illuminated, have good contrast, and are relatively small in size.

   The original quality of an image is just as important as how you scan or retouch it. Images that are murky or fuzzy in print will be even worse when viewed on a computer screen.

2. **Preview the image.**

   Most digital cameras let you preview images so that you can decide whether to keep or delete individual pictures before downloading to your computer. If you're working with a scanner, scanning programs let you make a quick *preview scan* of an image so that you can get an idea of what it looks like before you do the actual scan. When you press the Preview button, you hear a whirring sound as the optical device in the scanner captures the image. A preview image appears on-screen, surrounded by a rectangle made up of dashes, as shown in Figure 5-5.

Figure 5-5:
The software lets you crop a preview image to make it smaller and reduce the file size.

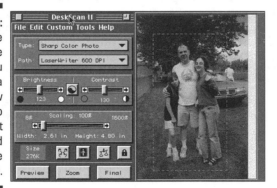

3. **Crop the image.**

   Cropping an image is a good idea because it highlights the most important contents and reduces the file size. Reducing the file size of an image should always be a primary goal – the smaller the image, the quicker it appears in someone's browser window. *Cropping* means that you resize the box around the image in order to select the portion of the image that you want to keep and leave out the parts of the image that aren't essential.

Almost all scanning and graphics programs offer separate options for cropping an image and reducing the image size. By cropping the image, you eliminate parts of the image you don't want, which *does* reduce the image size. But it doesn't reduce the size of the objects within the image. Resizing the overall image size is a separate step, which enables you to change the dimensions of the entire image without eliminating any contents.

4. **Select an input mode.**

   Tell the scanner or graphics program how you want it to save the visual data – as colour, line art (used for black-and-white drawings), or greyscale (used for black-and-white photos).

5. **Set the resolution.**

   In Chapter 2, we note that digital images are made up of little bits (dots) of computerised information called *pixels*. The more pixels per inch, the higher the level of detail. When you scan an image, you can tell the scanner to make the dots smaller (creating a smoother image) or larger (resulting in a more jagged image). This adjustment is called *setting the resolution* of the image. (When you take a digital photo, the resolution of the image depends on your camera's settings.)

How many dots per inch (dpi) do you want your image to be? When you're scanning for the Web, you expect your images to appear primarily on computer screens. Because many computer monitors can display resolutions only up to 72 dpi, 72 dpi – a relatively rough resolution – is an adequate resolution for a Web image. (By contrast, many laser printers print at a resolution of 600 dpi.) But using this coarse resolution has the advantage of keeping the image's file size small. Remember, the smaller the file size, the more quickly an image appears when your customers load your page in their Web browsers.

6. **Adjust contrast and brightness.**

   Virtually all scanning programs and graphics editing programs provide brightness and contrast controls that you can adjust with your mouse to improve the image. If you're happy with the image as is, leave the brightness and contrast set where they are. (You can also leave the image as is and adjust brightness and contrast later in a separate graphics program, such as Paint Shop Pro, which you can try out by downloading it from the Corel Web site (www.corel.co.uk).

7. **Reduce the image size.**

   The old phrase 'good things come in small packages' is never more true than when you're improving your digital image. If you're scanning an image that is 8" x 10" and you're sure that it needs to be about 4" x 5" when it appears on your Web page, scan it at 50 per cent of the original size. This step reduces the file size right away and makes the file easier to transport. That's really important if you have to put it on a floppy disk to move it from one computer to another.

8. **Scan away!**

   Your scanner makes a beautiful whirring sound as it turns those colours into pixels. Because you're scanning only at 72 dpi, the process shouldn't take too long.

9. **Save the file.**

   Now you can save your image to disk. Most programs let you do so by choosing File⇨Save. In the dialog box that appears, enter a name for your file and select a file format. (Because you're working with images to be published on the Web, remember to save either in GIF or JPEG format.)

Accommodating your viewers

Recent surveys show that broadband connections are taking over regular dialup connections. More people are using them because they're quicker and no longer cost the earth. But the many Web surfers who still have very slow Internet connections (or very low tolerances for waiting) may not have the bandwidth to display even ordinary images quickly enough. And, although it may be tempting to show off, you may as well forget about presenting such content as live video, teleconferencing, and other graphics files on the Web. After many minutes or even just seconds of waiting, the surfer is likely to hit the browser's Stop button, with the result that no graphics appear at all.

How do you prevent customers from blocking out your beautiful graphics and ruining the whole effect? Some alternatives include:

✔ Creating low-resolution alternatives to high-resolution graphics, such as thumbnails (postage-stamp sized versions of larger images)

✔ Cropping images to keep them small

✔ Using line art whenever possible, rather than high-resolution photos

By using the same image more than once on a Web page, you can give the impression of greater activity but yet not slow down the appearance of the entire page. Why? If you repeat the same image three times, your customer's browser has to download the image file only once. It stores the image in a storage area, called *disk cache,* on the user's hard drive. To display the other instances of the image, the browser retrieves the file from the disk cache, so the second and third images appear much more quickly than the first one did.

Users can also disable image display altogether so that they don't see graphics on any of the sites they visit. The solution: Always provide a simple textual alternative to your images so that, if the user has disabled the display of a particular image, a word or two describing that image appears in its place.

When you give your image a name, be sure to add the correct filename extension. Web browsers recognise only image files with extensions such as `.gif`, `.jpg`, or `.jpeg`. If you name your image product and save it in GIF format, call it `product.gif`. If you save it in JPEG format and you're using a PC, call it `product.jpg`. On a Macintosh, call it `product.jpeg`.

For more details on scanning images, check out *Scanning For Dummies,* 2nd Edition, by Mark Chambers (Wiley).

Creating a logo

An effective logo establishes your online business's graphic identity in no uncertain terms. A logo can be as simple as a rendering of the company name that imparts an official typeface or colour. Whatever text it includes, a logo is a small, self-contained graphic object that conveys the group's identity and purpose. Figure 5-6 shows an example of a logo.

A logo doesn't have to be a fabulously complex drawing with drop-shadows and gradations of colour. A simple, type-only logo can be as good work as well. Pick a typeface you want, choose your graphic's outline version, and fill the letters with colour.

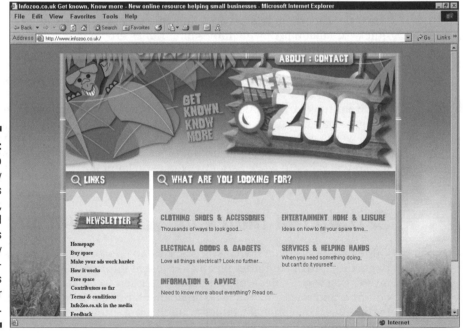

Figure 5-6:
A good logo effectively combines colour, type, and graphics to convey an organisation's identity or mission.

GIF versus JPEG

Web site technology and HTML may have changed dramatically over the past few years, but for the most part, there are only two types of images as far as Web pages are concerned: GIF and JPEG. Both formats use methods that compress computer image files so that the visual information contained within them can be transmitted easily over computer networks. (PNG, a third format designed a few years ago as a successor to GIF, is appearing online more and more, but it still isn't as widely used as GIF.)

GIF stands for Graphics Interchange Format. GIF is best suited to text, line art, or images with well-defined edges. Special types of GIF allow images with transparent backgrounds to be interlaced (broken into layers that appear gradually over slow connections) and animated. JPEG (pronounced 'jay-peg') stands for Joint Photographic Experts Group, the name of the group that originated the format. JPEG is preferred for large photos and continuous tones of grayscale or colour that need greater compression.

Extreme Web Pages: Advanced Layouts

People who have some experience creating Web sites typically use frames and tables. On the other hand, they may be right up the street of an adventurous type who wants to start an online business. So this section includes some quick explanations of what tables and frames are so that you know where to start when, and if, you decide you do want to use them.

We should point out that learning HTML is almost like learning a foreign language. Of course, you don't to speak HTML, but you do have to know it well if you want to get by. If you're taking the HTML route, as opposed to paying a designer or using standard WISYWIG software, then you must spend at least a few weeks getting to know it well before you have a crack at creating your Web site. Remember: People are put off easily by poor design and functionality, so yours has to work perfectly when you launch it.

Setting the tables for your customers

Tables are to designers what statistics are to sports fans. In the case of a Web page, they provide another means to present information in a graphically interesting way. Tables were originally intended to present tabular data in columns and rows, much like a spreadsheet. But by using advanced HTML techniques, you can make tables a much more integrated and subtle part of your Web page.

Because you can easily create a basic table by using Web page editors, such as Dreamweaver and FrontPage, starting with one of these tools makes sense. Some adjustments with HTML are probably unavoidable, however, especially if you want to use tables to create blank columns on a Web page (as we explain later in this section). Here is a quick rundown of the main HTML tags used for tables:

- ✔ `<TABLE>` `</TABLE>` encloses the entire table. The `BORDER` attribute sets the width of the line around the cells.

- ✔ `<TR>` `</TR>` encloses a table row, a horizontal set of cells.

- ✔ `<TD>` `</TD>` defines the contents of an individual cell. The `HEIGHT` and `WIDTH` attributes control the size of each cell. For example, the following code tells a browser that the table cell is 120 pixels wide:

```
<TD WIDTH=120> Contents of cell </TD>
```

A quick HTML primer

Thanks to Web page creation tools, you don't have to master HyperText Markup Language in order to create your own Web pages, although some knowledge of HTML is helpful when it comes to editing pages and understanding how they're put together.

HTML is a markup language, not a computer programming language. You use it in much the same way that old-fashioned editors marked up copy before they gave it to typesetters. A markup language allows you to identify major sections of a document, such as body text, headings, title, and so on. A software program (in the case of HTML, a Web browser) is programmed to recognise the markup language and to display the formatting elements that you have marked.

Markup tags are the basic building blocks of HTML as well as its more complex and powerful cousin, eXtensible Markup Language (XML). Tags enable you to structure the appearance of your document so that, when it's transferred from one computer to another, it will look the way you described it. HTML tags appear within carrot-shaped brackets. Most HTML commands require a *start tag* at the beginning of the

section and an *end tag* (which usually begins with a backslash) at the end.

For example, if you place the HTML tags `<B>` and `</B>` around the phrase 'This text will be bold', the words appear in bold type on any browser that displays them, no matter if it's running on a Windows-based PC, a UNIX workstation, a Macintosh, a palm device that's Web enabled, or any other computer.

Many HTML commands are accompanied by *attributes,* which provide a browser with more specific instructions on what action the tag is to perform. In the following lines of HTML, `SRC` is an attribute that works with the `<IMG>` tag to identify a file to display:

```
<IMG SRC="house.jpg">
```

Each attribute is separated from an HTML command by a single blank space. The equal sign (=) is an operator that introduces the value on which the attribute and command will function. Usually, the value is a filename or a directory path leading to a specific file that is to be displayed on a Web page. The straight (as opposed to curly) quotation marks around the value are essential for the HTML command to work.

Don't forget that the cells in a table can contain images as well as text. Also, individual cells can have different colours from the cells around them. You can add a background colour to a table cell by adding the BGCOLOR attribute to the <TD> table cell tag.

The clever designer can use tables in a hidden way to arrange an entire page, or a large portion of a page, by doing two things:

- ✔ Set the table border to 0. Doing so makes the table outline invisible, so the viewer sees only the contents of each cell, not the lines bordering the cell.

- ✔ Fill some table cells with blank space so that they act as empty columns that add more white space to a page.

An example of the first approach, that of making the table borders invisible, appears in Figure 5-7, David Nishimura's Vintage Pens Web site (www. vintagepens.com), where he sells vintage writing instruments.

Figure 5-7:
This page is divided into table cells, which give the designer a high level of control over the layout.

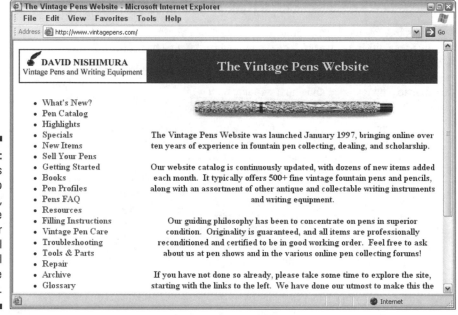

Framing your subject

Frames are subdivisions of a Web page, each consisting of its own separate Web document. Depending on how the designer sets up the Web page, visitors may be able to scroll through one frame independently of the other frames on the same page. A mouse click on a hypertext link contained in one frame may cause a new document to appear in an adjacent frame.

Simple two-frame layouts such as the one used by one of Greg's personal favourite Web sites, Maine Solar House (see Figure 5-8), can be very effective. A page can be broken into as many frames as the designer wants, but you typically want to stick with only two to four frames because they make the page considerably more complex and slower to appear in its entirety.

Frames fit within the BODY section of an HTML document. In fact, the <FRAMESET> </FRAMESET> tags actually take the place of the <BODY> </BODY> tags and are used to enclose the rest of the frame-specific elements. Each of the frames on the page is then described by <FRAME> </FRAME> tags.

Figure 5-8: This site uses a classic two-frame layout: A column of links in the narrow frame on the left changes the content in the frame on the right.

Only the more advanced Web page creation programs provide you with menu options and toolbar buttons that enable you to create frames without having to enter the HTML manually. Most of the popular Web page editors do this, including Adobe Dreamweaver and HotDog Professional by Sausage Software. See each program's Help topics for specific instructions on how to implement framing tools.

Breaking the grid with layers

Tables and frames bring organisation and interactivity to Web pages, but they confine your content to rows and columns. If you feel confined by the old up-down, left-right routine, explore layers for arranging your Web page content.

Layers, like table cells and frames, act as containers for text and images on a Web page. Layers are unique because you can move them around freely on the page – they can overlap one another, and they can 'bleed' right to the page margin.

Layers carry some big downsides: You can't create them with just any Web editor. Macromedia Dreamweaver is the Web editor of choice, and it's not free. (At time of writing, Dreamweaver Version 8 costs around £280-£300.) Layers are supported only by Versions 4.0 or later of Microsoft Internet Explorer or Netscape Navigator. However, Dreamweaver lets you create a layout in layers and then convert it to tables, which are supported by almost all browsers.

With Dreamweaver, you can draw a layer directly on the Web page you're creating. You add text or images to the layer and then resize or relocate it on the page by clicking and dragging it freely. The result is some innovative page designs that don't conform to the usual grid.

Hiring a Professional Web Designer

Part of the fun of running your own business is doing things yourself. So it comes as no surprise that many of the entrepreneurs we interviewed in the course of writing this book do their own Web page design, despite the extra time requirement and the fact that designers generally do it better! They discovered how to create Web sites by reading books or taking classes on the subject. But in many cases, the initial cost of hiring someone to help you design your online business can be a good investment in the long run. Dan, whose HTML is about as good as his Swahili, employed a Web design company to construct his Web site (www.infozoo.co.uk). The results are very professional and would take the average person a lot of time and expense to mimic. Keep in mind that after you pay someone to help you develop a look, you may be able to implement it in the future more easily yourself. For example:

- ✔ If you need business cards, stationery, brochures, or other printed material in addition to a Web site, hiring someone to develop a consistent look for everything at the beginning is worth the money.

- ✔ You can pay a designer to get you started with a logo, colour selections, and page layouts. Then you can save money by adding text yourself.

- ✔ If, like Greg (apparently), you're artistically impaired, consider the benefits of having your logo or other artwork drawn by a real artist.

Professional designers charge up to £100 per hour for their work (which is less than the average plumber). You can expect a designer to spend five or six hours to create a logo or template. But if your company uses that initial design for the foreseeable future, you're not really paying that much per year.

In this case, as in all others, ask friends and family to help first. Dan's got a couple of pals who are really artistic and have some technical knowledge, too. If you're in the same boat, then you can save some serious cash.

Chapter 6

Attracting and Keeping Customers

● ●

In This Chapter

▶ Creating compelling content through links and hooks

▶ Promoting your business by providing objective, useful information

▶ Making less do more through concise, well-organised content

▶ Writing friendly, objective prose that sells your products and services

▶ Inviting customer interaction with forms, e-mail, and more

● ●

*A*s writers, we know only too well the challenge of staring at a totally white piece of paper or a blank computer screen. It's at times like these that Greg remembers his teacher telling him to 'let it flow' and worry about editing after he'd let his creative juices flow. That's good advice up to a point, especially for something like a Web log (blog). But when it comes to a business Web site, you have to get it just right before you invite people to have a look. You need to present the *right* content in the *right* way to make prospective clients and customers want to explore your site the first time and then return down the road.

One of our primary points in this chapter is that you need to express your main message on your business site up front. We do the same by explaining what we consider to be general content rules for an online business. You should

✔ Remember that people who are online get bored quickly

✔ Make it easy for visitors to find out who you are and what you have to offer

✔ Be friendly and informal in tone, concise in length, and clear in your material's structure

✔ Develop the all-important one-to-one-relationship with customers and clients by inviting dialogue and interaction, both with you and with others who share the same interests

In other words, you need to be straightforward about who you are and where you're coming from on your business site. This chapter is obviously about writing for the Web. But the idea is not to be satisfied with generating just any old text. The goal is to craft exciting, well-organised, and easily digestible information. What follows is how to put these objectives into action.

Including Features That Attract Customers

Half the battle with developing content for a business Web site is knowing what shoppers want and determining strategies for giving it to them. Identifying your target audience helps you devise a message that will make each potential customer think you're speaking directly to him or her. But you also should keep in mind some general concepts that can help you market successfully to all ages, both genders, and every socioeconomic group.

Studies of how people absorb the information on a Web page indicate that people don't really read the contents from top to bottom (or left to right, for that matter) in a linear way. In fact, most Web surfers don't *read* in the traditional sense at all. Instead, they browse so quickly that you'd think they're on a timer. They 'skip through pages' by clicking link after link. As more Internet users connect with broadband technologies, such as DSL and cable, they can absorb complex graphics and multimedia. On average, people stay on each Web page for just a few seconds, unless they find something that really grabs them. Next time you're online for half an hour or so, press the Back button and check out the Web pages you've visited; you'll be amazed at how many you've browsed.

In addition, lots of users are beginning to use palm devices, pocket PCs, Web-enabled cell phones, and even Internet-ready automobiles to get online. These new devices only add to the 'can't hang about' Web surfing trend. Because your prospective customers don't necessarily have tons of computing power or hours' worth of time to explore your site, the best rule is to keep it simple.

People who are looking for things on the Web are often in a state of hurried distraction. Think about a television watcher browsing during a commercial or a harried parent stealing a few moments on the computer while the baby naps, or even, dare we say, while at work when they're supposed to be concentrating on other things. Imagine this person surfing with one hand on a mouse, the other dipping tortillas into salsa. This person – your average customer – isn't in the mood to listen as you tell your fondest hopes and dreams for success, which started with selling sweets in the playground. Here's what this shopper is probably thinking:

'Look, I don't have time to read all this. My show is about to come back on, and I still need to go to the bathroom.'

'What's this? Why does this page take so long to load? And I paid good money to get a quick broadband! I swear, sometimes I wish the Web didn't have any graphics. Here, I'll click this. No, wait! I'll click that. Oh, no, now the baby is crying again.'

The following sections describe some ways to attract the attention of the distracted and get them to scroll down exactly where you want them to go.

Don't be shy about what you have to say

Don't keep people in suspense about what your business does. People in general, and Web users in particular, want to know what it does and why. Make it hard for them to find out, and they'll be off without giving your business a second thought. Answer the golden questions, on the other hand, and you're well on your way to retaining them:

- ✔ Who are you, anyway?
- ✔ All right, so what are you selling?
- ✔ Well, then, why do I want to buy it?
- ✔ Why should I choose your site to investigate rather than all the others out there?

A recent survey by BizRate (www.bizrate.co.uk) revealed that around three in ten consumers abandon online shopping trolleys (or fail to buy the goods they have selected online) without making a purchase.

Web surfers are opportunists and, in many cases, aren't particularly loyal. Many discover new sites as they trawl randomly through the Web. If they find something easier and quicker, they'll move on. When it comes to Web pages, it pays to put the most important components first: who you are, what you do, and how you stand out from any competing sites. If you can, illustrate these points without using words – make the product completely self-explanatory (think Google) or brilliantly designed so that people naturally want to find out more.

If you have a long list of items to sell, you probably can't fit everything you have to offer right on the first page of your site. Even if you could, you wouldn't want to: As in a television newscast, it's better to prioritise the contents of your site so that the *breaking stories,* or the best contents, appear at the top, and the rest of what's in your catalogue is arranged in order of importance.

Think long and hard before you use features that may scare people away instead of wowing them. We're talking about those *splash pages* that contain only a logo or short greeting and then reload automatically and take the visitor to the main body of a site. We also don't recommend loading up your home page with Flash animations or Java applets that take your prospective customers' browsers precious seconds to load.

Encourage visitors to click, click, click!

Imagine multitasking Web surfers arriving at your Web site with only a fraction of their attention engaged. Make the links easy to read and in obvious locations. Having a row of links at the top of your home page, each of which points the visitor to an important area of your site, is always a good idea (see Figure 6-1). Such links give visitors an idea of what your site contains in a single glance and immediately encourage viewers to click a primary subsection of your site and explore further. By placing an interactive table of contents right up front, you direct surfers right to the material they are looking for.

The links can go at or near the top of the page on either the left or right side. The Dummies.com home page, shown in Figure 6-2, has a few links just above the top banner, but also sports links down *both* the left and right sides.

Figure 6-1: Notice how real business. co.uk uses lots of clearly labelled buttons to draw users' attention.

Figure 6-2:
Putting at
least five or
six links
near the top
of your
home page
is clearly a
good idea!

If you want to be ranked highly by search engines (and who doesn't?), you have another good reason to place your site's main topics near the top of the page in a series of links. Some search services index the first 50 or so words on a Web page. If you can get lots of important keywords included in that index, the chances are better that your site will be ranked highly in a list of links returned by the service in response to a search. (See Chapter 13 for more on embedding keywords.)

Use the following steps to create links to local files on your Web site by using Netscape Composer, the free Web page editor that comes with the Netscape Communicator Web browser. The steps assume that you've started up the program and that the Web page you want to edit is already open.

1. **Select the text or image on your Web page that you want to serve as the jumping-off point for the link.**

   If you select a word or phrase, the text is highlighted in black. If you select an image, a black box appears around the image.

2. **Choose Insert⇨Link or press Ctrl+L.**

   The Link Properties dialog box appears, as shown in Figure 6-3.

3. **In the box beneath Link Location, enter the name of the file you want to link to if you know the filename.**

   If the page you want to link to is in the same directory as the page that contains the jumping-off point, you need to enter only the name of the Web page. If the page is in another directory, you need to enter a path relative to the Web page that contains the link (or click the Choose File button, locate the file in the Open HTML File dialog box, and click the Open button).

4. **Click OK.**

   The Link Properties dialog box closes, and you return to the Composer window. If you made a textual link, the selected text is underlined and in a different colour. If you made an image link, a box appears around the image.

Presenting the reader with links up front doesn't just help your search engine rankings, it also indicates that your site is content rich and worthy of a thorough look.

Tell us a little about yourself

One thing you need to state clearly as soon as possible on your Web site is who you are and what you do, or what people can get out of using your Web site. Technorati, the blog search engine, encapsulates what it does in a very slick way:

Who's saying what. Right now.

Can you identify your primary goal in a single sentence? If not, try to boil down your goals to two or three sentences at the most. Whatever you do, make your mission statement more specific and customer oriented than simply saying, 'Out to make lots of money!' Tell prospects what you can do for them; the fact that you have three kids in college and need to make money to pay their tuition isn't really their concern. Dan's mission statement on Infozoo.co.uk is 'Get known. Know more', which is meant to sum up his Web site's service of helping small businesses 'get known' and their customers 'know more' about some great services on offer.

Add a search box

One of the most effective kinds of content you can add to your site is a search box. A *search box* is a simple text-entry field that lets a visitor enter a word or phrase. By clicking a button labelled Go, Search, or something of the sort, the search term or terms are sent to the site, where a script checks an index of the site's contents for any files that contain the terms. The script then causes a list of documents that contain the search terms to appear in the visitor's browser window.

A search box invites visitors to interact instantly with your Web site. If you can find a Web host that will help you set up a search box, you don't have to mess around with computer scripts and indexing tools. (See the section, 'Make your site searchable', later in this chapter, for more information.)

Search boxes are commonly found on commercial Web sites. You usually see them at the top of the home page, right near the links to the major sections of the site. The Dummies.com page, shown in Figure 6-4, includes a search box in the upper right corner of the page.

Figure 6-4: Many surfers prefer using a search box to clicking links.

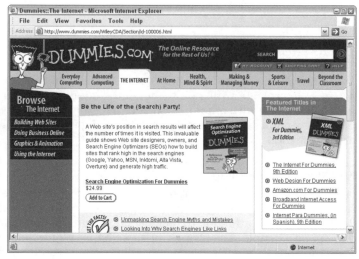

Although Greg's always looking for freelance writing jobs, even he has to admit that you don't really need to hire a professional to make a Web site compelling. You're not writing an essay, a term paper, or a book here. Rather, you need to observe only a few simple rules:

✔ Provide lots of links and hooks that readers can scan.

✔ Keep everything concise!

The key word to remember is *short*. Keep sentences brief and snappy. Limit paragraphs to one or two sentences in length. You may also want to limit each Web page to no more than one or two screens in length so that viewers don't have to scroll down too far to find what they want – even if they're on a laptop or smaller Internet appliance.

Making your content scannable

When you're writing something on paper, whether it's a letter to your Mum or your shopping list, contents have to be readable. Contents on your Web site, on the other hand, have to be scannable. This principle has to do with the way people absorb information online. Eyes that are staring at a computer screen for many minutes or many hours tend to jump around a Web page, looking for an interesting bit of information on which to rest. In this section, we suggest ways to attract those tired eyes and guide them toward the products or services you want to provide.

We're borrowing the term *scannable* from John Morkes and Jakob Nielsen of Sun Microsystems, who use it in their article 'Concise, Scannable, and Objective: How to Write for the Web' (www.useit.com/papers/webwriting/writing.html). We're including a link to this article (which was written eons ago in Web terms, but still holds true) in the Internet Directory on this book's Web site, along with other tips on enriching the content of your Web pages. See the section of the Directory called 'Developing Compelling Content' for more information.

Point the way with headings

One hard-to-miss Web page element that's designed to grab the attention of your readers' eyes is a heading. Every Web page needs to contain headings that direct the reader's attention to its most important contents. This book provides a good example. The chapter title (we hope) piques your interest first. Then the section headings and subheadings direct you to more details on the topics you want to read about.

Most graphics designers we've worked with label their heads with letters of the alphabet: 'A', 'B', 'C', and so on. In a similar fashion, most Web page editing tools designate top-level headings with the style Heading 1. Beneath this heading, you place one or more Heading 2 headings. Beneath each of those, you may have Heading 3 and, beneath those, Heading 4. (Headings 5 and 6 are too small to be useful, in our opinion.) The arrangement may look like the following.

```
Miss Cookie's Delectable Cooking School (Heading 1)
  Kitchen Equipment You Can't Live Without (Heading 2)
  The Story of a Calorie Counter Gone Wrong (Heading 2)
  Programmes of Culinary Study (Heading 2)
  Registration (Heading 3)
  Course Schedule (Heading 3)
```

You can energise virtually any heading by telling your audience something specific about your business. Instead of 'Ida's Antique Shop', for example, say something like 'Ida's Antique Shop: The Perfect Destination for the Collector and the Crafter'. Instead of simply writing a heading like 'Stan Thompson, Pet Grooming', say something specific, such as 'Stan Thompson: We Groom Your Pet at Our Place or Yours'.

Become an expert list maker

Lists are simple and effective ways to break up text and make your Web content easier to digest. They're easy to create and easy for your customer to view and absorb. For example, suppose that you import your own decorations, and you want to offer certain varieties at a discount during various seasons. Rather than bury the items you're offering within an easily overlooked paragraph, why not divide your list into subgroups of sale items so that visitors will find what they want without being distracted?

The following example shows how easy lists are to implement if you use Adobe Dreamweaver, a popular Web page creation tool that you can test for yourself for a 30-day trial period by downloading the program from the Macromedia Web site (www.adobe.com/uk/products/dreamweaver). You have your Web page document open in Dreamweaver, and you're at that point in the page where you want to insert a list. Just do the following:

1. **Type a heading for your list and then select the entire heading.**

   For example, you may type and then select the words *This Month's Specials*.

2. **Choose Text⇨Paragraph Format.**

   A list of paragraph styles appears as a submenu next to the Paragraph Format submenu.

3. **Click a heading style, such as Heading 3, to select it from the list of styles.**

   Your text is now formatted as a heading.

4. **Click anywhere in the Dreamweaver window to deselect the heading you just formatted.**

5. **Press Enter to move to a new line.**

6. **Type the first item of your list, press Enter, and then type the second item on the next line.**

   Repeat until you've entered all the items of your list.

7. **Select all the items of your list (but not the heading).**

8. **Choose Text⇨List⇨Unordered List.**

   A bullet appears next to each list item, and the items appear closer together on-screen so that they look more like a list. That's all there is to it! Figure 6-5 shows the result.

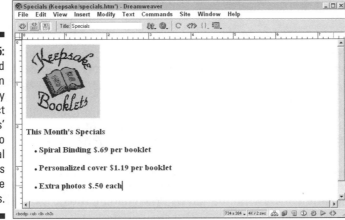

Figure 6-5:
A bulleted list is an easy way to direct customers' attention to special promotions or sale items.

Most Web editors let you vary the appearance of the bullet that appears next to a bulleted list item. For example, you can make it a hollow circle rather than a solid black dot, or you can choose a rectangle rather than a circle.

Lead your readers on with links

We mean for you to interpret your headings literally, not figuratively. In other words, we're not suggesting that you make promises on which you can't deliver. Rather, you should do anything you can to lead your visitors to your site and then get them to stay long enough to explore individual pages. You can accomplish this goal with a single hyperlinked word that leads to another page on your site:

<u>More . . .</u>

We see this word all the time on Web pages that present a lot of content. At the bottom of a list of their products and services, businesses place that word in bold type: **More . . .** and we're always interested in finding out what more they could possibly have to offer me.

Magazines use the same approach. On their covers you'll find taglines that refer you to the kinds of stories that you'll find inside. You can do the same kind of thing on your Web pages. For example, which of the following links is more likely to get a response?

<u>Next</u>

<u>Next: Paragon's Success Stories</u>

Whenever possible, tell your visitors what they can expect to encounter as a benefit when they click a link. Give them a tease – and then a big pay-off for responding.

Your Web page title: The ultimate heading

When you're dreaming up clever headings for your Web pages, don't overlook the 'heading' that appears in the narrow title bar at the very top of your visitor's Web browser window: the *title* of your Web page.

The two HTML tags `<TITLE>` and `</TITLE>` contain the text that appears within the browser title bar. But you don't have to mess with these nasty HTML codes: All Web page creation programs give you an easy way to enter or edit a title for a Web page. In Dreamweaver, you follow these steps:

1. **With the Web page you're editing open in the Dreamweaver window, choose Modify⇨Page Properties.**

   The Page Properties dialog box appears.

2. **In the Title text box, enter a title for your page.**

3. **Click OK.**

   The Page Properties dialog box closes, and you return to the Dreamweaver window. The title doesn't automatically appear in the title area at the top of the window. When you view the page in a Web browser, however, the title is visible.

If you have the Toolbar open, you can also simply type the title in the Title box and press Enter. In either case, make the title as catchy and specific as possible, but make sure that the title is no longer than 64 characters. An effective title refers to your goods or services while grabbing the viewer's attention. If your business is called Myrna's Cheesecakes, for example, you may make your title 'Smile and Say Cheese! with Myrna's Cakes' (40 characters).

Enhance your text with well-placed images

You can add two kinds of images to a Web page: an *inline image,* which appears in the body of your page along with your text, or an *external image,* which is a separate file that visitors access by clicking a link. The link may take the form of highlighted text or a small version of the image called a *thumbnail.*

The basic HTML tag that inserts an image in your document takes the following form:

```
<IMG SRC="URL">
```

This tag tells your browser to display an image (<IMG>) here. "URL" gives the location of the image file that serves as the source (SRC) for this image. Whenever possible, you should also include WIDTH and HEIGHT attributes (as follows) because they help speed up graphics display for many browsers:

```
<IMG HEIGHT=51 WIDTH=48 SRC="target.gif">
```

Most Web page editors add the WIDTH and HEIGHT attributes automatically when you insert an image. Typically, here's what happens:

1. **You click the location in the Web page where you want the image to appear.**

2. **Then you click an Image toolbar button or choose Insert⇨Image to display an image selection dialog box.**

3. **Next you enter the name of the image you want to add and click OK.**

   The image is added to your Web page. (For more information, see Chapter 5.)

A well-placed image points the way to text that you want people to read immediately. Think about where your own eyes go when you first connect to a Web page. Most likely, you first look at any images on the page; then you look at the headings; and finally, you settle on text to read. If you can place an image next to a heading, you virtually ensure that viewers will read the heading.

Freebies: Everyone's favourite

No matter how much money you have in the bank, you're bound to respond to a really good deal. If you want sure-fire attention, use one of the following words in the headings on your online business site's home page:

- ✔ Free
- ✔ New
- ✔ Act (as in Act Now!)
- ✔ Sale
- ✔ Discount
- ✔ Win (although this word can sound like a scam if used in the wrong context)

Contests and sweepstakes

The word *free* and the phrase *Enter Our Contest* can give you a big bang for your buck when it comes to a business Web page. In fact, few things are as likely to get viewers to click into a site as the promise of getting something for nothing.

Giveaways have a number of hidden benefits, too: Everyone who enters sends you personal information that you can use to compile a mailing list or prepare marketing statistics. Giveaways get people involved with your site, and they invite return visits – especially if you hold contests for several weeks at a time.

Of course, in order to hold a giveaway, you need to have something to *give away*. If you make baskets or sell backpacks, you can designate one of your sale items as the prize. If you can't afford to give something away, offer a big (perhaps 50 per cent) discount.

You can organise either a sweepstakes or a contest. In our definition, a *sweepstake* chooses its winner by random selection; a *contest* requires participants to compete in some way. The most effective contests on the Internet tend to be simple. If you hold one, consider including a Rules Web page that explains who is eligible, who selects the winner, and any rules of participation.

Be aware of the laws and regulations that cover sweepstakes and contests. Such laws often restrict illegal lotteries, as well as the promotion of alcoholic drinks, cigarettes, drugs, or weapons. Telemarketing is sometimes prohibited in connection with a contest. Following are some other points to consider:

- ✔ Unless you're sure that it's legal to allow Web surfers from other countries to participate, you're safest limiting your contest to UK residents only.

- ✔ On the contest rules page, be sure to clearly state the starting and ending dates for receiving entries. These dates protect you if someone claims they entered the competition on time, but didn't.

> ✔ Don't change the ending date of your contest, even if you receive far fewer entries than you had hoped for.
>
> ✔ Define the rules of the contest clearly. Include exactly what the prize is, how many you'll give away, and when you'll announce the winner.

If you do hold a contest, announce it at the top of your Web page and hint at the prizes people can win. Use bold and big type to attract the attention of your visitors.

Expert tips and insider information

Giveaways aren't just for businesspeople in retail or wholesale salespeople who have merchandise they can offer as prizes in a contest. If your work involves professional services, you can give away something just as valuable: your knowledge. Publish a simple newsletter that you e-mail to subscribers on a periodic basis. (See Chapter 12 for instructions on how to do so.) Or answer questions by e-mail. Some Web page designers (particularly college students who are just starting out) work for next to nothing initially, until they build a client base and can charge a higher rate for their services.

Make your site searchable

Search boxes let visitors instantly scan the site's entire contents for a word or phrase. They put visitors in control right away and get them to interact with your site. They're popular for some very good reasons.

We recommend some sort of search utility for e-commerce sites. However, adding a search box to your site doesn't make much sense if you have only five to ten pages of content. Add search capability only if you have enough content to warrant searching. If your site has a sales catalogue driven by a database, it makes more sense to let your customers use the database search tool instead of adding one of the site search tools that we describe in this section.

The problem is that search boxes usually require someone with knowledge of computer programming to create or implement a program called a CGI script to do the searching. Someone also has to compile an index of the documents on the Web site so that the script can search the documents. An application such as ColdFusion can do it, but it's not a program for beginners.

You can get around having to write CGI scripts to add search capabilities to your site. Choose one of these options:

✔ **Let your Web host do the work:** Some hosting services will do the indexing and creation of the search utility as part of their services.

✔ **Use a free site search service:** The server that does the indexing of your Web pages and holds the index doesn't need to be the server that hosts your site. A number of services will make your site searchable for free. In exchange, you display advertisements or logos in the search results you return to your visitors.

✔ **Pay for a search service:** If you don't want to display ads on your search results pages, pay a monthly fee to have a company index your pages and let users conduct searches. FreeFind (`www.freefind.com`) has some economy packages, a free version that forces you to view ads, and a professional version priced at £10 per month for a site of 1,000 pages or less. SiteMiner (`siteminer.mycomputer.com`) charges just over £10 per month for up to 1,500 pages, but lets you customise your search box and re-index your site whenever you add new content.

Judy Vorfeld went beyond having a simple Search This Site text box on her Office Support Services Web site. She has one at `www.ossweb.com/search.html`, which makes use of Google's search engine. But as you can see in Figure 6-6, she also provides a separate sitemap page that provides a list of links to her site's most important contents.

Figure 6-6: A Search This Site text box or sitemap page lets visitors instantly match their interests with what you have to offer.

You say you're up to making your site searchable, and you shudder at the prospect of either writing your own computer script or finding and editing someone else's script to index your site's contents and actually do the searching? Then head over to Atomz (www.atomz.com) and check out the hosted application Atomz Search. If your site contains 500 pages or less, you can also add a search box to your Web page that lets visitors search your site. Other organisations that offer similar services include:

- PicoSearch (www.picosearch.com)
- Webinator (www.thunderstone.com/texis/site/pages/webinator.html)

Writing Unforgettable Text

Quite often, business writing on the Web differs from the dry, linear report writing one is called upon to compose (or worse yet, read) in the corporate world. So you have the chance to express the real you: You're online, where sites that are funny, authors who have a personality, and content that's quirky are most read.

Striking the right tone

When your friends describe you to someone who has never met you, what do they say first? Maybe it's your fashion sense or your collection of salt and pepper shakers. Your business also has a personality, and the more striking you make its description on your Web page, the better. Use the tone of your text to define what makes your business unique and what distinguishes it from your competition.

Getting a little help from your friends

Blowing your own trumpet is a fine technique to use in some situations, but you shouldn't go overboard with promotional prose that beats readers over the head. Web readers are looking for objective information they can evaluate for themselves. An independent review of your site or your products carries far more weight than your own ravings about how great your site is. Sure, you know your products and services are great, but you'll be more convincing if your offerings can sell themselves, or you can identify third parties to endorse them.

What's that you say? *Wired* magazine hasn't called to do an in-depth interview profiling your entrepreneurial skills? Yahoo! hasn't graced you with the coveted glasses icon (indicating, in the estimation of Yahoo!'s Web site reviewers, a cool site worthy of special attention) on one of its long index pages? Take a hint from what we and our colleagues do when we're writing computer books such as the one you're reading now: We fire up our e-mail and dash off messages to anyone who may want to endorse our books: our mentors, our friends, and people we admire in the industry.

People should endorse your business because they like it, not simply because you asked for an endorsement. If they have problems with your business setup, they can be a great source of objective advice on how to improve it. Then, after you make the improvements, they're more likely than ever to endorse it.

Satisfied customers are another source of endorsements. Approach your customers and ask whether they're willing to provide a quote about how you helped them. If you don't yet have satisfied customers, ask one or two people to try your products or services for free and then, if they're happy with your wares, ask permission to use their comments on your site. Your goal is to get a pithy, positive quote that you can put on your home page or on a page specifically devoted to quotes from your clients.

Don't be afraid to knock on the doors of celebrities, too. Send e-mail to an online reporter or someone prominent in your field and ask for an endorsement. People love to give their opinions and see their names in print. You just may be pleasantly surprised at how ready they are to help you.

Sharing your expertise

Few things build credibility and ensure return visits like a Web site that presents inside tips and goodies you can't get anywhere else. The more you can make your visitors feel that they're going to find something on your site that is rare or unique, the more success you'll have.

Tell what you know. Give people information about your field that they may not have. Point them to all sorts of different places with links.

Building an online presence takes time

Judy Vorfeld, who goes by the *nom de Net* Webgrammar, knows all about finding different ways to attract a regular clientele. And she knows how important it is to have good content in a business Web site. She started the online version of her business Office Support Services (www.ossweb.com) from her home in Arizona in early 1998. She now has a second business site (www.editingandwriting services.com) and a third (www.web grammar.com), which serves as a resource for students, educators, writers, and Web developers.

Q. What would you describe as the primary goal of your online business?

A. To help small businesses achieve excellent presentation and communication by copyediting their print documents, books, and Web sites.

Q. How many hours a week do you work on your business site?

A. Three to six hours, which includes my syndicated writing tips, surveys, and newsletter, Communication Expressway (www.ossweb. com/ezine-archive-index.html).

Q. How do you promote your site?

A. Participating in newsgroups, writing articles for Internet publications, adding my URLs to good search engines and directories, moderating discussion lists and forums for others, offering free articles and tips on my sites, and networking locally and on the Web.

Q. Has your online business been profitable financially?

A. I continue to break even and am able to upgrade hardware and software regularly. I rarely raise my rates because my skills seem best suited to the small business community, and I want to offer a fee these people can afford.

Q. Who creates your business's Web pages?

A. Basic design is done by a Web designer, and I take over from there. I want the ability to make extensive and frequent changes in text and design. I do hire someone to format my ezine pages, graphics, and programming.

Q. What advice would you give to someone starting an online business?

A. I have a bunch of suggestions to give, based on my own experience:

- ✔ **Network.** Network with small business people who have complementary businesses and with those who have similar businesses. Also, network by joining professional associations participating in the activities. Volunteer time and expertise. Link to these organisations from your site.

- ✔ **Join newsgroups and forums.** Study Netiquette first. Lurk until you can adequately answer a question or make a comment. Also, keep on the lookout for someone with whom you can build up a relationship, someone who may mentor you and be willing to occasionally scrutinise your site, a news release, and so on. This person must be brutally honest, but perhaps you can informally offer one of your own services in return.

- ✔ **Learn Web development and the culture.** Even if you don't do the actual design, you have to make decisions on all the offers you receive regarding how to make money via affiliate deals, link exchanges, hosts, Web design software, and so on. It's vital that you keep active online and make those judgments yourself, unless you thoroughly trust your webmaster. Find online discussion lists that handle all areas of Web development and keep informed.

✔ **Include a Web page that shows your business biography or profile.** Mention any volunteer work you do, groups to which you belong, and anything else you do in and for the community. You need to paint as clear a picture as possible in just a few words. Avoid showcasing your talents and hobbies on a business site unless they are directly related to your business.

✔ **In *everything* you write, speak to your visitors.** Use the word 'you' as much as possible. Avoid the words 'I', 'we', and 'us'. You, as a businessperson, are there to connect with your visitors. You can't give them eye contact, but you can let them know that they matter, that they are (in a sense) the reason for your being there.

✔ **Become known as a specialist in a given field.** Be someone who can always answer a question or go out and find the answer. Your aim is to get as many potential clients or customers to your site as possible, not to get millions of visitors. Forget numbers and concentrate on creating a site that grabs the attention of your target market.

✔ **Get help.** If you can't express yourself well with words (and/or graphics) and know little about layout, formatting, and so on, hire someone to help you. You'll save yourself a lot of grief if you get a capable, trustworthy editor or designer.

She concludes: 'Don't start a business unless you are passionate about it and willing to give it some time and an initial investment. But when you do start, there are resources everywhere – many of them free – to help people build their businesses successfully.'

Inviting Comments from Customers

Quick, inexpensive, and *personal:* These are three of the most important advantages that the Web has over traditional printed catalogues. The first two are obvious pluses. You don't have to wait for your online catalogue to get printed and distributed. On the Web, your contents are published and available to your customers right away. Putting a catalogue on the Web eliminates (or, if publishing a catalogue on the Web allows you to reduce your print run, dramatically reduces) the cost of printing, which can result in big savings for you.

But the fact that online catalogues can be more personal than the printed variety is perhaps the biggest advantage of all. The personal touch comes from the Web's potential for *interactivity.* Getting your customers to click links makes them actively involved with your catalogue.

Getting positive e-mail feedback

Playing hide and seek is fun when you're amusing your baby niece, but it's not a good way to build a solid base of customers. In fact, providing a way for your customers to interact with you so that they can reach you quickly may be the most important part of your Web site.

Add a simple *mailto* link like this:

Questions? Comments? Send e-mail to info@mycompany.com

A mailto link gets its name from the HTML command that programmers use to create it. When visitors click the e-mail address, their e-mail program opens a new e-mail message window with your e-mail address already entered. That way, they have only to enter a subject line, type the message, and click Send to send you their thoughts.

Most Web page creation programs make it easy to create a mailto link. For example, if you use Dreamweaver, follow these steps:

1. **Launch and open the Web page to which you want to add your e-mail link.**

2. **Position your mouse arrow and click at the spot on the page where you want the address to appear.**

    The convention is to put your e-mail address at or near the bottom of a Web page. A vertical blinking cursor appears at the location where you want to insert the address.

3. **Choose Insert⇨Email Link.**

    The Insert Email Link dialog box appears.

4. **In the Text box, type the text that you want to appear on your Web page.**

    You don't have to type your e-mail address; you can also type *Webmaster, Customer Service,* or your own name.

5. **In the EMail box, type your e-mail address.**

6. **Click OK.**

    The Insert Email Link dialog box closes, and you return to the Dreamweaver Document window, where your e-mail link appears in blue and is underlined to signify that it is a clickable link.

Other editors work similarly but don't give you a menu command called Email Link. For example, in World Wide Web Weaver, a shareware program for the Macintosh, you choose Tags⇨Mail. A dialog box called Mail Editor appears.

Enter your e-mail address and the text you want to appear as the highlighted link, and then click OK to add the mailto link to your page.

The drawback to publishing your e-mail address directly on your Web page is that you're virtually certain to get unsolicited e-mail messages (commonly called *spam*) sent to that address. Hiding your e-mail address behind generic link text (such as 'Webmaster') may help reduce your chances of attracting spam.

Creating Web page forms that aren't off-putting

You don't have to do much Web surfing before you become intimately acquainted with how Web page forms work, at least from the standpoint of someone who has to fill them out in order to sign up for Web hosting or to download software.

When it comes to creating your own Web site, however, you become conscious of how useful forms are as a means of gathering essential marketing information about your customers. They give your visitors a place to sound off, ask questions, and generally get involved with your online business.

Be clear and use common sense when creating your order form. Here are some general guidelines on how to organise your form and what you need to include:

- ✔ **Make it easy on the customer:** Whenever possible, add pull-down menus with pre-entered options to your *form fields* (text boxes that visitors use to enter information). That way, users don't have to wonder about things such as the level of detail you expect them to include in their address.

- ✔ **Validate the information:** You can use a programming language called JavaScript to ensure that users enter information correctly, that all fields are completely filled out, and so on. You may have to hire someone to add the appropriate code to the order form, but it's worth it to save you from having to call customers to verify or correct information that they missed or submitted incorrectly.

- ✔ **Provide a help number:** Give people a number to call if they have questions or want to check on an order.

- ✔ **Return an acknowledgement:** Let customers know that you have received their order and will be shipping the merchandise immediately or contacting them if more information is needed.

As usual, good Web page authoring and editing programs make it a cinch to create the text boxes, check boxes, buttons, and other parts of a form that the user fills out. The other part of a form, the computer script that receives the data and processes it so that you can read and use the information, is not as simple. See Chapter 12 for details.

Not so long ago, you had to write or edit a scary CGI script in order to set up forms processing on your Web site. But an alternative recently turned up that makes the process of creating a working Web page form accessible to nonprogrammers. Web businesses, such as BOCC E-forms (www.bocc.co.uk/products) and FormMail.To (www.formmail.to), can lead you through the process of setting up a form and provide you with the CGI script that receives the data and forwards it to you.

Providing a guest book

The basic idea of a guestbook is not all that new and exciting. You have probably gone to plenty of special events where they ask you to sign in and write a little something about the guests of honour, the place where the party is being held, or the occasion marked by the event you're attending. But a guestbook on your Web site can add a whole other dimension to your business, making your customers feel that they're part of a thriving community. When you provide a guestbook or comments page on one of your business's Web pages, your clients and other visitors can check out who else has been there and what others think about the site.

If you set out to create your own Web page guestbook from scratch, you'd have to create a form, write a script (fairly complicated code that tells a computer what to do), test the code, and so on. Thankfully, an easier way to add a guestbook is available: You simply register with a special Web business that provides free guestbooks to users. One such organisation, Smart Guestbook (www.smartgb.com), offers a guestbook service that is free to use and doesn't come with pop-ups or similarly annoying advertising.

To sign up, you just have to fill in a few details, such as your Web site's domain name, a title for your guestbook, and your business type. Then all you do is click Create Guestbook and presto!

Another useful service, which is only marketed in the United States – but you can use over here – is Html Gear run by Lycos (htmlgear.lycos.com/specs/guest.html). Again, if you register with Html Gear's service, you can have your own guestbook right away with no fuss. (Actually, Html Gear's guestbook program resides on one of its Web servers; you just add the text-entry portion to your own page.) Here's how to do it:

1. **Connect to the Internet, start up your Web browser, and go to `htmlgear.lycos.com/specs/guest.html`.**

2. **Scroll down the page and click the Get This Gear! link.**

   You go to the Network Membership page.

3. **Click the Sign Me Up! button and follow the instructions on subsequent pages to register for the guestbook and other software on the Html Gear site.**

   The program asks you to provide your own personal information, choose a name and password for your guestbook, enter the URL of the Web page on which you want the guestbook to appear, and provide keywords that describe your page.

   After you register, a page entitled Gear Manager appears.

4. **Click Add Gear and then click Get Gear, which is next to Guest Gear.**

   After a few seconds, a page called Create Guest Gear appears. This page contains a form that you need to complete in order to create the guest-book *text-entry fields* (the text boxes and other items that visitors use to submit information to you) to your Web page.

5. **Fill out the Create Guest Gear form.**

   The form lets you name your guestbook and customise how you want visitors to interact with you. For example, you can configure the guest-book to send you an e-mail notification whenever someone posts a message.

6. **When you're done filling out the form, click Save & Create.**

   The Get Code page appears. A box contains the code you need to copy and add to the HTML for your Web page.

7. **Position your mouse arrow at the beginning of the code (just before the first line, which looks like this: `<!-- \/ GuestGEAR Code by htmlgear.com \/ ->`), press and hold down your mouse button, and scroll across the code to the last line, which reads: `<!-- /\ End GuestGEAR Code /\ -->`.**

   The code is highlighted to show that it's been selected.

8. **Choose Edit⇨Copy to copy the selected code to your computer's Clipboard.**

9. **Launch your Web editor, if it isn't running already, and open the Web page you want to edit in your Web editor window.**

   If you're working in a program (such as Dreamweaver or HotDog Pro) that shows the HTML for a Web page while you edit it, you can move on to Step 10. If, on the other hand, your editor hides the HTML from you, you have to use your editor's menu options to view the HTML source for your page. The exact menu command varies from program to program. Usually, though, the option is contained in the View menu. In FrontPage, for example, you click the HTML tab at the bottom of the window. The HTML for the Web page you want to edit then appears.

10. **Scroll down and click the spot on the page where you want to paste the HTML code for the guestbook.**

    How do you know where this spot is? Well, you have to add the code in the BODY section of a Web page. This is the part of the page that is contained between two HTML tags, <BODY> and </BODY>. You can't go wrong with pasting the code just before the </BODY> tag – or just before your return e-mail address or any other material you want to keep at the bottom of the page. The following example indicates the proper placement for the guestbook code:

    ```
    <HTML>
    <HEAD>
    <TITLE>Sign My Guestbook</TITLE>
    </HEAD>
    <BODY>
    The body of your Web page goes here; this is the part
           that appears on the Web.
    Paste your guestbook code here!
    </BODY>
    </HTML>
    ```

11. **Choose Edit⇨Paste.**

    The guestbook code is added to your page.

12. **Close your Web editor's HTML window.**

    Exactly how you do so varies depending on the program. If you have a separate HTML window open, click the close box (X) in the upper-right corner of the HTML window, if you are working in a Windows environment. (If you're working on a Mac, close the window by clicking the close box in the upper-left corner of the window that displays the HTML.)

    The HTML code disappears, and you return to your Web editor's main window.

13. **Choose File⇨Save to save your changes.**

14. **Preview your work in your Web browser window.**

    The steps involved in previewing also vary from editor to editor. Some editors have a Preview toolbar button that you click to view your page in a Web browser. Otherwise, launch your Web browser to preview your page as follows:

    - If you use Netscape Navigator, choose File⇨Open Page, click the name of the file you just saved in the Open Page dialog box, and then click Open to open the page.

    - If you use Internet Explorer, choose File⇨Open, click the name of the file you just saved in the Open dialog box, and then click Open to open the page.

    The page opens in your Web browser, with a new Guestbook button added to it, as shown in Figure 6-7.

Now, when visitors to your Web page click the Sign My Guestbook link, they go to a page that has a form they can fill out. Clicking the View My Guestbook link enables visitors to view the messages that other visitors have entered into your guestbook.

The problem with adding a link to a service that resides on another Web site is that it makes your Web pages load more slowly. First, your visitor's browser loads the text on your page. Then it loads the images from top to bottom. Besides this, it has to make a link to the Html Gear site in order to load the guestbook. If you decide to add a guestbook, images, or other elements that reside on another Web site, be sure to test your page and make sure that you're satisfied with how long the contents take to appear. Also make sure to use the 'Moderation' feature that enables you to screen postings to your guestbook. That way, you can delete obscene, unfair, or libellous postings before they go online.

Figure 6-7:
Add a
guestbook
link to your
Web page.

Chit-chatting that counts

You've accomplished a lot by the time you've put your business online. Hopefully, you're already seeing the fruits of your labour in the form of e-mail enquiries and orders for your products or services.

That's all good, but this is no time to rest on your laurels. After visitors start coming to your site, the next step is to retain those visitors. A good way to do so is by building a sense of community by posting a bulletin-board-type discussion area.

A *discussion area* takes the form of back-and-forth messages on topics of mutual interest. Each person can read previously posted messages and either respond or start a new topic of discussion. For an example of a discussion area that's tied to an online business, visit the Australian Fishing (www. ausfish.com.au) discussion areas, one of which is shown in Figure 6-8.

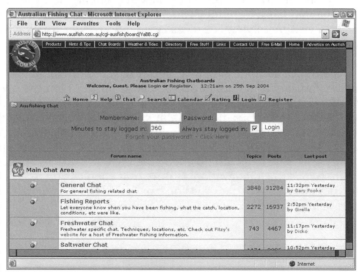

Figure 6-8:
A discussion area stimulates interest and interaction among like-minded customers.

The talk doesn't have to be about your own particular niche in your business field. In fact, the discussion will be more lively if your visitors can discuss concerns about your area of business in general, whether it's flower arranging, boat sales, tax preparation, clock repair, computers, or whatever.

How, exactly, do you start a discussion area? The first step is to install a special computer script on the computer that hosts your Web site. (Again, discussing this prospect with your Web hosting service beforehand is essential.)

When visitors come to your site, their Web browsers access the script, enabling them to enter comments and read other messages.

Here are some specific ways to prepare a discussion area for your site:

✔ Install Microsoft FrontPage, which includes the scripts you need to start a discussion group. You can't download a trial version, but you can get the 2003 version for around £120 on Amazon.

   www.microsoft.com/uk/office/frontpage/howtobuy/
   default.mspx

✔ Copy a bulletin board or discussion-group script from either of these sites:

   • Extropia.com (www.extropia.com/applications.html)

   • Matt's Script Archive (www.worldwidemart.com/scripts)

✔ Start your own forum on a service such as HyperNews, by Daniel LaLiberte, or install the HyperNews program yourself (www.hypernews.org/HyperNews/get/hypernews.html).

Chapter 7

Building in Security Up Front

*W*hether the perceived threat is from terrorists or roving gangs of teenage hoodlums, everyone seems to be on heightened security alert these days. And when you're an online businessperson, you face some real concerns that involve your own equipment and data, as well as the welfare of your customers.

The whole idea of security can seem intimidating. After all, you need to protect your business from the viruses and other hack attacks that are proliferating at a rate of knots. Ironically, always-on broadband Internet connections are partly to blame, because they're especially vulnerable to these intrusions. Fortunately, you can take some down-to-earth measures, most of which involve nothing more than good old common sense. You don't need to spend lots of money to make your information and that of your all-important customers secure.

Some measures are easy to put into practice and are especially important for home-based businesspeople. Others are technically challenging to implement on your own. But even if you have your Web host or a consultant do the work, you need to familiarise yourself with Internet security schemes. Doing so gives you the ability to make informed decisions about how to protect your online data. You can then take steps to lock your virtual doors so that you don't have to worry that your cyberstock is easy pickings for hackers and other bogeymen.

Practising Safe Business

If you work from home, you'd be forgiven for thinking that your safety concerns are the same as when you're watching TV on a Saturday afternoon. Unfortunately, this isn't the case. In law, you now have greater responsibility for yourself and the people you employ. You've got equipment to take care of, possibly stock, as well as lots of precious data to keep safe. Luckily, it doesn't take a brain surgeon to stay on the right side of employment law and keep your business interests secure.

We all know what a drag commuting can be, and working from your home-based business sounds like an ideal solution. But beware, distractions are everywhere. When Dan started work on InfoZoo.co.uk he made an agreement with his former managing director to keep using his old desk space, just so he could concentrate on getting the job done. When Greg works from home he's pestered by all manner of interruptions, mainly phone calls from relatives who assume that he isn't busy. So, knowing all too well that it's easier said than done, here are some simple steps that can help you set more clearly defined boundaries between work and domestic life, even when it all happens under the same roof.

When the computer is a group sport

Even if you're of a certain age, it's probably hard to comprehend that not so very long ago, there was one telephone per household and even that was connected to a party line shared by a number of other families. Now it seems everyone thinks they're entitled to their own computers. We haven't reached that level of paradise yet, but there is a lot to be said for having at least two separate machines in your home – one for personal use and one for business use. The idea is that you set up your system so that you have to log on to your business computer with a username and password. (For suggestions on how to devise a good password that's difficult to crack, see the section 'Picking passwords that are hard to guess', later in this chapter.)

If you have only one computer, passwords can still provide a measure of protection. Windows gives you the ability to set up different user profiles, each associated with its own password. You can assign a different profile to each member of your family. You can even make a game out of selecting profiles: Each person can pick his or her own background colour and desktop arrangement for Windows. User profiles and passwords don't necessarily protect your business files, but they convey to your family members that they should use their own software, stick to their own directories, and not try to explore your company data.

You can also set up different user profiles for your copy of Netscape Communicator. That way, your kids won't receive your business e-mail while they're surfing the Internet because you'll have different e-mail inboxes. If you're on Windows, choose Start➪Programs➪Netscape Communicator➪ Utilities➪User Profile Manager. If you use Outlook Express for e-mail, choose File➪Identities➪Add New Identity to create an identity and assign a password to it.

 Folder Guard, a program by WinAbility Corporation (`www.winability.com/folderguard`), enables you to hide or password-protect files or folders on your computer. The software works with Windows 95/98/Me/2000/XP. You can choose from the Standard version, which is intended for home users, or the Professional version, which is designed for business customers. A 14-day trial version is available for download from the WinAbility Web site; if you want to keep the Standard version of Folder Guard, you have to pay about £22.

Your call centre

Even thrifty guys like us consider it a necessity, not a luxury, to get a separate phone line for business use (even if it's your mobile phone rather than a land line). Having a devoted phone line not only makes your business seem more serious, but also separates your business calls from your personal ones. Additionally, if you need a phone line to connect to the Net, you then have a choice of which line to use for your modem.

The next step is to set up your business phone with its own answering machine or voice mail. On your business voice mail, identify yourself with your business's name. This arrangement builds credibility and makes you feel like a real business owner. You can then install privacy features, such as caller ID, on your business line as needed.

 Even though we've resigned ourselves to paying for multiple phone lines, we're still constantly on the lookout for the best deal possible. One place Dan goes to for tips and news on telephone service, not only for small businesses but also for personal use, is SimplySwitch.com. This Web site offers price comparisons of landlines, mobile phone networks, and while you're at it, gas, electricity, credit cards, and even mortgages. SimplySwitch also offers a call centre service so that you can talk to a real person.

Preparing for the worst

When you're lying awake at night, you can be anxious about all sorts of grim disasters: flood, fire, theft, computer virus, you name it. Prevention is always better than cure, so the following sections outline steps you can take to prevent problems. But, should a problem arise, you also find ways to recover more easily.

Insurance . . . the least you can do

We can think of ways to spend money that are a whole lot more fun than paying insurance premiums. But there we are every month, writing cheques to protect ourselves in case something goes wrong with our houses, cars, even ourselves. And yes, there's another item to add to the list: protecting our business investment by obtaining insurance that specifically covers us against hardware damage, theft, and loss of data. You can also go a step farther and obtain a policy that covers the cost of data entry or equipment rental that would be necessary to recover your business information.

It is important that you take stock of everything that you consider an asset for your business and make sure that it's all covered by your policy. This will probably add to your standard home insurance, but it's worth it if the worst happens. Here are some specific strategies:

- ✔ Make a list of all your hardware and software and how much each item cost and store a copy of it in a place such as a fireproof safe or safety-deposit box, preferably in a different building to where your business is located.

- ✔ Take photos of your computer setup in case you need to make an insurance claim and put them in the same safe place.

- ✔ Save your electronic files on CD-ROM or DVD and place the disc in a safe storage location, such as a safety-deposit box.

Investigate the many options available to you for insuring your computer hardware and software. Your current homeowner's or renter's insurance may offer coverage, but make sure that the money amount is sufficient for replacement. You may also want to take a look at a business insurance search engines and brokers that can give you some ideas of which provider best suits your needs. Try `www.thebroker.co.uk` or `www.insurancewide.com`.

Consider the unthinkable

The Gartner Group estimates that two out of five businesses that experience a major disaster will go out of business within five years. We'd guess that the three that get back up on their feet and running quickly are those that already had recovery plans in place. Even if your company is small, you need to be prepared for big trouble – not only for terrorist attacks, but natural disasters such as floods, hurricanes, or tornadoes. A recovery effort may include the following strategies:

- ✔ **Backup power systems:** What will you do if the power goes out and you can't access the Web? Consider a battery backup system such as APC Back-UPS Office (`www.apcc.co.uk`). It instantly switches your computers to battery power when the electricity goes out so that you can save your data and switch to laptops. Even more important, make sure that your ISP or Web host has a backup power supply so that your store can remain online in case of a power outage. Having a laptop, as well as a PC, can help, too. Simply switch to your laptop in the event of a power cut, and you'll get an extra couple of hours (depending on the machine's battery life) to bridge the power gap.

✔ **Data storage:** This is probably the most practical and essential disaster recovery step for small or home-based businesses. Back up your files on a computer that's not located in the place where you physically work. At the very least, upload your files periodically to the Web space that your hosting service gives you. Also consider storing your files with an online storage service. (See the section on online storage space in this book's Internet Directory for suggestions, including one free storage option.)

✔ **Telecommunications:** Having some alternate method of communication available in case your phone system goes down ensures that you're always in touch. The obvious choice is a mobile phone. Also set up a voice mailbox so that customers and vendors can leave messages for you, even if you can't answer the phone.

Creating a plan is a waste of time if you don't regularly set aside time to keep it up to date. Back up your data on a regular basis, purchase additional equipment if you need it, and make arrangements to use other computers and offices if you need to – in other words, *implement* your plan. You owe it not only to yourself but also to your customers to be prepared in case of disaster.

Antivirus protection without a needle

Antivirus group Sophos says only 0.4 per cent of e-mails are infected with viruses, well down on just a year ago. But it identified 2,000 new threats in August 2006 alone, bringing the total number of recognised malware programs to more than 186,000. As an online businessperson, you're going to be downloading files, receiving disks from customers and vendors, and exchanging e-mail with all sorts of people you've never met. Surf safely by installing antivirus programs such as:

✔ **Norton Internet Security 2006 by Symantec Corporation (go to `www.symantecstore.com` and select UK site):** This application, which includes an antivirus program and a firewall and lists for £49.99, automates many security functions and is especially good for beginners. A standalone version, Norton Anti-Virus, is available for £39.99, but we recommend the full-featured package, which includes a firewall that will block many other dangerous types of intrusions, such as Trojan horses.

✔ **AVG AntiVirus by GriSoft (`www.grisoft.com`):** Many users who find Norton Internet Security too intrusive (it leaves lots of files on your computer and consumes a great deal of memory) turn to this product, which comes in a free version as well as a more full-featured version for just under £20.

- **Sophos Anti-Virus Small Business Edition (www.sophos.com):** Another popular free program, Sophos is a British-based company with a global reach. You can't buy its products through its Web site, but it gives you a directory of shops where you can.

- **Internet Security Suite by McAfee (go to www.mcafeestore.com and select the United Kingdom store):** This is the leading competitor to Norton Anti-Virus. This is its most comprehensive program and costs ₤49.99. You can get lesser packages for between ₤20 and ₤45. Check out the Web site and assess what they've got on offer.

Low- and high-tech locks

If you play the word game with a Web surfer or Web site and say 'security', you're likely to get a response such as 'encryption'. But security doesn't need to start with software. The fact is, all the firewalls and passwords in the world won't help you if someone breaks into your home office and trashes it or makes off with the computer that contains all your files.

Besides insuring your computer equipment and taking photos in case you need to get it replaced, you can also invest in locks for your home office and your machines. They may not keep someone from breaking into your house, but they'll at least make it more difficult for intruders to carry off your hardware.

Here are some suggestions for how to protect your hardware and the business data your computers contain:

- **Lock your office:** Everyone has locks on the outer doors of their house, but go a step further and install a deadbolt lock on your office door.

- **Lock your computers:** Avanquest (www.avanquest.co.uk) offers a variety of computer locking systems for both desktop and laptop computers.

- **Mark your modem:** Unbeknownst to someone who's up to no good, an innovative theft recovery system called CompuTrace can be installed on your hard drive. Then, if your computer is stolen, the software is activated. When the thief connects its internal modem to a phone line, the authorities are notified. The system works with other types of Internet connections as well, including DSL and cable modems. CompuTrace Plus (www.eurotracking.co.uk) is offered by Eurotracking and costs home office users £25.50 for one year of monitoring.

- **Make backups:** Be sure to regularly back up your information on Zip drives or similar storage devices. Also consider signing up with a Web-based storage service where files can be transferred from your computer. That way, if your computers and your extra storage disks are lost for whatever reason, you'll have an online backup in a secure location. Look into Safe Data Storage Ltd (www.safedatastorage.co.uk); its prices start at £5 per month for 1GB of compressed data.

This is another area that demands your attention on a regular basis. Viruses change all the time, and new ones appear regularly. The antivirus program you install one day may not be able to handle the viruses that appear just a month later. You may want to pick an antivirus program that gives free regular updates. Also check out www.reviewcentre.com and take a look at the antivirus software reviews. People seem to feel quite passionate about this and they don't hold back in their opinions!

Greg loves gadgets, and few things get him more excited than hand-held devices, laptops, and other portable computing devices. Yet those are the items that he seems to have the most trouble keeping track of, literally and figuratively. At the very least, you should make the device's storage area accessible with a password. You can also install protection software designed especially for mobile devices, such as VirusScan PDA by McAfee (www.mcafee.com/uk/smb/products/mobile_security/mobile_security_smb.html).

Installing Firewalls and Other Safeguards

You probably know how important a firewall is in a personal sense. It filters out unwanted intrusions such as executable programs that hackers seek to plant on your file system so they can use your computer for their own purposes. When you're starting an online business, the objectives of a firewall become different: You're protecting not just your own information but also that of your customers. In other words, you're quite possibly relying on the firewall to protect your source of income as well as the data on your computers.

Just what is a firewall, exactly? A *firewall* is an application or hardware device that monitors the data flowing into or out of a computer network and that filters the data based on criteria that the owner sets up. Like a porter in the reception of a block of flats, a firewall scans the packets (small, uniform data segments) of digital information that traverse the Internet, making sure that the data is headed for the right destination and that it doesn't match known characteristics of viruses or attacks. Authorised traffic is allowed into your network. Attack attempts or viruses are either automatically deleted or cause an alert message to appear to which you must respond with a decision to block or allow the incoming or outgoing packets.

Keeping out Trojan horses and other unwanted visitors

A *Trojan horse* is a program that enters your computer surreptitiously and then attempts to do something without your knowledge. Some people say that such programs enter your system through a 'back door' because you don't immediately know that they've entered your system. Trojan horses may come in the form of an e-mail attachment with the filename extension .exe (which stands for *executable*). For example, Dan recently received an e-mail that purported to be from a US-based company and that claimed it contained a security update. The attachment looked innocent enough, but had he saved the attachment to his computer, it would have used it as a staging area for distributing itself to many other e-mail addresses.

He didn't run into trouble, however. A special firewall program we installed, called Norton Internet Security, recognised the attachment and alerted him to the danger. We highly recommend that anyone who, like us, has a cable modem, DSL, or other direct connection to the Internet install one right away. Take a look at PC Advisor Magazine's Web site (www.pcadvisor.co.uk/downloads), which lists antiviral software (free and not so free) that you may like to try out.

Cleaning out spyware

You've also got to watch out for software that 'spies' on your Web surfing and other activities and that reports them back to advertisers, potentially invading your privacy. Ad-Aware isn't a firewall exactly, but it's a useful program that detects and erases any advertising programs you may have downloaded from the Internet without knowing it. Such advertising programs may be running on your computer, consuming your processing resources and slowing down operations. Some *spyware programs* track your activities as you surf the Web; others simply report that they've been installed. Many users regard these spyware programs as invasions of privacy because they install themselves and do their reporting without your asking for it or even knowing they're active.

When Greg ran Ad-Aware the first time, he detected a whopping 57 programs he didn't know about that were running on his computer and that had installed themselves when he connected to various Web sites or downloaded software. As you can see in Figure 7-1, when he ran Ad-Aware while he was working on this chapter, sure enough, it found four suspicious software components running.

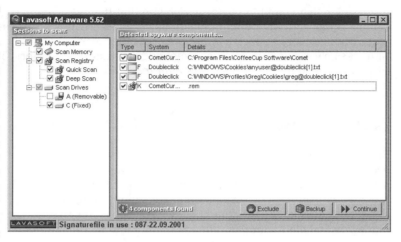

Figure 7-1:
Ad-Aware,
produced by
Swedish
company
Lavasoft,
deletes
advertising
software
that, many
users
believe, can
violate your
privacy.

We recommend Ad-Aware; you can download a version at www.lavasoft.
de/purchase/business, the cheapest version is $28.45 (about £15).

Positioning the firewall

These days, most home networks are configured so that the computers on
the network can share information, as well as the same Internet connection.
Whether you run a home-based business or a business in a discrete location,
you almost certainly have a network of multiple computers. A network is far
more vulnerable than a single computer connected to the Internet: A network
has more entry points than a single computer, and more reliance is placed on
each of the operators of those computers to observe good safety practices.
And if one computer on the network is attacked, there is the real potential for
the others to be attacked as well.

You are probably acquainted with software firewalls, such as Norton Personal
Firewall or McAfee Firewall (www.mcafee-uk.co.uk/mcafee). Software
firewalls protect one computer at a time. In a typical business scenario,
however, multiple computers share a single Internet connection through a
router that functions as a gateway. Many network administrators prefer a
hardware firewall – a device that functions as a filter for traffic both entering
and leaving it. A hardware firewall may also function as a router, but it can
also be separate from the router. The device is positioned at the perimeter
of the network where it can protect all the company's computers at once.
Examples of hardware are the Symantec Gateway Security 1600 Series (one
example is at enterprisesecurity.symantec.com/landingpages/
YB/1600_mini_uk.cfm), and the SonicWall TZ170 (www.sonicwallon
line.co.uk).

Companies that want to provide a Web site that the public can visit as well as secure e-mail and other communications services create a secure sub-network of one or more specially hardened (in other words, secured because all unnecessary services have been removed from them) computers. This kind of network is sometimes called a *Demilitarised Zone* or DMZ.

Keeping your firewall up to date

Firewalls work by means of attack *signatures* (also called *definitions*), which are sets of data that identify a connection attempt as a potential attack. Some attacks are easy to stop: They've been attempted for years, and the amateur hackers who attempt intrusions don't give much thought to them. The more dangerous attacks are new ones. They have signatures that have emerged since you installed your firewall.

You quickly get a dose of reality and find just how serious the problem is by visiting one of the Web sites that keeps track of the latest attacks, such as e-security company Sophos (`www.sophos.com/security`). US-based intrusion detection Web site DShield has reported that the 'survival time' for an unpatched computer (a computer that has security software that has not been equipped with the latest updates called *patches*) after connecting it to the Internet was only 16 minutes. That means such a computer only has 16 minutes before someone tries to attack it. If that doesn't scare you into updating your security software, we don't know what will.

Using Public Keys to Provide Security

The conversations Greg overhears as he drives his pre-teen daughters and their friends to events leave no doubt in his mind that different segments of society use code words that only their members can understand. Even computers use encoding and decoding to protect information they exchange on the Internet. The schemes used online are far more complex and subtle than the slang used by kids, however. This section describes the security method that is used most widely on the Internet, and the one you're likely to use yourself: Secure Sockets Layer (SSL) encryption.

The keys to public-key/ private-key encryption

Terms like *SSL* and *encryption* may make you want to reach for the remote, but don't be too quick to switch channels. SSL is making it safer to do business online and boosting the trust of potential customers. And anything that makes shoppers more likely to spend money online is something you need to know about.

The term *encryption* refers to the process of encoding data, especially sensitive data, such as credit-card numbers. Information is encrypted by means of complex mathematical formulas called *algorithms.* Such a formula may transform a simple-looking bit of information into a huge block of seemingly incomprehensible numbers, letters, and characters. Only someone who has the right formula, called a *key,* which is itself a complex mass of encoded data, can decode the gobbledygook.

Here's a very simple example. Suppose that your credit-card number is `12345`, and you encode it by using an encryption formula into something like the following: `1aFgHx203gX4gLu5cy`.

The algorithm that generated this encrypted information may say something like: 'Take the first number, multiply it by some numeral, and then add some letters to it. Then take the second number, divide it by x, and add y characters to the result', and so on. (In reality, the formulas are far more complex than this example, which is why you usually have to pay a licence fee to use them. But you get the general idea.) Someone who has the same formula can run it in reverse, so to speak, in order to decrypt the encoded number and obtain the original number, `12345`.

In practice, the encoded numbers that are generated by encryption routines and transmitted on the Internet are very large. They vary in size depending on the relative strength (or uncrackability) of the security method being used. Some methods generate keys that consist of 128 bits of data; a *data bit* is a single unit of digital information. These formulas are called *128-bit keys.*

Encryption is the cornerstone of security on the Internet. The most widely used security schemes, such as the Secure Sockets Layer protocol (SSL), the Secure Electronic Transactions protocol (SET), and Pretty Good Privacy (PGP), all use some form of encryption.

With some security methods, the party that sends the data and the party that receives it both use the same key (this method is called *symmetrical encryption*). This approach isn't considered as secure as an asymmetrical encryption method, such as public-key encryption, however. In public-key encryption, the originating party obtains a licence to use a security method. (In the following section, we show you just how to do so yourself.) As part of the licence, you use the encryption algorithm to generate your own private key. You never share this key with anyone. However, you use the private key to create a separate public key. This public key goes out to visitors who connect to a secure area of your Web site. As soon as they have your public key, users can encode sensitive information and return it to you. Only you can decode the data – by using your secret, private key.

Getting a certificate without going to school

On the Internet, how do you know that people are who they say they are when all you have to go on is a URL or an e-mail address? The solution in the online world is to obtain a personal certificate that you can send to Web site visitors or append to your e-mail messages.

How certificates work

A *certificate,* which is also sometimes called a Digital ID, is an electronic document issued by a certification authority (CA). The certificate contains the owner's personal information as well as a public key that can be exchanged with others online. The public key is generated by the owner's private key, which the owner obtains during the process of applying for the certificate.

In issuing the certificate, the CA takes responsibility for saying that the owner of the document is the same as the person actually identified on the certificate. Although the public key helps establish the owner's identity, certificates do require you to put a level of trust in the agency that issues it.

A certificate helps both you and your customers. It assures your customers that you're the person you say you are, plus it protects your e-mail communications by enabling you to encrypt them.

Obtaining a certificate from VeriSign

Considering how important a role certificates play in online security, it's remarkably easy to obtain one. You do so by applying and paying a licensing fee to a CA. One of the most popular CAs is VeriSign, Inc. (`www.verisign.co.uk`), which lets you apply for a range of SSL certificates that range in price from £259 for a basic one-year licence, to several thousands of pounds for more complicated packages.

A VeriSign Secure Site certificate, which you can use to authenticate yourself in e-mail, news, and other interactions on the Net, costs £259 plus VAT per year, but you can get a better deal signing up for longer terms, and you can try out a free certificate for secure e-mail IDs for 60 days. Follow these steps to obtain your Digital ID:

1. **Go to the VeriSign, Inc. Digital IDs for Secure E-Mail page at** `www.verisign.co.uk/products-services/security-services/pki/pki-security/email-digital-id/index.html`.

2. **Click the Buy Now button whether you're certain you want an ID or you only want the trial version.**

   The Digital ID Enrollment page appears.

3. **Click Buy Now near the bottom of the page.**

   A page may appear (if you don't have JavaScript support) that asks you to identify the Web browser you use most often, and that you want to associate with the Digital ID. Click the browser you want. An application form for a Digital ID appears.

4. **Complete the application form.**

   The application process is pretty simple. The form asks for your personal information and a challenge phrase that you can use in case anyone is trying to impersonate you. It also requires you to accept a license agreement. (You don't need to enter credit-card information if you select the 60-day trial option.)

5. **Click the Accept button at the bottom of the screen.**

   A dialog box appears asking you to confirm your e-mail address. After you confirm by clicking OK, a dialog box appears asking you to choose a password. When you enter a password and click OK, VeriSign uses your password to generate a private key for you. The private key is an essential ingredient in public-key/private-key technology.

6. **Click OK to have your browser generate your private key.**

   A page appears asking you to check your e-mail for further instructions. In a few minutes, you receive a message that contains a Digital ID PIN.

7. **In your e-mail program, open the new message from VeriSign Customer Support Department.**

8. **Use your mouse to highlight the PIN and then choose Edit⇨Copy to copy the PIN.**

9. **Go to the URL for Digital ID Services that's included in the e-mail message and paste your PIN in the text box next to Enter The Digital ID Personal Identification Number (PIN).**

10. **Click Submit.**

    The certificate is generated, and the Digital IDF Installation and Registration Page appears.

11. **Click the Install button.**

    The ID from VeriSign downloads, and you're now able to view it with your browser. Figure 7-2 shows Greg's certificate for Netscape Navigator. (Copying this ID, or anyone else's, is pointless because this is only your public key; the public key is always submitted with your private key, which is secret.)

Figure 7-2:
A personal
certificate
assures
individuals
or Web sites
of your
identity.

After you have your Digital ID, what do you do with it? For one thing, you can use it to verify your identity to sites that accept certificate submissions. Some sites that require members to log in use secure servers that give you the option of submitting your certificate rather than entering the usual user-name and password to identify yourself. You can also attach your Digital ID to your e-mail messages to prove that your message is indeed coming from you. See your e-mail program's Help files for more specific instructions.

You can't encrypt or digitally sign messages on any computer other than the one to which your certificates are issued. If you're using a different computer than the one you used when you obtained your certificates, you must contact your certificate issuer and obtain a new certificate for the computer you're now using. Or, if your browser allows transfers, you can export your certificate to the new computer.

Keeping Other Noses Out of Your Business

Encryption isn't just for big businesses. Individuals who want to maintain their privacy, even while navigating the wilds of the Internet, can install special software or modify their existing e-mail programs in order to encode their online communications. You may not need to use software like this, but if you deal in sensitive data, then it's a must.

The TechWorld Web site (www.techworld.com/security/features/index.cfm?featureid=993) presents some good tips and strategies for personal protection on the Internet.

Encryption software for the rest of us

PGP (Pretty Good Privacy), a popular encryption program, has been around about as long as the Web itself. PGP lets you protect the privacy of your e-mail messages and file attachments by encrypting them so that only those with the proper authority can decipher the information. You can also digitally sign the messages and files you exchange, which assures the recipient that the messages come from you and that the information has not been tampered with. You can even encrypt files on your own computer.

PGP (`www.pgp.com/products/desktop/index.html`) is a personal encryption program. PGP offers a range of *plug-ins,* applications that work with other programs to provide added functionality. You can integrate the program with popular e-mail programs such as Microsoft Outlook (although Netscape Messenger is notably absent from the list of supported applications).

In order to use PGP Personal Privacy, the first step is to obtain and install the program. For a price list or more information about the 30-day free trial, go to the Web site at `www.pgp.com`. After you install the program, you can use it to generate your own private-key/public-key pair. After you create a key pair, you can begin exchanging encrypted e-mail messages with other PGP users. To do so, you need to obtain a copy of their public keys, and they need a copy of your public key. Because public keys are just blocks of text, trading keys with someone is really quite easy. You can include your public key in an e-mail message, copy it to a file, or post it on a public-key server where anyone can get a copy at any time.

After you have a copy of someone's public key, you can add it to your *public keyring,* which is a file on your own computer. Then you can begin to exchange encrypted and signed messages with that individual. If you're using an e-mail application supported by the PGP plug-ins, you can encrypt and sign your messages by selecting the appropriate options from your application's toolbar. If your e-mail program doesn't have a plug-in, you can copy your e-mail message to your computer's Clipboard and encrypt it there by using PGP built-in functions. See the PGP User's Guide files for more specific instructions.

Encrypting e-mail messages

You can use your existing software to encrypt your mail messages rather than have to install a separate program such as PGP. In the following sections, we describe the steps involved in setting up the e-mail programs that come with the biggest browser package, Microsoft Internet Explorer, to encrypt your messages.

If you use Outlook, Microsoft's e-mail program that you get as standard with the computer's Office suite, you can use your Digital ID to do the following:

✔ **Send a digital signature:** You can digitally shrink-wrap your e-mail message by using your certificate in order to assure the recipient that the message is really from you.

✔ **Encrypt your message:** You can digitally encode a message to ensure that only the intended party can read it.

To better understand the technical details of how you can keep your e-mail communications secure, read the Digital ID User Guide, which you can access at www.verisign.com/stellent/groups/public/documents/guides/005326.pdf.

After you have a digital ID, in order to actually make use of it, you need to follow these steps in Internet Explorer:

1. **After you obtain your own Digital ID, the first step is to associate it with your e-mail account by choosing Tools⇨Accounts.**

   The Internet Accounts dialog box appears.

2. **Select your e-mail account and click Properties.**

   The Properties dialog box for your e-mail account appears.

3. **Click the Security tab to bring it to the front.**

4. **Click the Select button in the Signing Certificate section; then when the Select Default Account Digital ID dialog box appears, select your Digital ID.**

5. **Click OK to close the Select Default Account Digital ID dialog box; then click OK to close the Properties dialog box and click Close to close the Internet Accounts dialog box.**

   You return to the main Outlook window.

6. **To send a digitally signed e-mail message to someone, click Create Message.**

   The New Message dialog box appears.

7. **Click either or both of the security buttons at the extreme right of the toolbar, as shown in Figure 7-3.**

   The Sign button enables you to add your Digital ID. The Encrypt button lets you encrypt your message.

8. **Finish writing your message and then click the Send button.**

   Your encrypted or digitally signed message is sent on its way.

Figure 7-3:
When you
click the
Sign and
Encrypt
buttons,
your
message
goes out
encrypted
and with
your
certificate
attached.

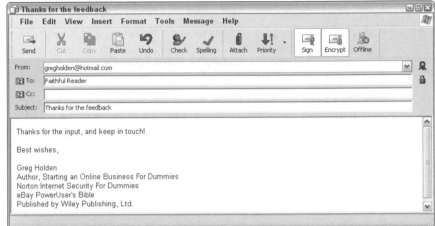

Figure 7-3:
When you
click the
Sign and
Encrypt
buttons,
your
message
goes out
encrypted
and with
your
certificate
attached.

The preceding steps show you how to digitally sign or encrypt an individual message. You have to follow these steps every time you want to sign or encrypt a message. On the other hand, by checking one or more of the options (Encrypt Contents and Attachments for All Outgoing Messages and Digitally Sign All Outgoing Messages) on the Security tab of the Options dialog box, you activate Outlook Express's built-in security features for *all* your outgoing messages. (You can still 'turn off' the digital signature or encryption for an individual message by deselecting the Sign or Encrypt buttons in the toolbar of the New Message dialog box.)

Picking passwords that are hard to guess

You put a lot of effort into picking the names of your kids and pets, and now you get to choose passwords. But the point of creating a password is to make it difficult for thieves to figure out what it is. That is true whether you're protecting your own computer, downloading software, subscribing to an online publication, or applying for a certificate (as we explain earlier in this chapter).

One method for choosing a password is to take a familiar phrase and then use the first letter of each word to form the basis of a password. For example, the old phrase 'Every Good Boy Deserves Fruit' would be EGBDF. Then, mix uppercase and lowercase, add punctuation, and you wind up with eGb[d]f. If you *really* want to make a password that's hard to crack, add some numerals as well, such as the last two digits of the year you were born: eGb[d]f48.

Whatever you do, follow these tips for effective password etiquette:

- **Don't use passwords that are in a dictionary:** It takes time but not much effort for hackers to run a program that tries every word in an online dictionary as your password. So if it's in the dictionary, they will eventually discover it.

- **Don't use the same password at more than one site:** It's a pain to remember more than one password, not to mention keeping track of which goes with what. Plus, you tend to accumulate lots of different passwords after you've been online for a while. But if you use the same password for each purpose and your password to one site on the Internet is compromised, all your password-protected accounts are in jeopardy.

- **Use at least six characters:** The more letters in your password, the more difficult you make the life of the code-crackers.

When it comes to passwords, duplication is not only boring but also dangerous. It's especially important not to reuse the same password that you enter to connect to your account on a commercial service such as AOL, Pipex, or Tiscali as a password to an Internet site. If a hacker discovers your password on the Internet site, that person can use it to connect to your AOL or CompuServe account, too – and you'll have to pay for the time they spend online.

A mouthful of protection with authentication

Authentication is a fun word to try to say quickly ten times in a row, and it's also another common security technique used on the Web. This measure simply involves assigning approved users an official username and password that they must enter before gaining access to a protected network, computer, or directory.

Most Web servers allow you to set up areas of your Web site to be protected by username and password. Not all Web hosts allow this, however, because it requires setting up and maintaining a special password file and storing the file in a special location on the computer that holds the Web server software. If you need to make some content on your business site (such as sensitive financial information) available only to registered users, talk to your Web host to see whether setting up a password-protected area is possible.

Chapter 8

Monitoring and Improving Your Business

*O*ne of the many advantages of doing business online is the ease with which you can shift your shop's focus. With a bricks-and-mortar outlet, changing the business's name, address, or physical appearance can be labour-intensive and expensive. On the Web, however, you can rebuild your shop's *front door* (your home page) in a matter of minutes, while, in theory, you can revamp your sales catalogue in under an hour.

Because it's relatively easy to make changes to your Web site, you have no excuse for not making regular improvements and updates to what you're offering. Giving the shop an overhaul doesn't just mean changing the colours or the layout on your Web site, which is the part of your operation that customers notice. It also means jazzing up back-office functions that customers don't see, such as inventory management, invoices, labels, packing, and shipping. This chapter examines different ways to test, check, and revise your Web site based on its current performance so that you can boost your revenue and increase sales as well as make your Web site more usable.

Bolstering Your Infrastructure

Every business has its foundations – some elements that give it a presence in the marketplace or in the place where it is physically located. For a traditional, bricks-and-mortar business, this foundation may be an address or phone number, or the building in which the merchandise is presented and the employees work. That's how the post office gets mail to the business, and how the customers find the stuff you want to sell.

For an online business, your infrastructure is made up of the domain name that forms your Web address, and the Web server that presents your Web site files – which, in turn, present the merchandise you have for sale. Your server makes your site available, and your URL gives your customers a way to find you: Together, they're the equivalent of your high street address and the physical space you rent. Over time, you may have to change your domain name – say, if customers complain that your site is too hard to find or your URL is too long. You may also need to find a new Web server in order to keep your business running efficiently if any of the following occur:

- ✔ Your pages slow down.
- ✔ Customers complain that your forms don't work.
- ✔ You run out of storage space on your server, and your host wants to charge you armfuls of cash for more space.

Other regular upgrades need to be made to your domain and/or your Web server, as described in the following sections.

Renewing your domain name

As described in Chapter 3, you have a choice of two different types of domain names: One that is relatively short (for example, mynewebusiness.co.uk) and one that is long-winded and difficult to recall off the top of your head (myinternetprovider.co.uk/~mynewebusiness). Even though the first type of domain name is obviously preferable, many individuals who are creating their first Web sites start with the longer one. They get a certain amount of Web server space along with their monthly access account from their Internet Service Provider. Their natural inclination is to use the directory space they're given (which has a long URL like the latter example) just to get the site started.

Does this sound like you? There's nothing wrong with doing things the easiest way possible when you're a beginner, but be aware that your businesses will evolve as it grows. Before long, you'll need to find a domain name that more accurately fits your business or is easier to remember.

Making your own name a domain

Even if you don't make it active right away, it's a good idea to lock up a name to give you the option of using it in the future. For example, creating a personal Web site may well still be on your to-do list. But, if your name is Joe Bloggs, you may want to purchase the domain name joebloggs.co.uk for future use. If you don't, you may eventually have to deal with cyber squatters – the scourge of domain name buyers.

Cyber squatters are businesses that make money by buying up lots of domain names, knowing that at some point in the future, someone will want the domain name enough to buy it at a premium price. If your ideal domain name is owned by a cyber squatter or by another business, you may have to come up with a variation on your original name. When Greg was looking for domain names, for example, he was unable to buy `Holden.com` because a car manufacturer in Australia was already using it. However, he was lucky enough to find `gregholden.com` and snapped it up straight away – even though, at the time, he didn't have a home page of his own. You should be doing the same for your own name or your business's name right now.

Deciding which top-level domain name to use

Where does a business like yours get the easy-to-remember addresses you need? You purchase them from one of the approved domain name registrars. A *registrar* is a business that has been designated as having the responsibility for keeping track of the names registered in one of the top-level domains. Originally, there were six domains, but as `.com`, `.co.uk`, and others became crowded, alternatives were eventually approved. The list of available domains is growing all the time, but the originals are still the most recognisable, so ideally you should try for a `.com`, `.co.uk`, `.net`, or `.info`. The total list of domains is bewildering, so we include a scaled down version in Table 8-1.

A *top-level domain* (TLD) is one of the primary categories into which addresses on the Internet are divided. It's the part of a domain name that comes after the dot, such as `com` in `.com`. A *domain name* includes the part that comes before the dot, such as `wiley` in `wiley.co.uk`. A fully qualified domain name includes the host name – for example, `www.wiley.com` or `infozoo.co.uk`.

Table 8-1	Top-Level Domain Names		
Domain Name	*Primary Use*	*In Original Six Domains?*	*Good for Online Businesses?*
`.biz`	Businesses	No	Yes
`.com`	Companies or individuals involved in commerce	Yes	Yes
`.co.uk`	Same as above, but for business located in the UK	No	Yes
`.gov.uk`	Government agencies	Yes	No
`.info`	Sites that provide information about you, your ideas, or your organisation	No	Yes

(continued)

Table 17-1 *(continued)*			
Domain Name	**Primary Use**	**In Original Six Domains?**	**Good for Online Businesses?**
.name	Any individual	No	No
.net	Network providers	Yes	Potentially
.org	Not-for-profit organisations	Yes	No
.pro	Licensed professionals	No	Potentially

Some of the newer domain names, of course, haven't really taken off. They were created in order to provide alternatives for organisations that couldn't find names in the original domains. In reality, it has forced big companies and other organisations to keep buying up domain names to prevent others from trading on their good name.

A perfect example of why this is necessary occurred when Pricewaterhouse Coopers, an accountancy firm, changed the name of its consulting arm to Monday. To spread the word, it bought the domain name www.introducing monday.com. It didn't buy the co.uk equivalent, however, which was promptly snapped up by a group of tricksters with too much time on their hands. They created a Web site mocking the new name, a fact which helped to destroy the rebrand.

Having said that, one or two of the newer domains have gathered popularity. In particular, the .info name has taken off. According to its registry service, Afilias (www.afilias.info), it is the sixth largest domain on the Internet, with around half a million sites. Because virtually every business needs to put information about itself online, the .info domain is a good alternative if your first-choice domains aren't available.

Certain domains are 'restricted' only to particular types of individuals or organisations. For example, .gov.uk is restricted to government-funded groups, while .org.uk is restricted to noncommercial organisations, such as lobbies, trade unions, and so on. In actual practice, businesses don't observe such restrictions very strictly. The .net domain, which was originally intended for network service providers such as ISPs and Web hosts, is commonly used by businesses that can't find their ideal name in the .com or .co.uk domains, for example. You aren't limited to one domain, either.

Registering domain names related to yours

Even if you already have a domain name, it makes sense to pay a nominal fee to lock up a related name. That way, other businesses or cyber squatters can't attempt to register a domain that's like yours and possibly steal some of your visits. For example, Dan owns www.infozoo.co.uk, but he doesn't own www.infozoo.com. To go about registering such a domain, follow these steps:

1. **Start up your Web browser and go to a recognised domain name provider, such as Nominet, Easyspace, Ukreg, or 123-reg.**

   The home page for your choice opens.

2. **All domain name providers allow you to check whether your domain name is available, so type the name in the space provided and click Go.**

   In most cases, you see a screen saying 'Yes it's available' or 'No it's not'.

   If the domain name isn't available, the provider should offer alternative TLDs. If not, simply search again.

   If your domain is available, then snap it up as quickly as possible! Providers accept switch and credit cards, and domains vary in price from around £8 to around £25, depending on whether they're national (.co.uk) or international (.com).

Most organisations that sell domain names also offer servicing such as hosting and design. If you're just starting out and are keen to get going with your Web site then give it some thought, if not ignore these.

Nominet may be the best-known registrar, but it's not the least expensive. You'll save money by shopping around for domain name registrars. A simple search using the phrase 'domain names' can turn up hundred of options.

Finding a new Web server

You should always consider the option of finding a new Web host if you aren't happy with the one you have. Chances are you're on a server that shares space with lots of other individuals and Web sites. If some of the organisations that share space on your server start streaming audio or video or experience heavy traffic, the performance of your Web site will likely suffer. You may even experience Web site downtime, too. In either case, you should arrange with your hosting service to find a better Web server to house your site or find another host altogether.

One upgrade you may consider is renting a *dedicated computer* – a computer on which yours is the only Web site. This option is far more expensive than a shared hosting account, but after you've developed a customer base and have the resources, it may be worth it. Also consider the following factors that you may find with another host:

✔ **File transfer capability:** The amount of data, in gigabytes, megabytes, or kilobytes, of information that you're allowed to transfer each month before you're charged an additional fee. Successful e-commerce sites can quickly pile up thousands of page views per month, and if you go over your limit, you can get a shock when your bill arrives.

✔ **Marketing services:** Some Web hosting services help you advertise your online business. For example, Easyspace (www.easyspace.com) offers business directory listings and search engine optimisation to improve your business's marketing reach.

✔ **Technical support:** When you're just starting an online business, you'll probably have questions you just can't answer or problems you can't solve on your own. Therefore, you should choose a host that can provide you with round-the-clock tech support.

Another option you have open to you, if you have a broadband Internet connection (and you should!), is setting up your own Web server. This option gives you total control over the management of your Web site. That sounds really nice, but keep in mind that it also means that if something goes wrong, it's your responsibility to get things up and running again. If you're ambitious and technically able, you should consider the popular (not to mention free) Web server program Apache (www.apache.org).

Setting up and running a Web site in this way is not for beginners. If your kids unplug or crash the computer on which your Web site is running, your business goes offline, which can cost you money. If your computer runs slowly or doesn't have enough memory, your site's performance may suffer. It's generally best for beginners to leave the hosting to professionals. Web hosts have the ability to purchase and maintain the best hardware available and have technicians on call to solve problems round the clock. If you leave the hosting to someone else, you have more time to focus on essentials such as building inventory, maintaining the content on your site, and providing good customer service.

Performing Basic Web Housekeeping

To be better prepared to maintain and improve your Web site, you should visit it yourself on a regular basis. In fact, you should be the first one to view your pages when they go online; after that, you need to revisit as often as you can to make sure that your photos display correctly and that your links take you where you want them to go. Other helpful tips are described in the following sections.

All Web browsers are not created equally in the way that they handle colours, fonts, and other Web page elements. Be sure to visit your site by using different browsers in order to confirm that things work the way you want in all cases. At the very least, check your site with Microsoft Internet Explorer and Netscape Navigator; you may also want to use a popular alternative browser called Firefox (www.mozilla.com).

Making sure that your site is organised

One of the basic principles of e-commerce is that products must be easy to find. The way you organise your Web site defines whether customers find your products easily or get caught up in an impromptu game of hide and seek. The people who make a living writing about and designing Web sites call this *usability*. As long as the Web has existed, experts have been studying what makes a Web site usable. Most agree on the following essential characteristics:

- **Keep it logical.** Create an organised path through your site that leads to your shopping trolley and checkout area.

- **Keep it simple.** Each one of your Web pages should do one thing and one thing only.

- **Keep it searchable.** Shoppers who are in a hurry want to jump past all your sales categories, enter a product name in a search box, and go straight to a page of search results which satisfy their enquiry. Give them the chance to do it.

- **Keep it navigable.** The best Web sites offer plenty of points at which users can return to the home page, check out, or navigate back to a broad category.

You can add a search box to your site and have your pages indexed by a service such as FreeFind (www.freefind.com), which is free if you consent to display ads in your search results, or as little as £3 a month for ad-free results.

Make sure that your site has a logical page flow. How many Web pages do your customers have to click through before making their purchases? The general rule 'the fewer the better' applies. Your goal is to lead shoppers into your site and then encourage them to search through your sales catalogue.

Adding navigational links

Another reason to review your e-commerce Web site is to evaluate the number of navigational buttons or other links you give your visitors. The most common options are a row of buttons or links across the top of the page and a column along the left side of the page. These spots are the most obvious places to put such links, but by no means the only types of navigational aids you can add. Your goal should be to provide three types of links when the customer is viewing a sales item:

- Links that make it easy to 'back out' of the category the customer is in by following links to the previous level

- A link to your site's home page

✔ Links to other parts of your site so that the shopper doesn't need to return to the home page continually when they want to explore new parts of your site

Make a map of your Web site

When it comes to your e-commerce Web site, a site map can help you make your site easier to navigate. A *site map* is a graphical representation of your Web site – a diagram that graphically depicts all the pages in the site and how they connect to one another. It is not necessary to provide a map if your site is small (say, only a few pages), but it can help if your site has lots of different areas to explore. Some Web page editing programs, such as Microsoft FrontPage, have a site map function built into them. As you create pages and link them to one another, a site map is created. The following figure shows the site map on the left side of the window and a list of files on the right.

Keep in mind that you don't have to invest in a fancy (and expensive) software program in order to create a site map. You can also create one the old-fashioned way, using a pencil and paper. Or you can draw boxes and arrows, using a computer graphics program you're familiar with. The point is that your site map can be a useful design tool for organising the documents within your site.

If your sales are sluggish, make sure that your customers can actually find what they are looking for. Take a typical product in your sales catalogue and then visit your own site to see how many clicks someone would need to make in order to find it. Then see how many clicks they'd need to complete its purchase. Eliminating any unnecessary navigational layers (such as category opening pages) will make your site easier to use.

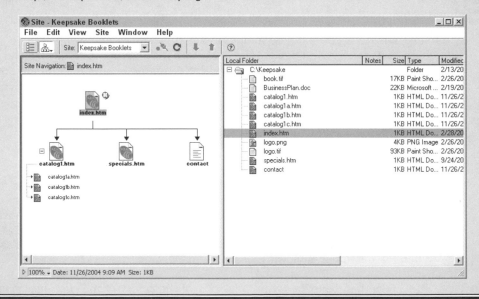

Amazon.co.uk, shown in Figure 8-1, shows a range of useful links that appear on a catalogue page. Along the top, the shopper sees a row of buttons leading to different areas within the site; in the middle of the page, links appear to related items and to other categories within the site.

Ensuring that your site is searchable

The single most useful type of navigational aid is a *search box* – a text box into which visitors enter keywords to search your catalogue by product name or number. Here again, you have different options for adding such a box to your site:

- **The hard way:** You create a Web page with a text box. You write a script that will process the data submitted by visitors. The server that hosts your site needs to be able to process such scripts. Usually, this requirement means it has to have the programming language present.

  For example, if a script is written in the programming language Perl, the host needs to have Perl running on the server. Not all hosts allow the execution of scripts on their servers, however; check with yours to make sure.

- **The less hard way:** You create a Web page with a text box, but you borrow a script so that you don't have to write your own. You can use the popular Simple Search form at Matt's Script Archive (`www.script archive.com`).

- **The Microsoft way:** Most Web hosts allow the use of a set of programs called the FrontPage Server Extensions. If you have FrontPage, you can use it to create your own searchable site index.

- **The easy way:** You sign up with a service that indexes your site – in other words, scours your Web pages and records their contents – and provides you with a search box that you can add to your site.

- **The alternative way:** You get your Web site designed and built for you by a professional company, at a cost. In your brief to them, you stipulate that you'd like users to search through your products. They'll do the rest for you.

Because the 'easy way' is the one that doesn't require any programming and is easiest for beginners, we describe it in more detail. Services that make other people's Web sites searchable usually provide two options. One is free, but the results that appear when someone searches your site have advertisements displayed as well. The other isn't free, but the search results *are* ad-free. These days, shoppers are so accustomed to seeing ads displayed all over the Web that they probably won't be put off if some appear in your search results. So we wouldn't be reluctant to choose the free search option if it is available.

Figure 8-1:
Highly
visible links
show the
customer
exactly
what's
on offer.

Picosearch makes it easy to place a search box on a Web site, either on a free, ad-supported basis or on a monthly subscription basis. Go to the site's home page at www.picosearch.com and follow these steps to use the free service:

1. **Type your site's URL and your e-mail address in the boxes supplied, and click Submit.**

   The Site Search New Account Setup page appears.

2. **Type your name and a password in the boxes supplied.**

3. **Type the URLs for the pages you want to serve as entry points to your site.**

4. **Adjust the options for indexing and *spidering* (the amount of searching that can be done).**

   If you're in doubt about which options to choose, just leave the defaults for now; you can change them later.

5. **Scroll to the bottom of the New Account Setup page, select the check box that says you agree to the terms of the Picosearch licence, and click OK, Build My FREE Search Engine!**

A page appears informing you that your Web site is being indexed. You'll also receive at least two e-mails from Picosearch. You need to click a link in the first e-mail in order to complete the registration for your free account. (The second tells you that your site is being indexed.) A third e-mail (which can take up to 24 hours to arrive) tells you the indexing is done.

6. **Click the link supplied in the first message from Picosearch; when the Select A Plan page appears, click Subscribe next to Free Plan.**

   A page appears informing you that your registration is complete and reminding you to view another e-mail message. This message instructs you on how to add the all-important search box to your Web page.

7. **Open the message and copy the code for your search box by dragging the mouse pointer across all the following and pressing Ctrl+C:**

```
<!-- Begin Picosearch Code -->
[code follows]
<!-- End Picosearch Code -->
```

8. **Open the code for your Web page in a Web page editor or a text editor such as Notepad. Position the text cursor at the spot where you want the search box to appear and then press Ctrl+V to paste the copied code.**

   The text is added to your Web page code.

9. **Save your Web page code and upload the new Web page to your Web server.**

After you've uploaded your page, open it in your Web browser to view the box. Greg's Web site search box is shown in Figure 8-2.

Do a search on your page to see how the service works. As you can see from Figure 8-3, ads are included in a search of Greg's Web site. But because Greg searched for the term *eBay,* the ads are at least related to the topic – in other words, the ads are keyword-based.

A search of your Web site is only as effective as the most recent index of your pages and their contents. If you revamp or improve your Web site (as you should periodically), you need to have your site re-indexed by your search service. Picosearch allows its customers to re-index their site manually at any time – in other words, you go to the Picosearch Web site and request that your site be re-indexed. But if you pay a monthly fee for Picosearch instead of using the free version, you can schedule automatic re-indexing so that you don't have to worry about requesting a new survey of your site on your own.

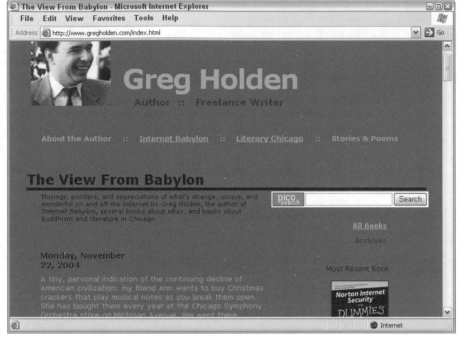

Figure 8-2:
Free site
search
services
index your
Web site
contents
and provide
you with a
searchable
text box.

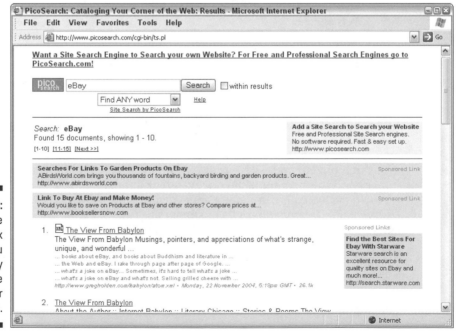

Figure 8-3:
A free
search box
requires you
to display
Google-type
ads in your
results.

Whenever you sign up for 'free' services and submit an e-mail address, you are liable to receive unsolicited commercial e-mail (that is, *spam*) at that address. One solution is to not use your primary e-mail address for such registrations. Instead, set up an address specifically for this purpose and then cancel it when it becomes overrun by too much spam.

Taking your site for a test run

After you've enhanced your Web site with navigational aids, search boxes, and other changes, you need to visit it yourself to make sure that everything works the way you want. You not only need to make sure that your site creates a good visual impression, but also watch out for any problems you have to undo, such as:

- Background colours that are too similar to the colour of your body text and that make it hard to read

- Images that aren't cropped closely enough, which makes them bigger in file size than they need to be (which, in turn, makes them appear on screen too slowly)

- Pages that are overcrowded, with insufficient room between columns or between images and text

- Errors in spelling or grammar

- Type that's too small and can't be read easily by older viewers

- Copyright notices or 'This site was last updated on . . .' messages that are old and out of date

- Factual statements that are no longer accurate

It makes sense to perform such evaluations when you change your site. But you should test things whenever you move files from your computer to your Web server. In order to know how to best make improvements, it is important to continue to test and make evaluations.

If you want an entertaining rundown of bad Web design features to avoid on your own site, visit Web Pages That Suck (`www.webpagesthatsuck.com`). Author Vincent Flanders includes a feature called Mystery Meat Navigation that shows how *not* to guide visitors through your Web site.

Managing Goods and Services

Shoppers on the Web are continually in search of The New: the next new product, the latest price reduction, the latest must-know information and up-to-the-minute headlines. As a provider of content, whether in the form of words or images or products for sale, your job is to manage that content to keep it fresh and available. You also need to replenish stock as it's purchased, handle returns, and deal with shipping options.

Sourcing goods

Sourcing is a fancy term for buying items at a really low price so that you can sell them for a profit. For a small business just starting out on the Internet, sourcing isn't an easy prospect. Lots of online businesses advertise themselves as wholesale sellers. Many say they will *drop-ship* their merchandise – in other words, ship what's purchased directly from their wholesale facility so that you never actually have to handle them and may never see them.

Sound too good to be true? In some cases, it is, and you should always exercise a healthy dose of caution when you're looking for wholesale suppliers. The eBay sellers we've talked to who have faithful, reliable wholesalers guard the identities of those suppliers jealously. They usually find such suppliers only by word of mouth: Rather than answering an ad or visiting a Web site, they ask someone who knows someone who . . . you get the idea.

If you aren't in the business of selling goods or services that you manufacture yourself, you need to find a steady stream of merchandise that you can sell online. Your goal is to find a wholesaler who can supply you with good-quality items at rock-bottom prices; you can mark up the prices and make a profit while keeping the prices low enough to make them attractive. Generally, the best wholesale items are small objects that can be packed and shipped inexpensively. On eBay, things like cheap watches, t-shirts, jewellery, and other small gift items are commonly sold by PowerSellers, along with the occasional antique or collectible. Here are a few general rules for finding items you can sell:

- ✔ **Try them out yourself.** Purchase a few items yourself to start with or ask the wholesaler for samples. (Resist any attempts by the wholesaler to sell you, say 10,000 items at a supposedly dirt-cheap price straight off the bat.) Take a few of the items for a test drive. It's easier to convince others to buy what you like yourself.

- ✔ **Try to sell many small, low-priced items rather than a few large ones.** Instead of computers or printers, consider selling computer memory chips or printer ink cartridges, for example.

✔ **Ask for references.** Talk to businesspeople who have already worked with the supplier. Ask how reliable the supplier is and whether the prices are prone to fluctuate.

When looking for merchandise to sell, try to build on your own hobbies and interests. If you collect model cars, try to develop a sideline selling parts, paints, and components online. You'll find the process more enjoyable when you're dealing in things you love and know well.

Handling returns

Your returns policy depends on the venue where you make your sales. If you sell primarily on eBay, you should accept returns, if only because many of the most experienced and successful sellers do, too. That doesn't mean you need to accept every single item that is returned. Most businesses place restrictions on when they will receive a return and send a refund. The items must be returned within 30 days; the packages must be unopened; the merchandise must not be damaged; and so on.

Adding shipping rates

As part of creating a usable e-commerce catalogue, you need to provide customers with shipping costs for your merchandise. Shipping rates can be difficult to calculate. They depend on your own geographic location as well as the location where you're planning to ship. If you are a small-scale operation and you process each transaction manually, you may want to ship everything a standard way (for example, via Royal Mail). Then you can keep a copy of your shipper's charges with you and calculate each package's shipping cost individually.

Maintaining inventory

Shoppers on the Web want things to happen instantly. If they discover that you've run out of an item they want, they're likely to switch to another online business instead of waiting for you to restock your shop. With that in mind, obey the basic principle of planning to be successful: Instead of ordering the bare minimum of this or that item, make sure that you have enough to spare. In other words, too much inventory initially is better than running out early.

Rely on software or management services to help you keep track of what you have. If you feel at ease working with databases, record your initial inventory in an Excel spreadsheet from Microsoft. This step forces you to record each sale manually in the database so that you know how many items are left. You can connect your sales catalogue to your database by using a program such as ColdFusion from Macromedia. Such a program can update the database on the fly as sales are made. But you may need to hire someone with Web programming experience to set the system up for you and make sure it actually works.

If you sign up with a sales management provider like Marketworks (`www.marketworks.com/uk`), inventory is tracked for you automatically. Marketworks is popular with eBay.co.uk auction sellers, but there's no reason why you can't establish an account with back-end functions such as payment, invoices, and inventory management for any online business. Whether you do the work yourself or hire an outside service, you have to be able to answer basic questions such as

- ✔ **When should you reorder?** Points in your business cycle at which you automatically reorder supplies (when you get down to two or three items left, for example).

- ✔ **How many do you have in stock right now?** You need to forecast not only for everyday demand but also in case a product gets hot or the holiday season brings about a dramatic increase in orders. Know when stuff will be in demand (sunglasses in summer, for example) and buy accordingly.

An e-commerce hosting service may also be able to help you with questions that go beyond the basics, such as the past purchasing history of customers. Knowing what customers have purchased in the past means you can suggest additional items your customers may want. But in the early stages, make sure that you have a small cushion of additional inventory – you don't want demand to outstrip supply early on – that may dent your reputation just when you're trying to establish a good one!

Part III
Running and Promoting Your Online Business

'We only started our eBay business, webuyoldmasters.co.uk, this morning and the response has been amazing.'

In this part . . .

Going into business doesn't mean going it alone. For one thing, you don't necessarily want to quit your day job right away. You aren't ready to start making money online 24/7 and maintain the infrastructure that goes with an online business. Signing up with a well-known hosting service is like renting office space in a mall, except that in this case, your virtual landlord gives you a jump-start. In this part, you discover how to start making money with the help of online business stalwarts such as eBay. You also discover how to accept payments, provide top-notch service, and get on the radar of search engines.

Chapter 9

Easing the Shopping Experience

● ●

In This Chapter

▶ Understanding the purchasing needs of online consumers

▶ Obtaining technical help and support from your Web host

▶ Choosing one of the major e-commerce hosting services

▶ Evaluating the performance of your Web site

▶ Gaining benefits by working with Application Service Providers (ASPs)

● ●

*N*othing can compare to the emotional thrill you feel when you start your own new business and get it online. Nothing, that is, but the real excitement of getting paid for what you do. A pat on the back is nice, but it's even better to receive the proverbial cheque in the mail or have funds transferred to your business account.

When you're in an online business, financial transactions involve two important elements. First, you must take more care than a bricks-and-mortar shopkeeper to reassure the customer (and make sure that they pay you promptly). You also need to protect your money. It's nice to know that, because e-commerce has been around for a few years, you have your choice of experts, services, and online tools that make your job easier. Even though independence may be one of the factors that you like most about running your own online business, you have plenty of demands on your time, and getting help is a sensible idea.

For example, the technical side of starting up a site doesn't have to be your concern. You don't have to spend years studying to be a programmer. Plenty of gizmos are available to help you create Web pages, make links, keep your books, and do other tasks online.

Time is on your side in this case because the range of software 'shortcuts' is becoming larger and more user friendly. You can create forms that will process data and send it to you. You can keep track of your business expenses online, create banner ads and animations, hold videoconferences, and more. In this chapter, we suggest practices that will reduce your business time-to-market as well as ways to share information more efficiently. Every hour you save by taking advantage of these services is an hour you can spend on another part of your business, or perhaps even relaxing.

Here is a short list of what you need to do to be a successful e-commerce businessperson: set up the right atmosphere for making purchases, provide options for payment, and keep sensitive information private. Oh, and don't forget that your main goal is to get goods to the customer safely and on time.

Attracting and Keeping Online Customers

You've heard it before, but we can't emphasise enough the importance of understanding the needs and habits of online shoppers and doing your best to address them. When it comes to e-commerce, a direct correlation exists between meeting the needs of your customers and having a healthy balance in your bank account.

See your merchandise

Customers may end up buying an item in a brick-and-mortar shop, but chances are that they saw it online first. In fact, they often aren't interested until they read a detailed description and reviews. More and more shoppers are assuming that legitimate shops will have a Web site and an online sales catalogue.

'It's not enough to just say we have this or that product line for sale. Until we actually add an individual item to our online shop, with pictures and prices, we won't sell it,' says Ernie Preston, who helped create an 84,000-item online catalogue for a bricks-and-mortar tool company profiled later in this chapter. 'As soon as you put it in your online catalogue, you'll get a call about it. Shopping on the Web is the convenience factor that people want.'

Don't hesitate to post as many items as possible on your online catalogue and don't scrimp on the amount of detail that you include about each item. Two great examples are ASOS (www.asos.com) and Pixmania (www.pixmania.co.uk). The first site is great because you can see exactly what you're getting (in different colours and at different angles), and the second site offers splendid descriptions of the stuff you're looking for. For more and more businesses, having an online catalogue is becoming an integral, not peripheral, part of their identity.

Tell me that the price is right, right now

Customers may have a lot of questions to ask you, but what they want to know first and foremost is how much an item costs. Be sure to put the cost right next to the item that you're presenting. Searching through a price list will lose the competitive edge of speed and convenience, which is what Web shoppers want most. They don't have the patience to click through several pages. Chances are that they're comparison shopping and in a hurry.

The rise of price comparison Web sites like Kelkoo.co.uk, PriceRunner.co.uk, and SimplySwitch.co.uk have changed the way people shop. They can check out the cheapest price for almost any product. Leave out the price, or make it hard to find, and your customers will leave your Web site in droves.

Microsoft Office, the widely used suite of applications that includes Word, Excel, and PowerPoint, gives you access to clip art images that help highlight sales items. Figure 9-1 shows an example of how you can edit an HTML Web page file with Word by inserting an image from the Clip Art pane. (You can find more clip art images at the Microsoft Office Clip Art and Media Centre, `office.microsoft.com/en-gb/default.aspx`.)

Font menu   Clip Art task pane

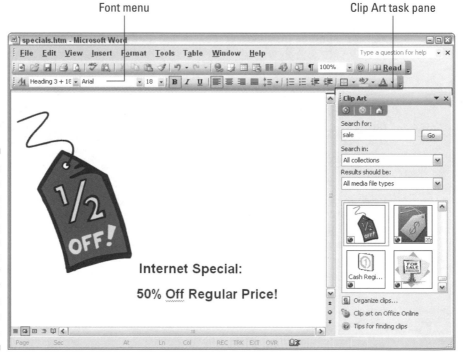

Figure 9-1: Use graphics to call attention to the information your customer wants the most: the price.

Show me that 1 can trust you!

Trust is the foundation on which every good relationship is built, and building trust is especially important for an online business. Electronic commerce is still in its early days, and many customers still have fears:

- ✔ How do I know that someone won't intercept my name, phone number, or credit-card information and use the data to make unauthorised purchases?
- ✔ How can I be sure that your online business will actually ship me what I order and not 'take the money and run'?
- ✔ Can I count on you not to sell my personal information to other businesses that will flood me with unwanted e-mail?

To get an in-depth look at how customers shop online and what constitutes 'good' and 'bad' shopping for many people, consult *Buying Online For Dummies* (Wiley), by Joseph Lowery.

How do you build trust online? If you run an eBay.co.uk shop, you have the advantage of being able to display a feedback rating, and customers can look up comments left on the site by the people with whom you have done business. If you're not on eBay.co.uk, the best way to reassure people is to publish comments from satisfied customers. If you're really savvy, you'll have generated some press coverage (local usually, but national/international if you're very good), and the fact that you have been profiled by a newspaper or Web site will add to your legitimacy. Failing that, you need to state your policies clearly and often. Don't overdo it, though. Constantly reiterating that you will keep information safe and that you honestly really, really will send them their purchased goods will arouse suspicion rather than trust. If you plan to accept credit-card orders, be sure to get an account with a Web host that provides a *secure server,* which is software that encrypts data exchanged with a browser.

Official recognition is another good way to settle customers' nerves. TrustUK (`www.trustuk.org.uk`) is one organisation that can help. To get your hands on one of its 'e-hallmarks', you must go through a fairly arduous (though straightforward) process. First, you have to check that your business qualifies and then you must complete an application form, print and post the form (or send it by e-mail), and get it to TrustUK headquarters. You can see the full process by following this link: `www.trustuk.org.uk/default.asp?option=7`.

Give me the essentials; show me the products

Remember that one of the big advantages of operating a business online is space. You have plenty of room in which to provide full descriptions of your sale items. Be clever with your descriptions, however, and try not to bore people. Remember that people stick on a Web page for a few moments unless something grabs them, so make your words jump out of the screen. Whatever you do, don't bang on about how great your products are and don't tell people stuff they already know. Customers (and people in general) hate being patronised. Here are some suggestions of how to provide information that your customer may want:

- ✔ If you sell clothing, include a page with size and measurement charts, display plenty of photos, and use a model (a person or a dummy) to model the clothes. People like to see how things fit, and they can't do that if you display them folded up.

- ✔ If you sell food, provide weights, ingredients, and nutritional information. More importantly, be very clear about what they actually get for their money. Don't just say hamper – £35. Give some pertinent details about what goes in it!

- ✔ If you sell Web design, artwork, calligraphy, poetry, or anything else that needs to 'be seen', provide samples of your work, links to Web pages you've created, and testimonials from satisfied clients.

- ✔ If you're a musician, publish a link to a short sound file of your work. Dan's in an events band, and its Web site features MP3s (music files) so that potential customers can get an idea of the type of music and how well they play.

Don't be reluctant to tell people ways that your products and services are better than others. Estate agents and auctioneers are very good at selling the quality of the things they are selling. Check out www.foxtons.com and www.sothebys.co.uk for examples of how businesses play up their products.

Looking for a Good Web Host: The 411

Time and again, we hear successful entrepreneurs extol the virtues of the companies that enable their businesses to go online. Why all the praise? Some Web hosting services or ISPs go beyond the basic tasks of providing space on a Web server and keeping the server functioning smoothly.

Finding the right hosting company is one of the most important parts of building an online Web site that works. Whether you're building the site yourself, or getting a professional to do it, it's worth snooping for recommendations and referrals. Choosing a host that no one has recommended is unwise. No matter what type of Web site you run, you'll be handing over a substantial amount of money to your host – so make sure that they're worth it.

At RealBusiness.co.uk, Dan recently asked readers for hosting companies they would recommend. The top four businesses were as follows:

- ✔ **Open-Minded Solutions** (`www.openmindedsolutions.co.uk`) got top marks from several of the respondents.

- ✔ **1and1Internet** (`www.1and1.co.uk`) was noted for its reasonable pricing and strong customer service.

- ✔ **FastHosts** (`www.fasthosts.co.uk`) was said to be technically reliable with good phone support (Dan recommends these guys, too).

- ✔ **Global Gold** (`www.globalgold.co.uk`) received the thumbs up for great customer service.

Before you sign up with a host, check out customer service options. Specifically, find out when service staff are available by telephone. Also ask whether telephone support costs extra. If you're working alone and don't have a technical person you can call, being able to speak to a technical support person about a problem you're encountering on your site can be invaluable.

It may seem surprising to think of your Web host as one of the reasons for your success. After all, you do most of the work. At the most basic level, a hosting service is just a company that provides you with space on a server. You call them only when you have a problem or a billing question. At least, that's how most people look at their Web host.

However, whether you use the server space given to you by your ISP or sign with a full-time Web host, the relationship can be much more.

For example, FastHosts (`www.fasthosts.co.uk`) comes in for a lot of praise from novices and experts alike. It was created by an entrepreneur during the height of the dotcom boom when hosting companies were charging a fortune for their services. FastHosts strives to be cost-effective but reliable – and on the whole, it has achieved that goal. Basic hosting packages start at just £3.99 a month. But for a little extra (between £7.99 and £15.99 a month), you can command extra services that rise above standard deals:

✔ **Multiple server hosting:** Basically, this feature means your Web site will almost certainly never go down. Because it's hosted across numerous servers, if one suffers a blip, then another one will seamlessly take over.

✔ **TrafficDriver:** FastHosts makes extra effort to get your Web site to the top of the world's most popular search engines, such as Google and Yahoo!.

✔ **Advanced password protection:** This feature helps if you run a membership-based organisation or if you want to confirm your service to a few paying customers. The passwords and logins are stored in a directory where you can add or delete at will.

✔ **Thirty-day money back guarantee:** This one is a very nice extra. If you're not totally happy with the service (and Dan reckons you probably will be), you can get your money back without quibble. Setup is free, and you can activate your account just about instantly.

Don't get locked in to a two- or three-year contract with a Web host. Go month to month or sign a one-year contract. Even if you're initially happy with your host, a shorter contract gives you a chance to back out and go elsewhere if the company takes a turn for the worse or your needs change.

Domain name registration

People frequently get confused when Greg tries to explain how to register a domain name and how to 'point' the name at the server that hosts their Web sites. This area is a perfect place for an ISP to help you. In addition to giving you an Internet connection and Web server space, some ISPs also function as domain name registrars: The ISP provides a service that enables anyone to purchase the rights to use a domain name for one, two, or more years. It's a kind of one-stop shopping: You can set up your domain name, and, if the same company hosts your site, you can easily have the name associated with your site instead of having to go through an extra step or two of pointing the name at the server that holds your site.

By *pointing* your domain name at your server, we mean the following: You purchase the rights to a domain name from a registrar. You then need to associate the name with your Web site so that when people connect to your site, they won't have to enter a long URL, such as `username.home.mindspring.co.uk`. Instead, they'll enter `www.mybusiness.co.uk`. To do so, you tell the registrar that your domain name should be assigned to the IP address of your server. Your ISP or Web host tells you the IP address to give to the registrar.

When you're registering your site, don't focus solely on the `.com` or `.co.uk` domains. Some new domains have been made available that can provide you with alternate names in case your ideal `.com` name is unavailable. Even if you do get a `.com` name (`.com` is still the most recognisable and desirable domain name extension), you may want to buy up the same name with `.co.uk`, `.net`, `.biz`, `.info`, or `.tv` at the end so that someone else doesn't grab it.

Marketing utilities

Some people are great at promotion and marketing. Others excel at detail work. Only a few lucky people can do both kinds of business tasks well and enjoy it. If, like Greg, your promotional talents are a bit weak, find a hosting service that can help you get noticed.

Some hosts, such as Streamlinenet.co.uk (`www.streamlinenet.co.uk`), give you access to a variety of marketing services if you sign with it as your host. The services are a mix of free and paid for. Probably the best bit is that you get £25 toward Google Adwords and £25 toward Mirago search (`www.mirago.co.uk`) with your account. If you get several recommendations for a good hosting service, and you can't decide which one to go with, it's worth looking at what's thrown in free – it may help you get off the ground more quickly.

Catalogue creators

Some of the biggest Web hosts give you software that enables you to create an online sales catalogue by using your Web browser. In other words, you don't have to purchase a Web design program, figure out how to use it, and create your pages from scratch.

On the downside, a Web-based catalogue creation tool doesn't give you the ultimate control over how your pages look. You probably can't pull off fancy layout effects with tables or layers. (See Chapter 5 for more on using tables and layers to design your site's Web pages.) On the plus side, however, if you have no interest in Web design and don't want to pay a designer, you can use one of these tools to save time and money by getting your pages online quickly all by yourself.

Database connectivity

If you plan on selling only 5, 10, or even 20 or so items at a time, your e-commerce site can be a *static* site, which means that every time a customer makes a sale, you have to manually adjust inventory. A static site also requires you to update descriptions and revise shipping charges or other details by hand, one Web page at a time.

In contrast, a *dynamic* e-commerce site presents catalogue sales items 'on the hoof' (dynamically) by connecting to a database whenever a customer requests a Web page. Suppose, for example, that a customer clicks a link for shoes. On a dynamic site, the customer sees a selection of footwear gathered instantly from the database server that's connected to the Web site. The Web page data is live and up to date because it's created every time the customer makes a request.

If you need to create a dynamic Web site, another factor in choosing a Web host is whether it supports the Web page and database software that you want to use. If you use a database program such as MySQL, for example, you may want to sign up with a Web host that allows you to run SQL Server on one of its servers.

Payment plans

Handling real-time online transactions is one of the most daunting of all e-commerce tasks. Some Web hosts can facilitate the process of obtaining a merchant account and processing credit-card purchases made online. FastHosts.co.uk, for one, says you can make direct payments into your UK account at no extra cost.

BT eShop (`www.btbroadbandoffice.com/internetapplications/ itplanding`), one of the best-known Web hosts, has a hosting plan especially for business beginners hoping to set up e-commerce Web sites. The service is incredibly simple and costs only £25 a month plus VAT (with no set up fees) for a fully functioning 'e-tail' Web site. Of course, for this money, you're not going to set the world on fire with your design or functionality – but it's perfect for a part-time or hobby business.

Once you've designed and built your Web site from a template, you're able to add up to 1,000 different products to sell. BT has recently done a deal with PayPal, so you can use this simple (though some would say pricey) payment platform on your site. However, eShop is compatible with a range of payment systems that you can integrate through its Web site.

In any case, you still have to set up your Web site, catalogue, and shopping trolley pages, and you still have to ship out your items and answer your customers' questions. But having your Web host provide you with the sales and payment tools, along with the availability to answer your questions, removes part of the burden.

Boosting Business through Efficient Communication

In the earlier sections of this chapter, we show you how ISPs can help you create catalogues, process payments, obtain domain names, and perform other business tasks. However, sometimes the tasks that aren't directly related to marketing and sales can actually enable you to improve your profit margin by giving you more time to do marketing and sales. If you can use the Internet to communicate with vendors, co-workers, and other business partners, you increase efficiency, which, in turn, enables you to take care of business.

Efficiency involves getting everyone on the same page and working together, if not at the same time, at least at the *right* time.

A less intrusive tool for getting people together is an online *personal information manager* (PIM). An online PIM provides the tools, such as a calendar, an address book, a to-do list, and e-mail, so that members of a workgroup can co-ordinate their schedules.

An example of an online PIM is ScheduleOnline (`www.scheduleonline.com`). ScheduleOnline received high marks from the online news service CNET and VNUNET, particularly for its calendar, which enables multiple users to share lists of tasks and meetings, as shown in Figure 9-2. Users can invite others to meetings (guests confirm with a single click), send meeting announcements by e-mail, and check for conflicts to ensure that everyone's schedule has an opening during the time selected.

Collaboration boosts efficiency

Health Decisions (www.healthdec.com), a clinical research and development company based in Chapel Hill, North Carolina, manages its internal operations plus an office in Oxford, England, by taking advantage of the Internet. The company posts its company's benefits, travel, and orientation information for new employees on its intranet. Staff can also purchase travel vouchers and record purchases made with company credit cards online.

Improved communication and workflow – thanks to e-mail, the intranet, and access to the wider Internet – enables the company's 80 staff members to collaborate and communicate with the aid of only two administrative staff. Health Decisions doesn't even have a receptionist.

CEO Michael Rosenberg estimates that Health Decisions would require five to seven additional people if it used conventional communications. He believes the company's intranet is saving them about £90,000 to £125,000.

'A lot of the administrative questions you get are very predictable. How do I check the status of my 401K plan or enter time for a project? We try to put it all on our intranet. Why pay someone to do these repetitive tasks when we can put the relevant information on the intranet, and people can access the data quickly. We save time; the employee saves time. I look on it as a means of empowering people.'

The Internet also enables Health Decisions to handle critical procedures far more quickly when compared with industry standards:

- The time required to collect and enter data into a database is only a matter of minutes, in contrast to industry averages of anywhere between several hours and several months.

- The error rate for databases is less than 1 per 10,000 database fields, compared with about 5 per 1,000 incurred by other companies.

- The time required to submit a 10,000-page regulatory application is three months, compared with about a year for companies that don't collaborate online.

Health Decisions conducts tests of pharmaceutical drugs. Such tests are expensive and collect an extensive amount of data. It's critical for staff to get the data in the system quickly and get the information in the field. When a study has been completed, Health Decisions uses standard forms stored on its intranet to present the data, which is then submitted via the Internet.

'We typically deal with project teams scattered around the globe, and our system is designed to collect, digest, and share information widely. While a study is still being done, we can tell how it's progressing because the data is put on the intranet in real time in a database,' says Rosenberg. 'We set up a Web site for each study. At other organisations, it may take a week to gather the data. On the Net, you can do it instantly. Ultimately, we have shown that we can reduce typical drug development timelines by 20 per cent or more.'

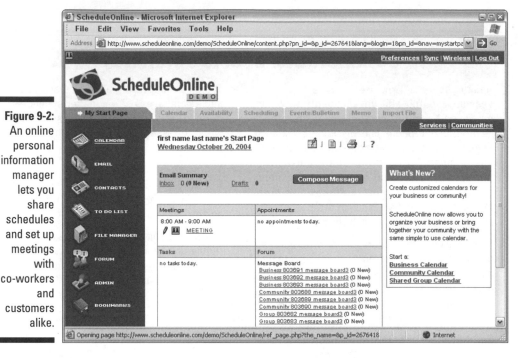

Figure 9-2:
An online
personal
information
manager
lets you
share
schedules
and set up
meetings
with
co-workers
and
customers
alike.

Making Sure That Your Web Site Is Up to Scratch

It's tempting to just get your Web site online and then forget about it. It's up to your hosting service or ISP to monitor traffic and make sure that everything's up and running. That's their job, right?

It *is* their job, to be sure, but unless you keep an eye on your site and its availability to your customers, you may not be aware of technical problems that can scare potential business away. If your site is offline periodically or your server crashes or works slowly, it doesn't just waste your customers' time – it can cut into your sales directly. Luckily, some shortcuts help you monitor your Web site, and they don't take a lot of time and effort or technical know-how.

If your site doesn't work well, you can find another site whose pages load more quickly. Outages can be costly, too. Dan knows of a techie who until recently was responsible for keeping a popular bank's Web site up and running. He was paid an extra $20,000 a year to be on 24-hour call in case the site went down. That's how much companies value consistent 'up time'. *Internet*

Week reported back in 1999 that if the Dell Computer site was down for just one minute, it would cost the hardware giant £5,000. Back then, a 90-minute outage would have cost the company nearly a million dollars – you can probably multiply that figure several times nowadays, such is big companies' reliance on the Net.

Using software to monitor performance

A number of programs are available for anywhere up to a few hundred pounds that continually keep an eye on your Web site and notify you of any problems. Such programs take effort to install. But the effort required to get them up and running has a big benefit – you know about setbacks at least as soon as your customers do, if not before.

WebCheck is a tool that monitors the performance of your Web site. It automatically checks your site and alerts you if your site goes down or if a page has been accidentally renamed or deleted. You configure WebCheck to check your site's URLs; you can have the program load the URLs once a minute, or even once every second. (Faster checking may slow down your site's performance, however.) You can be notified by e-mail, fax, pop-up browser window, or Taskbar icon. You can download WebCheck from the IT Utils Web site (www.itutils.com).

Another application, SiteScope, by Mercury Interactive Corp, runs on Microsoft Windows 2003 or 2000 Server or Windows NT 4.0 and checks sites every five to ten minutes.

You don't have to install your own software in order to monitor your Web site's performance, of course. You can sign up with a company that offers such monitoring as a service. In this case, you use the company's software, which resides on its computers, not yours. For example, Site Confidence (www.siteconfidence.co.uk) provides an online service that checks your site's logins, search facility, upload speeds, and e-mail servers periodically to see whether everything is working correctly. The company offers several levels of service to suit most budgets. That means smaller businesses like yours can probably cut a deal.

Dealing with service outages

Ideally, your Web host will provide a page on its Web site that keeps track of its network status and records any recent problems. One site monitoring notification (from a program you install yourself or one that you 'rent' as a service from an ASP – see the next section 'Outsourcing Your Business Needs') probably shouldn't be cause for concern. However, when you receive a *series* of notifications, call your Web hosting service and talk to its technical staff. Be courteous, but specific. Tell technical support exactly what the problems are/were. You may even want to print the reports you receive so that you can be aware of the exact nature of the problems. Regular service outages no longer have any excuse; plenty of service providers out there promise that your site will almost never go down. To avoid these problems, go for a host that has good track record and a long list of satisfied customers.

If the problem with your site is a slow response to requests from Web browsers rather than a complete outage, the problem may be that your server is slow because you're sharing it with other Web sites. Consider moving from shared hosting to a different option. In *colocation,* you purchase the server on which your files reside, but the machine is located at your Web host's facility rather than at your own location. Your site is the only one on your machine. You also get the reliability of the host's technical support and high-speed Internet connection.

If you really need bandwidth, consider a *dedicated server*. In this case, you rent space on a machine that is dedicated to serving your site. This arrangement is far more expensive than sharing a Web server, and you should choose it only if the number of visits to your site at any one time becomes too great for a shared server to handle. You know a shared server is becoming overtaxed if your site is slow to load. Discuss the situation with your host to see whether a move to a dedicated server makes sense.

Outsourcing Your Business Needs

One of the most effective ways to save time and money doing business online is to let someone else install and maintain the computer software that you use. *Outsourcing* is now a common method of business, but in terms of e-commerce, it refers to the practice of using an online service to perform various tasks for you, such as Web hosting, form creation, or financial record keeping, rather than installing software and running it on your own computer. Outsourcing isn't anything mysterious, however: It simply refers to the practice of having an outside company provide services for your business.

One of the companies that provides Web-based services on an outsourced basis is called an *Application Service Provider* (ASP). An ASP is a company that makes business or other applications available on the Web. You and your colleagues can then use those applications with your Web browser instead of having to purchase and install special software. For example, when you fill out a form and create a shop Web page on eBay.co.uk, you're using eBay as an ASP. Rather than create your Web page on your own computer by using a program, such as Microsoft FrontPage, you use an application on the eBay.co.uk site and store your Web page information there.

How ASPs can help your company

You have to pay a monthly fee to use an ASP's services. You may incur installation fees, and you may have to sign a one- or two-year contract. In return, ASPs provide a number of benefits to your company. Here are the kinds of business processes they can help you perform:

- **Payroll and administration:** Moorepay (www.moorepay.psmda.co.uk), a division of Northgate Information Solutions, is a small business specialist originated in the 1960s – so it has a pretty healthy track record. Its FirstPay tool is an easy to operate Web-based payroll solution, aimed specifically at people like you. Like with most services of this type, the cost depends on how many people you employ, which gives you a chance to haggle.

- **Tech support:** ComponentControl (www.componentcontrol.com), a 55-person company with offices in San Diego and New York, licenses software that enables aerospace companies to locate and trade aviation parts. Instead of having to travel all over the country to solve every problem that users encounter with its software, ComponentControl's tech support staff use an online application called DesktopStreaming that enables them to 'see' the problem a customer is encountering. ComponentControl can also show customers how to use the software from its own offices, which saves on travel costs and has reduced the time to solve problems by 30 per cent.

- **Online form creation:** FormSite.com (www.formsite.com) is a leader in creating a variety of forms that can help online shoppers provide such essential functions as subscribing to newsletters or other publications, asking for information about your goods and services, or providing you with shipping or billing information. The sample pizza order form shown in Figure 9-3 is an example of the type of form that this particular ASP can help you create.

- **Marketing and survey data gathering online:** LeadMaster (www.leadmaster.com) calls itself a 'Web-based data mining tool'. You store your customer information with LeadMaster, and LeadMaster provides you with an online database that you can access any time with your Web browser. It enables you to develop mailing lists based on your customer database. You can use LeadMaster's online tools to do sales forecasting and develop surveys that give you a better idea of what your customers need and want.

Figure 9-3:
An ASP like
FormSite.
com lets you
create a
database-
backed
Web page
feature,
such as a
feedback
form,
without
having to
purchase,
install, and
master a
database
program.

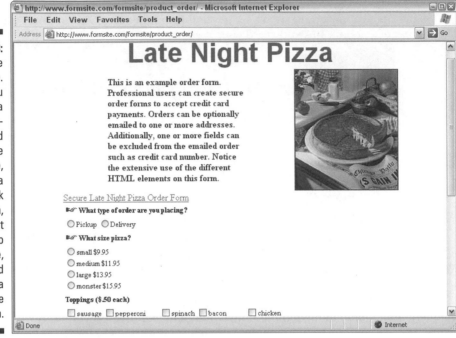

Although ASPs can help you in many ways, they require research, interviewing, contract review, and an ongoing commitment on your part. When does the extra effort make sense? We illustrate the potential pluses and minuses of outsourcing in Table 9-1.

Table 9-1	Outsourcing Benefits and Risks
Pros	*Cons*
Time-saving: Saving time can save you money in the long run.	**ASPs are relatively new:** This is especially true in the UK. Many are startups, and they may not have much experience working with customers. Get some references before you sign a contract for service.

Pros	*Cons*
Better customer service: By outsourcing scheduling or other functions, businesses give customers more options for interacting with them online. Customers don't have to call or e-mail the company; in the case of online scheduling, customers can schedule or cancel appointments by accessing the company's online calendar.	**A contract is required:** When ASPs first began to appear in the late '90s, they spoke in terms of 'renting' software. These days, ASPs usually allow customers to try out their services for a while, but then offer long-term contracts. The terms of these contracts can range from one to three years. Don't get yourself locked in to a long-term arrangement that will prevent you from trying out cheaper or better alternatives down the road.
Greater Web site functionality: ASPs enable your site to provide better service to your customers and allow you to get more work done.	**ASPs face stiff competition:** Many ASPs have failed in recent years. Make sure that the companies that you sign agreements with will be around for a while by talking to current customers and reviewing CVs of senior staff and key employees. Scan the Web for any press releases or articles that serve as warning signs about the ASP's financial health.
Expanded scope: You don't have to become proficient in subjects that aren't part of your core business or expertise.	**Security risks:** The moment you hand over your business data to another online firm or give outside companies access to your internal network, you risk theft of data or virus infections from hackers. Make sure that the ASPs you work with use encryption and other Internet security measures. (See Chapter 7 for more on Web site security.)

In many cases, ASPs can provide a software solution and customise it to your needs. Outsourcing not only improves your company's bottom line, but also helps you convey your message to potential customers that you may never reach otherwise.

CASE STUDY

Videoconferencing: Being in two places at once

One of the best and most useful types of ASP-based services you can use is videoconferencing, which can allow you to hold live meetings with your customers or business partners by using a Web-based conferencing service. Videoconferencing works like this: Participants need a computer that's equipped with a microphone and a camera that takes live video of them while they're sitting in front of their computers. They connect to a central location on the Web – the conferencing service – by using their Web browsers. After they're connected to the same location on the server, they can communicate in real time.

Webex (www.webex.com/uk), a company specialising in events, training, and meetings conducted online, supports a whopping 25,000 customers worldwide. On average, it supports 30,000 meetings a day, but it has been known to deal with 150,000 at once during peak times. The point of all this is that you don't have to travel to meet with roaming employees, potential customers, and business partners. Big businesses can save millions of pounds a year on air, train, and fuel costs – but to you it may mean a tidy saving of a few hundred quid.

What's that you say? You think that videoconferencing is too difficult to set up and expensive to use? WebEx now offers a pay-as-you-go plan. You can use the company's services for a whopping 19p per user per minute. It's a great way to try out the service to see how it works for you. For more about using WebEx, check out *WebEx Web Meetings For Dummies* by Nancy Stevenson (Wiley).

Keep in mind, though, that the quality of any real-time activity on the Web depends on the speed of the participants' respective Internet connections. Because of time lags, videoconferencing is really ideal for users with direct connections, such as T1 or T3 lines, cable modems, or DSL connections.

TIP

ASPNews.com (www.aspnews.com) provides an overview of the current state of the ASP industry. The ASPNews.com staff publishes regular articles about ASPs and industry trends. The site also includes a directory of ASPs (linksmanager.com/aspnews). To check out a very good ASPNews.com article on what to look for in an ASP, go to the following URL:

```
www.aspnews.com/analysis/analyst_cols/article/0,,4431_
425751,00.html
```

Before you sign on the dotted line . . .

After you try out the software or (and any reputable ASP should let you try it out first), you usually need to sign a contract to keep using the service. This step is the time to slow down and read the fine print.

'It's a huge commitment for people to go into an ASP arrangement,' says Dana Danley, an analyst with Current Analysis. 'The lengths of contracts can range from 12 to 50 months. Sometimes you can choose the length of a contract, but most often you're offered standard terms. It's important not to get one that's too long. You don't even know for sure if the ASP will be around in three years, for instance.'

Don't rush, even if you're experiencing the time-to-productivity pressures, merger upheavals, or lack of IT resources that drive many companies to out-source. In the following list, we present some suggestions to help you get the service you should be getting:

- ✔ **Understand pricing schemes.** The pricing schemes that ASPs use to charge for their Web-based services are downright confusing. For example, some ASPs charge on a per-employee basis, which means you pay according to the number of individuals in your company. But others charge per-seat fees based on each registered user, not every employee. Still others charge per CPU, which means you're charged for each machine that runs the hosted application. Make sure that you understand what your prospective ASP plans to charge by asking questions and getting detailed information.

- ✔ **Pin down startup fees.** Virtually all ASPs charge a startup fee, also called a *service implementation fee,* when you sign the contract. Make sure that the fee covers installation and any customisation that you'll need.

- ✔ **Don't accept just any SLA.** Obtaining a *service level agreement* (SLA), a document that spells out what services you expect an ASP (or other vendor) to provide, is essential. But regard the SLA as a dynamic document. Think of SLA as standing for Stop, Look, and Adjust.

- ✔ **Avoid 'gotcha' fees.** Pricing arrangements are hardly standard with regard to ASPs. Some of the big hidden costs involve personalising or customising the service to adapt to legacy systems. Here are some questions you can ask in order to avoid wincing at 'gotchas' when you open up the bill from your ASP:

  - Is there an additional cost for customising or personalising the application?

  - Does it cost extra to back up my company's data and recover it if one of my computers goes down?

  - Is help desk support included in my monthly fee, or will you charge me every time I call with a question or problem?

✔ **Make sure that you have security.** Having information reside on some-one else's system is a double-edged sword. Putting this data on the Web makes it accessible from anywhere. But some huge security risks are associated with transmitting your information across the wide-open spaces of the Net. Make sure that your ASP takes adequate security measures to protect your data by asking informed questions, such as:

- Is my data protected by SSL encryption?

- Do you run a virtual private network?

- How often do you back up your customers' data?

If the answer to any of these questions seems inadequate, move on to the next ASP – plenty are out there, and competition among ASPs is fierce. So right now at least, it's a buyer's market, and you should be able to get what you want.

Chapter 10

Running a Business on eBay.co.uk

*H*ere's a quick quiz: Throughout the ups and downs of e-commerce in the 1990s and early 2000s, what marketplace has remained strong and continued to grow at a steady rate? As you probably know already, it's eBay – we say you probably know this piece of trivia because chances are you've already bought or sold some things yourself on the world's most popular auction site (or maybe this chapter's title gave you a hint).

There's a difference, though, between selling occasionally in order to make a few extra quid and doing what thousands have already done: selling on eBay.co.uk as a means of self-employment. eBay itself has estimated that as many as 450,000 individuals across the world run a business on the auction site full time. Countless others do it on a permanent part-time basis to earn a little sideline cash. Whatever the reason, you can't overlook eBay.co.uk as a way to get a first business off the ground. With eBay, you don't necessarily have to create a Web site, develop your own shopping trolley, or become a credit-card merchant: The auction site itself handles each of those essential tasks for you. But that doesn't mean that developing your own eBay business is easy. It takes hard work and a commitment, combined with the important business strategies described in this chapter. For a more in-depth assessment of starting and running a business on eBay.co.uk, check out Dan's book *Starting a Business on eBay.co.uk For Dummies* (by Wiley, 2006).

Running a business on eBay.co.uk doesn't necessarily mean that you depend on eBay as the sole source of your income. You may sell on eBay.co.uk part-time for some supplementary income each month. This chapter assumes that you want to sell regularly on eBay and build up a system for successful sales that can provide you with extra money, bill-paying money, or 'fun money'.

Understanding eBay.co.uk Auctions

In any contest, you have to know the ground rules. Anyone who has held a garage sale knows the ground rules for making a person-to-person sale. But eBay.co.uk strives to be different, and not just because auctions are the primary format – a rare way of selling in the UK, especially online. eBay.co.uk gives its members many different ways to sell, and each sales format has its own set of rules and procedures. It pays to know something about the different sales so that you can choose the right format for the item you have.

This section assumes that you have some basic knowledge of eBay.co.uk and that you have at least shopped for a few items and possibly won some auctions.

When it comes to putting items up for sale, eBay gets more complicated. You've got the following sales options:

✔ **Standard auctions:** This is the most basic eBay auction. You put an item up for sale, and you specify a starting bid (usually a low amount because you want to generate interest in your item). If you don't have a reserve price; the highest bidder at the end of the sale wins (if there is a highest bidder). Standard auctions and other auctions on eBay can last one, three, five, seven, or ten days. The ending time is precise: If you list something at 10:09 a.m. on a Sunday and you choose a seven-day format, the sale then ends at 10:09 a.m. the following Sunday.

✔ **Reserve auctions:** A *reserve price* is a price you specify as a minimum in order for a purchase to be successful. Any bids placed on the item being offered must be met or exceeded; otherwise, the sale will end without the seller being obligated to sell the item. You know if a reserve price is present by the message `Reserve Not Yet Met` next to the current high bid. When a bid is received that exceeds the reserve, this message changes to `Reserve Met`. The reserve price is concealed until the reserve is met.

✔ **Multiple-item auctions:** This type of sale, also known as a Dutch auction, is used by sellers who want to sell more than one identical item at the same time. The seller specifies a starting bid and the number of items available; bidders can bid on one or more items. But the question of who wins can be confusing. The bidders who win are the ones who have placed the lowest successful bid that is still above the minimum price, based on the number of items being offered. For example, suppose six items are offered, and ten bidders place bids. One bidder bids £20 for two items. Another bids £24 for one. Three others bid £18, two others bid £14, and three bid £10. The winners are the ones who bid £24, £20, and £18, respectively. The others lose out because only six items are available.

✔ **Fixed-price Buy It Now sales:** A Buy It Now price is a fixed price that the seller specifies. Fixed prices are used in all eBay.co.uk shops: The seller specifies that you can purchase the item for, say, £10.99; you click the Buy It Now button, agree to pay £10.99 plus shipping, and you instantly win the item.

✔ **Mixed auction/fixed price sales:** Buy It Now (BIN) prices can be offered in conjunction with standard or reserve auctions. In other words, even though bidders are placing bids on the item, if someone agrees to pay the fixed price, the item is immediately sold, and the sale ends. If a BIN price is offered in conjunction with a standard auction, the BIN price is available until the first bid is placed; then the BIN price disappears. If a BIN price is offered in conjunction with a reserve auction, the BIN price is available until the reserve price is met. After the BIN price disappears, the item is available to the highest bidder.

Those are the basic types of sales. You can also sell cars on eBay.co.uk Motors or even your home (check out `home-garden.listings.ebay.co.uk`). By knowing how eBay.co.uk sales work and following the rules competently, you'll gradually develop a good reputation on the auction site.

How you sell is important, but the question of exactly *what* you should sell is one you should resolve well before you start your eBay.co.uk business, just like in any business. Sell something you love, something you don't mind spending hours shopping for, photographing, describing, and eventually packing up and shipping. Sell something that has a niche market of enthusiastic collectors or other customers. More importantly, sell something that *isn't already there* or that there's clearly a lot of demand for. Do some research on eBay.co.uk to make sure that a thousand people aren't already peddling the same things you hope to make available.

Building a Good Reputation

In order to run a business on eBay.co.uk, you need to have a steady flow of repeat customers. Customer loyalty comes primarily from the trust that is produced by developing a good reputation. eBay.co.uk's feedback system is the best indicator of how trustworthy and responsive a seller is because past performance is a good indication of the kind of service a customer can expect in the future. Along with deciding what you want to sell and whether you want to sell on eBay.co.uk on a part- or full-time basis, you need to have the development of a good reputation as one of your primary goals.

Feedback, feedback, feedback!

eBay's success is due in large measure to the network of trust it has established among its millions of members. The feedback system, in which members leave positive, negative, or neutral comments for the people with whom they have conducted (or tried to conduct) transactions, is the foundation for that trust. The system rewards users who accumulate significant numbers of positive feedback comments and penalises those who have low or negative feedback numbers. By taking advantage of the feedback system, you can realise the highest possible profit on your online sales and help get your online business off the ground.

There probably aren't any scientific studies of how feedback numbers affect sales, but we've heard anecdotally from sellers that their sales figures increase when their feedback levels hit a certain number. The number varies, but it appears to be in the hundreds – perhaps 300 or so. The inference is that prospective buyers place more trust in sellers who have higher feedback numbers because they have more experience and are presumably more trustworthy. Those who have PowerSeller status, denoted by the PowerSeller icon, are even more trustworthy. (See the 'Striving for PowerSeller status' section, later in this chapter.)

Developing a schedule

One thing that can boost your reputation above all else on eBay.co.uk is timeliness. If you respond to e-mail enquiries within a few hours, or at most a day or two, and if you can ship out merchandise quickly, you're virtually guaranteed to have satisfied customers who leave you positive feedback. The way to achieve timely response is to observe a work schedule.

It's tedious and time consuming to take and retake photos, edit those photos, get sales descriptions online, and do the packing and shipping that's required at the end of a sale. The only way to come up with a sufficient number of sales every week is to come up with a system. And a big part of coming up with a system is developing a weekly schedule that spells out when you need to do all your eBaying. Table 10-1 displays a possible schedule .

Table 10-1	eBay Business Schedule	
Day of Week	*First Activity*	*Second Activity (optional)*
Sunday	Get seven-day sales online	Send end-of-sale notices
Monday	Packing	E-mails
Tuesday	Shipping	E-mails

Day of Week	First Activity	Second Activity (optional)
Wednesday	Plan garage sales	Take photos
Thursday	Go to garage sales	Prepare descriptions
Friday	More sales	Prepare descriptions
Saturday	Respond to buyer enquiries	Get some sales online

You'll notice that something is conspicuously missing from this proposed schedule: a day of rest. You can certainly work in such a day on Sunday (or whatever day you prefer). If you sell on eBay.co.uk part time, you can probably take much of the weekend off. But most full-time sellers (and full-time self-employed people in general) will tell you that it's difficult to find a day off, especially when it's so important to respond to customer e-mails within a day or two of their receipt. You don't have to do everything all by yourself, however. You can hire full- or part-time help, which can free up time for family responsibilities.

Creating an About Me page

One of the best ways to build your reputation on eBay.co.uk is to create a Web page that eBay makes available to each of its members free of charge called About Me. Your About Me page should talk about who you are, why you collect or sell what you do, and why you're a reputable seller. You can also talk about an eBay shop, if you have one, and provide links to your current auction sales. It takes only a few minutes to create an About Me page (not much longer than filling out the Sell Your Item form to get a sale online, in fact). If you want to include a photo, you should take a digital image and edit it in an image-editing program, such as Paint Shop Pro or Photoshop, just as you would any other image. But a photo isn't absolutely necessary. Kimberly King, the eBay seller profiled later in this chapter, has a simple About Me page (see Figure 10-1).

When you've decided what you want to say on your page, you need to save a digital photo if you want to include one. Then follow these steps:

1. **Click My eBay on the navigation bar at the top of virtually any eBay.co.uk page.**

   A login page appears.

2. **Type your User ID and password and click Sign In Securely.**

   The My eBay page appears.

Figure 10-1:
An About Me page can be simple; it can contain links to your eBay shop and your eBay auction sales.

3. **Click Personal Information under the My Account heading in the links on the left-hand side of the page.**

   The My eBay Account: Personal Information page appears.

4. **Scroll down to the About Me link and click Edit.**

   The About Me page appears.

5. **Look toward the bottom of the page and click Create Your Page.**

   The Choose Page Creation Option page appears.

6. **Leave the Use Our Easy Step-By-Step Process option selected and click Continue.**

   The About Me: Enter Page Content page appears.

7. **As indicated on the page, type a heading and text for your page. Label your photo and enter the URL for the photo in the Link to Your Picture text box. You can also type links to favourite pages and your own Web page if you have one. When you're done, click Continue.**

   The Preview and Submit page appears, as shown in Figure 10-2.

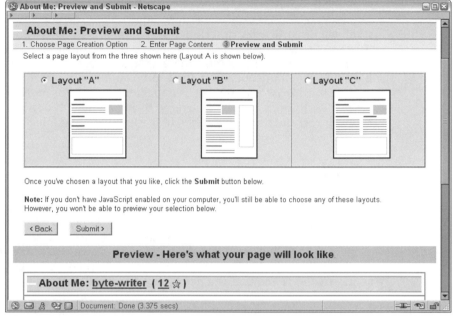

Figure 10-2:
Take a few
minutes to
proofread
your About
Me page
before
you post
it online.

8. **Choose one of three possible layouts for your page and preview your page content in the bottom half of the page. When you're finished, click Submit.**

   Your page goes online.

Like any Web page, you can change your About Me page at any time by following the preceding steps.

Another way to build a good reputation as a seller is to participate actively in eBay's discussion boards. Pay special attention to boards that pertain to the type of merchandise you buy and sell. Responding to questions from new users and offering advice based on your experience can boost your standing within the user community.

Preparing Sales Descriptions That Sell

How do you actually go about selling on eBay.co.uk? The aim is similar to other forms of e-commerce: You select merchandise, take photos, type descriptions, and put the descriptions online in a catalogue.

But there are some critical differences as well. You don't have to specify a fixed price on eBay.co.uk; you can set a starting bid and see how much the market will bear. All sales descriptions are not created equal, however. Many sellers would argue that clear, sharp photos are the most important part of a description and that, if you show the item in its best light, it will practically sell itself. We're of the opinion that a good heading and descriptions that include critical keywords are just as important as good photos. The art of creating descriptions is best discovered by inspecting other people's sales listings; the essentials are described in the following sections.

Details, details

The primary way of getting your sales online is eBay.co.uk's Sell Your Item form. You can access this form at any time by clicking Sell on the eBay navigation bar, which appears at the top of just about any page on the eBay.co.uk Web site. The Sell Your Item form is easy to use, so we don't take you through every little option. In this section, however, we do point out a few features you may overlook and that can help you get more attention for your sales.

The Sell Your Item form is by no means the only way to get eBay sales online. Many full- or part-time businesspeople use special software that allows them to upload multiple images at once or schedule multiple sales so they all start and end at the same time. The auction services Andale (uk.andale.com) and MarketWorks (www.marketworks-uk.co.uk/ebay-auction-software.asp) offer eBay.co.uk auction listing tools. In addition, eBay offers two programs you may find helpful:

- **Turbo Lister** (pages.ebay.co.uk/turbo_lister/index.html), which is free, provides sellers with design templates that they can use to add graphic interest to their sales descriptions.

- **Selling Manager** (pages.ebay.co.uk/selling_manager/index.html), a monthly subscription service, is sales and management software. It provides you with convenient lists that let you track what you have up for sale, which sales have ended, which items have been purchased, and what tasks you have yet to do – for example, sending e-mails to winning bidders or relisting items that didn't sell the first time.

Choosing a second category

One of the first things you do in the Sell Your Item form is to choose a sales category in which to list your item. We recommend using the search box at the top of the All Categories page. Enter a keyword and click Search. You're presented with some auctions and a detailed list of sales categories on the left hand side of the page. The best thing about the list is that it is ranked in order of the ones that are most likely to sell items matching your desired keywords. The categories near the top of the list are the ones to choose.

We also recommend paying an extra few pence or so (when you choose a second category, your listing fee is doubled) and listing the item in a second category – especially if the second category has a ranking that's almost as high as the first.

Focusing on your auction heading

The heading of an eBay sales description is the set of six or seven words that appears in a set of search results or in a set of listings in a category. In other words, it's the set of words that a potential customer initially sees when he or she is deciding whether to investigate a sale and possibly bid on it. Keep your heading short and specific. Include dates, colours, or model numbers if applicable. Try to pick one word that may attract a buyer, such as Rare, Hard-to-Find, Mint, New, or something similar.

Choosing a good ending time for your sale

With eBay sales, it's not the starting time that counts but the ending time that makes a difference. The more attention you can get at the end of a sale, the more likely you are to make a profit. Most sales get attention on weekends, when the majority of shoppers aren't working. The optimal time, in fact, is to have the sale end some time on a Saturday or Sunday afternoon.

Of course, bidders can come from all over the world, and what's early afternoon on a Sunday morning in London is the middle of the night in Australia. But don't worry too much about such distinctions: Pick an ending time that's convenient for eBay.co.uk shoppers in your own country to be present – not in the middle of a workday, but on the weekend.

To keep delivery costs down, you can specify that you'll only accept bids from people within the UK. Don't worry about getting your item seen by everybody in the world; this country alone has more than enough people!

Adding keywords

When you prepare an auction description, you don't have to make it overly lengthy. It's not the length that counts; it's the number of keywords you include. A *keyword* is a word or phrase that describes the item you have for sale and that prospective buyers are likely to enter in their eBay searches. If your description contains a keyword that someone enters, your sale will show up in search results. And just showing up in the search results is half the battle: If a buyer can find your item, he or she can then follow through with its purchase.

The more keywords you can add to your description, the more frequently that sale will be found by searchers. It's to your advantage, then, to think of all the terms that someone would use when looking for your item and add as many of those keywords to the heading and to the body of the description as you can. If you're selling an electric drill, for example, use keywords such as *cordless, electric, drill, Black & Decker,* or anything else a likely buyer may enter.

Upgrading your listings

Near the end of the Sell Your Item form, you get the option to specify whether you want to upgrade your listings. *Upgrade,* in this case, means adding graphic highlights that are intended to help your listing stand out from those around it, either in search results or on category pages. You can choose from the options shown in Table 10-2.

Table 10-2	Listing Upgrades	
Upgrade	*Description*	*Cost*
Highlight	A coloured strip is drawn across the auction title.	£2.50
Bold	The auction title is formatted in bold type.	75p
Gallery	A thumbnail image appears next to auction title.	15p
Gallery Featured Plus!	A Gallery image appears in a 'Featured Items' area at the top of Gallery pages.	£9.95
Home Page Featured	Your auction title is listed randomly along with other sales on eBay's home page.	£49.95

Of these, the single most cost-effective upgrade, in our opinion, is the Gallery thumbnail image, which costs only 15p and draws more attention to your sales listing – especially when you consider that most other listings around yours also have Gallery images. The Home Page may be expensive, but it gives you a chance of having your sale on eBay's home page and guarantees exposure for your sale on featured areas. Reserve this upgrade for big money sales, like a car or expensive furniture.

In eBay's early days, if you wanted a sale to end at a particular time (say, 7 p.m. on a Sunday, when lots of bidders are online), you had to physically be present to create the description at a certain time. For example, if you wanted such a sale to last seven days, you had to list it at precisely 7 p.m. the preceding Sunday. Now, you don't have to be physically present exactly a week, five days, three days, or one day before you want your sale to end: You can specify an ending time when you fill out the Sell Your Item form.

Note: Although it's free to register for an account on eBay.co.uk and free to fill out the Sell Your Item form, eBay charges you an Insertion Fee when you actually put an item up for sale. The Insertion Fee is based on the starting price of the auction. The fee is only 15p for a starting bid of 99p or less, which explains why many starting bids are less than £1. A Final Value Fee is also charged at the end of the auction, and it depends on the sale price. On a sale of £25, the Final Value Fee is 5.25 per cent of the final amount; at £700 it's 5.25 per cent of the initial £29.99, plus 3.25 per cent of the £30–£599, plus 1.75 per cent of remaining value. Complicated? Certainly! Luckily, eBay calculates it all for you. For a detailed explanation of the formula used to calculate fees, see `pages.ebay.co.uk/help/sell/fees.html`.

Include clear images

No matter how well written your auction's headings and description, all your work can quickly be undone by digital images that are dark, blurry, or slow to load because they're too large in either physical or file size. The same principles that you use when capturing digital images for your e-commerce Web site apply to images on eBay.co.uk:

- ✔ Make sure that you have clear, even lighting (consider taking your photos outdoors).
- ✔ Use your camera's auto-focus setting.
- ✔ Crop your images so that they focus on the merchandise being sold.
- ✔ Keep the file size small by adjusting the resolution with your digital camera or your image editing software.

Some aspects to posting images along with auction descriptions are unique to eBay:

- ✔ **Image hosting:** If you run a business on eBay.co.uk and have dozens, or even hundreds, of sales items online at any one time, you can potentially have hundreds of image files to upload and store on a server. If you use eBay Picture Services as your photo host, the first image for each sale is free. Each subsequent image costs 12p. It's worth your while to find an economical photo hosting service, such as FileHigh (`www.filehigh.com`) or Auctionpix (`www.auctionpix.co.uk`).
- ✔ **Close-ups:** If what you're selling has important details such as brand names, dates, and maker's marks, you need to have a camera that has *macro capability* – that is, the ability to get clear close-ups. Virtually all digital cameras have a macro setting, but it can be tricky to hold the camera still enough to get a clear image (you may need to mount the camera on a tripod). If you use a conventional film (not recommended) camera, you'll need to invest in a macro lens.

> ✔ **Multiple images:** You'll never hear an eBay shopper complaining that you included too many images with your auction listings. As long as you have the time and patience and an affordable image host, you can include five, six, or more views of your item (for big, complex objects such as cars and motorbikes, multiple images are especially important).

Be sure to crop and adjust the brightness and contrast of your images after you take them, using a program such as Paint Shop Pro by Jasc (www.jasc.com) or Adobe Photoshop Elements by Adobe Systems (www.adobe.com).

If you want to find out more about creating sales descriptions (and practically every aspect of buying or selling on eBay.co.uk, for that matter), take a look at Dan's book, *Starting a Business on eBay.co.uk For Dummies* (Wiley).

Be flexible with payment options

It may seem like payments are the most nerve-wracking part of a transaction on eBay.co.uk. They have been, in the past, but as time goes on, eBay provides more safeguards for its customers. That doesn't mean you won't run into the occasional bidder who doesn't respond after winning your auction, or whose cheque bounces. But as a seller, you have plenty of protections: If someone doesn't respond, you can relist your item; if someone's cheque bounces, you don't lose out on your sales item because you held on to it during the process of the cheque clearing process.

As an eBay.co.uk seller, you should accept the basic forms of payment. A PayPal account covers most of your customers, but some will want to pay by cheque, card, or a standard bank transfer. You can enable your customers to pay with a credit card, either by using your merchant credit-card account if you have one (see Chapter 11), or by using one of a handful of popular electronic payment services, which include eBay's own PayPal (www.paypal.com), Protx (www.protx.com), or WorldPay (www.worldpay.com). In the case of PayPal, you're charged a nominal fee (1.4 to 3.4 per cent of the amount plus a 20p fee) when a buyer transfers money electronically to your account.

You should generally not accept other forms of payment from buyers. Occasionally, a buyer insists on sending you cash in an envelope; you should insist, in turn, that the buyer sends a money order instead.

Providing Good Customer Service

When you make the decision to sell on eBay.co.uk on a regular basis, you need to develop a good reputation. Earlier in this chapter, we outline ways that you can do that. But one of the best ways to achieve this goal – providing a high level of customer service to your buyers – is an issue that warrants a separate discussion. The single best way to do *that* is to be responsive to e-mail enquiries of all sorts. Good customer service means checking your e-mail a few times a day and spending lots of time responding to your customers' questions. If you take days to get back to someone who asks you about the colour or the condition of an item you have for sale, it may just be too late for that person to bid. And slow response to a high bidder or buyer after the sale can make the buyer nervous and result in 'neutral' feedback – not a complaint about fraud or dishonesty, but a note about below-par service. Such feedback is considered as bad as a negative comment on eBay.co.uk.

Setting terms of sale

One aspect of good customer service is getting back to people quickly and communicating clearly and with courtesy. When you receive enquiries, you should always thank prospective customers for approaching you and considering the sale; even if they don't end up placing bids, you'll have spread goodwill, which hopefully you'll get back.

Another way to be good to your customers is to be clear about how you plan to ship your merchandise and how much it will cost. When you fill out the Sell Your Item form (which we discuss in the earlier section, 'Details, details'), you can specify either an *actual shipping cost* (a cost based on weight and the buyer's residence) or a *flat shipping fee* (a shipping fee you charge for all your items).

The moment you specify a shipping charge in the Sell Your Item form, you set eBay's automated Checkout system in motion. The Checkout system enables buyers to calculate their own shipping charges. The advantage to you, as the seller, is that you don't need to send your buyers a message stating how much they need to pay you.

Packing and shipping safely

One of the aspects of selling on eBay that is often overlooked (not by *buyers*) is the practice of packing and shipping. After sending payment for something, buyers often wait on tenterhooks, expecting to receive their items while dreading the prospect of an unresponsive seller who neglects to ship what has been purchased.

Besides the danger of fraud, there's the danger that the item you send will be damaged in transit. Be sure to use sturdy boxes when you ship and to adequately cushion your merchandise within those boxes. We've received boxes from sellers who stuffed the insides with bubble wrap and newspaper, and we were happy for the trouble. If you're shipping something particularly fragile, consider double-boxing it: Put it in a box, place the box in a larger one, and put cushioning material between the two. Your customers will be pleased to receive the merchandise undamaged, and you'll get good feedback as a result.

Place a thank-you note, business card, or even a small gift inside the box with your shipment. It will remind buyers that you're a trustworthy seller and let them know how to get in touch with you in the future.

Moving from Auctioneer to eBay.co.uk Businessperson

Few eBay.co.uk sellers start out proclaiming, 'I'm going to be a PowerSeller, and I'm going to sell full-time on eBay for a living!' Rather, they typically start out on a whim. They find an object lying around in a box, in the loft, or on a shelf, and they wonder: Will anyone pay money for this? Other sellers are existing businesses who join eBay.co.uk to earn some extra cash, many of whom soon realise it's not just a supplement but an essential component of their business.

For example, take Nick Talley, who runs the phenomenally popular eBay.co.uk shop iPosters. He gave up his courier business after 16 years because of rising bills and set up a Web site called `www.pop-culture.biz`.

Like many people he thought eBay.co.uk would provide a useful second source of income, but nearly 25,000 sales later, Nick is pulling in some very useful profits. Nick says, 'Good old-fashioned customer service, as well as in-demand products and a well-designed site, are the most essential components of any online business. But on eBay.co.uk, which brings together so many sellers in one place, this matters more than ever.'

Opening an eBay.co.uk shop

An *eBay.co.uk Shop* is a Web site within eBay's own voluminous Web empire. It's a place where sellers can post items for sale at fixed prices. The great advantage of having a shop is that it enables a seller to keep merchandise available for purchase for 30, 60, 90, or even an unlimited number of days at a time. It gives customers another way to buy from you, and it can significantly increase your sales, too. eBay itself, at a recent eBay Live event, made the claim that eBay shops brought about a 25 per cent increase in overall sales. (Kimberly King, a US-based PowerSeller profiled later in this chapter, says her shop accounts for perhaps 55 to 60 per cent of her sales.)

eBay.co.uk's own Education section is well worth a look. It describes how you can set up your shop, make it look good, sell effectively, and get it picked up by major search engines.

For more on getting your shop noticed, check out the following link: `pages.ebay.co.uk/education/SEO/SEO-eBay-Store/index.html`.

Striving for PowerSeller status

PowerSellers are eBay.co.uk's elite. Those members who have the coveted icon next to their names feel justifiably proud of their accomplishments. They have met the stringent requirements for PowerSellers, which emphasise consistent sales, a high and regular number of completed sales, and excellent customer service. Moving from occasional seller to PowerSeller is a substantial change. Requirements include:

- ✔ At least 100 unique feedback results – 98 per cent of which are positive
- ✔ A minimum of £750 of average gross monthly sales for three consecutive months
- ✔ A good standing record – achieved by complying with eBay Listing Policies
- ✔ A current account – achieved by contacting bidders within three business days and upholding the eBay Community Values

In return for the hard work required to meet these standards, PowerSellers do get a number of benefits in addition to the icon. These include priority e-mail support, free banner ads, a special discussion board just for PowerSellers, and invitations to eBay events. They also have the opportunity to become featured PowerSellers in the introductory section for eBayers who want to upgrade.

See an example of a featured PowerSeller here: `pages.ebay.co.uk/services/buyandsell/powersellers.html`.

The PowerSeller programme isn't just something you apply for. eBay.co.uk reviews your sales statistics and invites you to join the programme when you have met the requirements. You can find out more about the requirements and benefits of the PowerSeller programme at `pages.ebay.co.uk/services/buyandsell/powerseller/benefits.html`.

Finding lots of merchandise to sell

Moving up to PowerSeller status means an ongoing commitment to conducting a large number of sales, responding quickly to customers, and shipping efficiently. It also means finding a steady and reliable stream of merchandise to sell. When you need to get 50 or more items up for sale each week, car boot sales quickly become impractical for all but the most dedicated. Many PowerSellers manage to find sufficient stock by heading to antiques fairs, garage sales, and car bootathons in teams, showing up in the pre-dawn hours and waiting in line, and then buying as many things as they can grab. Others find a wholesale supplier who can provide them with low-cost items, such as figurines, coffee, or holiday decorations, in bulk.

PowerSeller keeps sales going with a little help from her friends

PowerSeller status is something that many eBay sellers strive for, and Kimberly King is no exception. After she started selling on a regular basis, she decided to try for the coveted icon. 'When I realised that I could do this, I had to do a little more research about what I was selling,' she says. 'Having not been in sales before, I found that there are some strategies you have to follow and some things you have to hunt for, like a wholesale supplier.'

Having a steady stream of merchandise to buy at wholesale and then resell on eBay.co.uk is important for PowerSellers, who are required to maintain at least £750 in gross sales each month in order to keep their PowerSeller icon. This requirement does put some pressure on a seller, King says. 'I do put some pressure on myself to keep my PowerSeller status. I feel I have to list a certain number of items and be available for people constantly. You have more people you are helping and working with.'

A housewife and mother, King has to fit her eBay activities in between errands, childcare, and many other responsibilities. Still, she manages to spend as much as six hours on the auction site each day. This is the level of commitment required from eBay.co.uk's top sellers, too – you can't just dip in and out! She takes her own photos of each of her sales items even though her wholesaler has offered stock photos because, she says, shoppers need to see exactly what they are buying. 'Right now I am striving to list ten sales online per day. It's hard to remember to do this yourself, so some other sellers and I have decided to be 'listing buddies'. We remind each other every day that we need to keep up our quota; that way, we're accountable to someone.'

Having items up for sale for a month or more at a time helps King maintain her PowerSeller sales quotas. 'If one of my kids is home from school sick and I can't do something that week, I have those sales in my store. It's not like I completely left eBay that week.'

One of the best sources of support and help has been the member-created discussion forums called eBay Groups. 'When you find something, you can post a message on one group asking, 'Hey I found this neat thing at a garage sale, does anyone know what this is?'' King says. 'Those discussion boards have been so helpful because you get information from really knowledgeable sellers.'

A good UK example of a dedicated PowerSeller is a woman known only as the_cd_collector. The business sells predominantly obscure and collectible CDs – by the bucket load! She became a PowerSeller in September 2005, after finding bits and bobs around the house to sell and gradually upscaling her selling activities,

just as many eBay.co.uk professionals do. Before she knew it, the_cd_collector was becoming a near full-time job, and she was forced to package and post items in her lunch hour. Special software packages like Turbo Lister and Selling Manager Pro helped speed up the process, but it's still plenty of hard work.

The_cd_collector believes customer service is all-important. She promises to answer queries within 24 hours and has a seven-day returns policy as standard. She says the benefits of this ethic are reflected in a large number of repeat customers. Her score of approaching 2,500, with 100 per cent positive feedback, is another strong indicator. This figure shows her shop in all its glory.

stores.ebay.co.uk/the-cd-collector

Finding a wholesale supplier

All the PowerSellers we've spoken to in recent years have assured us that it's not easy to find a reputable, reliable wholesaler. They urge other sellers to do their homework by getting references and talking to satisfied customers. Many wholesalers are primarily interested in taking sellers' money and not providing good service, they say. Often, finding wholesalers is a matter of word of mouth: You ask someone who knows someone, and so on. Kimberly King (the seller we profile in the 'PowerSeller keeps sales going with a little help from her friends' sidebar) used connections left over from her former management position at an herbal tea company to find a supplier.

'You're not going to find someone on eBay who is going to tell you their wholesaler,' she cautions. 'They're too valuable. My advice is to make sure to call and check out references; do everything you can to find out everything about a company. Some force you to make an initial order of maybe £500 minimum up front, knowing when you see the product you'll never order it again.'

Chapter 11

Accepting Payments

● ●

In This Chapter

▶ Anticipating your online customers' purchasing needs

▶ Applying for credit-card merchant status

▶ Finding shortcuts to processing credit-card data

▶ Providing shoppers with electronic purchasing systems

▶ Delivering your products and services

● ●

*S*tarting up a new business and getting it online is exciting, but believe us, the real excitement occurs when you get paid for what you do. Nothing boosts your confidence and tells you that your hard work is paying off like receiving the proverbial cheque in the post.

The immediacy and interactivity of selling and promoting yourself online applies to receiving payments, too. You can get paid with just a few mouse clicks and some important data entered on your customer's keyboard. But completing an electronic commerce (*e-commerce,* for short) transaction isn't the same as getting paid in a traditional retail store. The customer can't personally hand you cash or a cheque. Or, if a credit card is involved, you can't verify the user's identity through a signature or photo ID.

In order to get paid promptly and reliably online, you have to go through some extra steps to make the customer feel secure – not to mention protect yourself, too. Successful e-commerce is about setting up the right atmosphere for making purchases, providing options for payment, and keeping sensitive information private. It's also about making sure that the goods get to the customer safely and on time. In this chapter, we describe ways in which you can implement these essential online business strategies.

Sealing the Deal: The Options

As anyone who sells online knows, the point at which payment is transferred is one of the most eagerly awaited stages of the transaction. It's also one of the stages that's likely to produce the most anxiety. Customers and merchants who are used to dealing with one another face to face and who are accustomed to personally handing over identification and credit cards suddenly feel lost. On the Web, they can't see the person they're dealing with.

For some customers, paying for something purchased over the Internet is still fraught with uncertainty, even though security is improving. For merchants like you, it can still be nerve-wracking; you want to make sure that cheques don't bounce and purchases aren't being made with stolen credit cards.

Your goal, in giving your customers the ability to provide payments online, should be to accomplish the following:

- **Give the customer options.** Online shoppers like to feel that they have some degree of control. Give them a choice of payment alternatives: phone, cheque, and credit/debit cards are the main ones.

- **Keep their credit-card numbers secure.** Pay an extra fee to your Web host in order to have your customers submit their credit-card numbers or other personal information to a secure server – a server that uses Secure Sockets Layer (SSL) encryption to render it unreadable if stolen.

- **Make payment convenient.** Shoppers on the Web are in a hurry. Give them the Web page forms and the phone numbers they need so that they can complete a purchase in a matter of seconds.

Though the goals are the same, the options are different if you sell on eBay.co.uk or on a Web site other than eBay's (see Chapter 10). If you sell on eBay.co.uk, either through an auction or an eBay shop, you can take advantage of eBay's fraud protection measures: a feedback system that rewards honesty and penalises dishonesty; fraud insurance; investigations staff; and the threat of suspension. These safeguards mean that it's feasible to accept cash and personal cheques or money orders from buyers. If you don't receive the cash, you don't ship. If you receive cheques, you can wait until they clear before you ship.

On the Web, you don't have a feedback system or an investigations squad to ferret out dishonest buyers. You can accept cheques or money orders, but credit or debit cards are the safest and quickest option, and accordingly, they're what buyers expect. It's up to you to verify the buyer's identity as best you can in order to minimise fraud.

Enabling Credit-Card Purchases

Having the ability to accept and process credit-card transactions makes it especially easy for your customers to follow the impulse to buy something from you. You stand to generate a lot more sales than you would otherwise.

But although credit cards are easy for shoppers to use, they make *your* life as an online merchant more complicated. We don't want to discourage you from becoming credit-card ready by any means, but you need to be aware of the steps (and the expenses) involved, many of which may not occur to you when you're just starting out. For example, you may not be aware of one or more of the following:

- **Merchant accounts:** You have to apply and be approved for a special bank account called a *merchant account* in order for a bank to process the credit-card orders that you receive. If you work through a traditional bank, approval can take days or weeks. However, a number of online merchant account businesses are providing hot competition, which includes streamlining the application process.

- **Setup fees:** Fees can be high but they vary widely, and it pays to shop around. Some banks charge a merchant setup fee (up to a couple of hundred pounds). On the other hand, some online companies such as Smart Merchant (www.smartmerchant.co.uk) charge no setup fee, while others, like Nochex (www.nochex.com), charge only a nominal fee of £50.

- **Usage rates:** All banks and merchant account companies (PayPal included) charge a *usage fee.* Typically, this fee ranges from 1 to 4 per cent of each transaction. Plus, you may have to pay a monthly premium charge to the bank. Nochex asks for £50 upfront and then charges you 2.9 per cent plus 20p per transaction. However, if you sell regularly, you pay no monthly fee, and the charges come down.

For more advice about online payment software services, check out the following bCentral link: www.bcentral.co.uk/business-technology/your-company-website/online-payment-services.mspx.

You must watch out for credit-card fraud, where criminals use stolen numbers to make purchases. You, the merchant – not the issuing bank – end up being liable for most of the fictitious transactions. To combat this crime, before completing any transaction, verify that the shipping address supplied by the purchaser is the same (or at least in the same vicinity) as the billing address. If you're in doubt, you can phone the purchaser for verification – it's a courtesy to the customer as well as a means of protection for you. (See the later section, 'Verifying credit-card data'.)

Setting up a merchant account

The good news is that getting merchant status is relatively easy, as banks have come to accept the notion that businesses don't have to have an actual, physical shop front in order to be successful. Getting a merchant account approved, however, still takes time, and, of course, you have to pay for the privilege. Banks look more favourably on companies that have been in business for several years and have a proven track record, but they see the benefits of taking on newbies, too. When Dan was setting up www.InfoZoo.co.uk, he received letter after letter from his bank offering more services and enquiring when the first transactions would be made.

Traditional banks are reliable and experienced, and you can count on them being around for a while. The new Web-based companies that specialise in giving online businesses merchant account status welcome new businesses and give you wider options and cost savings, but they're new; their services may not be as reliable, and their future is less certain.

You can find more information about institutions that provide merchant accounts for online businesses at the following site: www.merchantaccountforum.com.

The list of merchant account providers is growing so long that knowing which company to choose is difficult. We recommend visiting Business Link's Web site (www.businesslink.gov.uk), which provides you with a good overview of what's required to obtain a merchant account.

MyTexasMusic.com, a family-run business we profile in Chapter 1, uses a Web-based merchant account company called GoEmerchant.com (www.goemerchant.com) to set up and process its credit-card transactions. This company offers a shopping trolley and credit-card and debit-card processing to businesses that accept payments online. MyTexasMusic.com chose to use GoEmerchant after an extensive search because it found that the company would help provide reliable processing, while protecting the business from customers who purchased items fraudulently.

One advantage of using one of the payment options set up by VeriSign Payment Services (www.verisign.com/products/payment.html) is that the system (which originated with a company called CyberCash) was well known and well regarded before VeriSign acquired it. We describe the widely used electronic payment company in the section 'Exploring Online Payment Systems', later in this chapter.

In general, your chances of obtaining merchant status are enhanced if you apply to a bank that welcomes Internet businesses, and if you can provide good business records proving that you're a viable, moneymaking concern.

Be sure to ask about the monthly rate that the bank charges for Internet-based transactions before you apply. Compare the rate for online transactions to the rate for conventional 'card-swipe' purchases. Most banks and credit-card processing companies charge 1 to 2 extra percentage points for online sales.

Do you use an accounting program such as QuickBooks or MYOB Accounting? The manufacturers of these programs enable their users to become credit-card merchants through their Web sites. See the 'Accounting Software' section of this book's online Internet Directory for more information.

Finding a secure server

A *secure server* is a server that uses some form of encryption, such as Secure Sockets Layer, which we describe in Chapter 7, to protect data that you receive over the Internet. Customers know that they've entered a secure area when the security key or lock icon at the bottom of the browser window is locked shut.

If you plan to receive credit-card payments, you definitely want to find a Web-hosting service that will protect the area of your online business that serves as the online store. In literal terms, you need secure server software protecting the directory on your site that is to receive customer-sent forms. Watertight security should be a given by now, but it's always good to make sure that your customers will be protected. Ask your host (or hosts you're considering) whether any extra charges apply.

Verifying credit-card data

Unfortunately, people are out there who try to use credit-card numbers that don't belong to them. The anonymity of the Web and the ability to shop anywhere in the world, combined with the ability to place orders immediately, can facilitate fraudulent orders, just as it can benefit legitimate ones.

Protecting yourself against credit-card fraud is essential. Always check the billing address against the shipping address. If the two addresses are thousands of miles apart, contact the purchaser by phone to verify that the transaction is legit. Even if it is, the purchaser will appreciate your taking the time to verify the transaction.

You can use software to help check addresses. Here are three programs that perform this service:

- CapScan (`www.capscan.com/products.htm`)
- Worldpay (`support.worldpay.com/fraud/body.html`)
- QAS, part of credit reporting company Experian (`www.qas.co.uk/products`)

Processing your orders

You can hire a company to automatically process credit-card orders for you. These companies compare the shipping and billing addresses to help make sure that the purchaser is the person who actually owns the card and not someone trying to use a stolen credit-card number. If everything checks out, they transmit the data directly to the bank.

Loads of different companies offer a range of payment-processing packages. Do a search on Google.co.uk for 'online payment processing' and get in contact with a few of the organisations that take your fancy. Dan recommends PayPal for ease of use and Protx for its low cost options. See the upcoming section on shopping trolley software for more information.

Keeping back-office functions personal

Mark Lauer knows the importance of credit-card verification and order processing. Yet he tries to make these functions as personal as possible in keeping with the spirit of online business.

Mark is president of General Tool & Repair, Inc., a power tool supplier based in Pennsylvania, in the United States. General Tool has been in business for ten years, and seven years ago, General Tool & Repair created a simple Web page on America Online to help promote the company. Within two weeks, an order was received from a customer in Florida.

Since then, Mark has expanded his e-commerce Web site with Microsoft Commerce Server, and he set up shop at `www.gtr.com`.

Mark estimates that General Tool's Web site receives between 10 and 40 orders each day, and average online sales amount to $35,000 to $45,000 per month. He believes the site takes the place of 50 salespeople. 'This is all business we never had until two years ago, so it's basically all extra sales for us,' he notes happily.

Q. How do you process credit-card orders?

A. Our customers send us the credit-card information through our Web site, and our secure server encrypts the data. But we don't process orders online. We first check to see if we have the item in stock, and, if we do, we process the order the next business day. That way, we don't 'slam' the customer's credit card without having the item ready to ship out.

Q. How do you verify the identity of customers who submit credit-card numbers to you?

A. We use a program called Authorizer by Atomic Software. The program lets you check the shipping address against the address of the credit-card owner. If the two addresses are in the same state, you're pretty sure that you can ship the item. Otherwise, you know that you'd better e-mail the card owner and tell the person there's a problem. Sometimes, a customer will want to purchase a gift and have it shipped out of state to a family member, and in this case you should also e-mail the customer just to be sure. We have since upgraded to the multimerchant version of Authorizer, which lets us accept several different types of credit cards.

Q. Do you get many fraudulent credit-card orders?

A. We don't get too many bogus orders. Normally, you can tell because they don't have the correct Ship To address. If we suspect something, we e-mail or call the customer to confirm. Additionally, Authorizer will detect fraudulent credit-card orders. Customers don't mind you being extra careful when dealing with their credit-card protection, by confirming that it is a legit order. This extra step has gained us many repeat customers.

Q. Whom do you use for shipping?

A. We get orders from countries like Japan and Finland, and all over the United States, too. If the customer is affiliated with the military, you're required to use the US Postal Service for shipping. If we're shipping to a business address, such as an office in New York City, we use United Parcel Service because they give the option of sending a package *signature required*, which, as it implies, requires someone to sign for an item before they deliver it. We add the UPS charge for signature required to the shipping charge, but we feel that it's worth it because we don't want any items to get lost because they were left without a signature. There have been many instances where a customer's neighbour, employee, or landlord has signed for their package without the customer's knowledge, so it really provides protection for all involved.

Q. How do you tell your customers about shipping options?

A. We offer customers three choices during the purchase process: UPS ground, second-day air, and next-day air. We also provide a comment area where shoppers can make shipping requests or provide us with special instructions regarding their orders. That way, they can choose. We don't add on flat-rate shipping or handling charges that may be excessive. There are only five of us here, and I can't justify charging someone $25 shipping and handling for a $3 part for a power tool. Our products vary a great deal in price and weight, and we haven't found a way to provide a flat rate for shipping that is fair to everyone, so each order is treated individually. This flexibility in shipping has proven to be a service that sets us apart from the 'Big Box' online power tool providers, and customers shop on our Web site because of it.

Automatic credit-card processing works so fast that your customer's credit card can be charged immediately, whether or not you have an item in stock. If a client receives a bill and is still waiting for an item that is on back order, the person can get very unhappy. For this reason, some business owners, such as Mark Lauer (profiled in the sidebar, 'Keeping back-office functions personal'), choose not to use them.

Exploring Online Payment Systems

A number of organisations have devised ways to make e-commerce secure and convenient for shoppers and merchants alike. These alternatives fall into one of three general categories:

✔ Organisations that help you complete credit-card purchases (for example, VeriSign Payment Services).

✔ Escrow services that hold your money for you in an account until shipment is received and then pay you, providing security for both you and your customers.

✔ Organisations that provide alternatives to transmitting sensitive information from one computer to another. A number of attempts to create 'virtual money' have failed. However, companies like Electracash (www.electracash.com) let customers make payments by directly debiting their cheque accounts.

In order to use one of these systems, you or your Web host has to set up special software on the computer that actually stores your Web site files. This computer is where the transactions take place. The following sections provide general instructions on how to get started with setting up each of the most popular electronic payment systems.

To work smoothly, some electronic payment systems require you to set up programming languages such as Perl, C/C++, or Visual Basic on your site. You also have to work with techy documents called *configuration files*. This is definitely an area where paying a consultant to get your business set up saves time and headaches and gets your new transaction feature online more efficiently than if you tackle it yourself. VeriSign, for example, provides support in setting up systems for its merchants; you can find an affiliate to help you or call the company directly. Visit the VeriSign Payment Processing page (www.verisign.com/products/payment.html) for links and phone numbers.

Which payment system is right for you? That depends on what you want to sell online. If you're providing articles, reports, music, or other content that you want people to pay a nominal fee to access, consider a micropayment system. The important things are to provide customers with several options for submitting payment and to make the process as easy as possible for them.

Reach for your wallet!

One of the terms commonly thrown around in the jargon of e-commerce is *wallet*. A wallet is software that, like a real wallet that you keep in your bag or pocket, stores available cash and other records. You reach into the cyberwallet and withdraw virtual cash instead of submitting a credit-card number.

Wallets looked promising a few years ago, but they have never really taken off. The idea is that a cybershopper who uses wallet software, such as Microsoft .NET Passport (www.passport.com), is able to pay for items online in a matter of seconds, without having to transfer credit-card data. What's more, some wallets can even 'remember' previous purchases you have made and suggest further purchases.

The problem with wallets is that shoppers just aren't comfortable with them. Credit cards are quick and convenient, and they've proven to be secure enough for most consumers. Consumers who are committed to using Microsoft's services can use .NET Passport, which offers a 'single sign-in' to register or make purchases on sites that support this technology. It also enables consumers to create a wallet that stores their billing and shipping information. (Credit-card numbers are stored in an offline database when users sign up for a .NET Passport.) Customers can then make purchases at participating sites with the proverbial single mouse click. In order for your online business Web site to support .NET Passport, you need to download and install the .NET Passport Software Development Kit (SDK) on the server that runs your Web site. You may need help in deploying this platform; a list of consultants, as well as a link to the SDK, is included on the .NET Passport home page.

Shopping trolley software

When you go to the supermarket or another retail outlet, you pick goodies off the shelves and put them in a shopping trolley. When you go to the cash till to pay for what you've selected, you empty the trolley and present your goods to the cashier.

Shopping trolley software performs the same functions on an e-commerce site. Such software sets up a system that allows online shoppers to select items displayed for sale. The selections are held in a virtual shopping trolley that 'remembers' what the shopper has selected before checking out.

Shopping trolley programs are pretty technical for nonprogrammers to set up, but if you're ambitious and want to try it, you can download and install a free program called PerlShop (www.perlshop.org). Signing up with a Web host that provides you with shopping trolley software as part of its services, however, is far easier than tackling this task yourself.

A shopping trolley is often described as an essential part of many e-commerce Web sites, and Web hosts usually boast about including a trolley along with their other businesses services. But the fact is that you don't *have* to use a shopping trolley on your site. Some shoppers are put off by them and are just as likely to abandon a purchase than follow through by submitting payment. Plenty of other e-businesses have users phone or fax in an order or fill out an online form instead.

PayPal

PayPal was one of the first online businesses to hit on the clever idea of giving business owners a way to accept credit- and debit-card payments from customers without having to apply for a merchant account, download software, apply for online payment processing, or some combination of these steps.

PayPal is essentially an *escrow service:* It functions as a sort of financial middleman, debiting buyers' accounts and crediting the accounts of sellers – and, along the way, exacting a fee for its services, which it charges to the merchant receiving the payment. The accounts involved can be credit-card accounts, checking accounts, or accounts held at PayPal into which members directly deposit funds. In other words, the person making the payment sets up an account with PayPal by identifying which account (credit card or debit card, for example) a payment is to be taken from. The merchant also has a PayPal account and has identified which debit- or credit-card account is to receive payments. PayPal handles the virtual 'card swipe' and verification of customer information; the customer can pay with a credit card without the merchant having to set up a merchant account.

PayPal is best known as a way to pay for items purchased on eBay. eBay, in fact, owns PayPal. But the service is regularly used to process payments both on and off the auction site. If you want to sell items (including through your Web site), you sign up for a PayPal Business or Premier account. You get a PayPal button that you add to your auction listing or sales Web page. The customer clicks the button to transfer the payment from his or her PayPal account to yours, and you're charged a transaction fee.

Setting up a PayPal account is free. Here's how you can set up a PayPal Business account:

1. **Go to the PayPal home page (`www.paypal.co.uk`) and click the Sign Up Now button.**

   You go to the PayPal Account Sign Up page.

2. **Click the button next to Business Account, choose your country of residence, and click Continue.**

   The Business Account Sign Up page appears.

3. **Follow the instructions on the registration form page and set up your account with PayPal.**

   After you've filled out the registration forms, you receive an e-mail message with a link that takes you back to the PayPal Web site to confirm your e-mail address.

4. **Click the link contained in the e-mail message.**

   You go to the PayPal – Password page.

5. **Enter your password (the one you created during the registration process) in the Password box and then click the Confirm button.**

   You go to the PayPal – My Account page.

6. **Click the Merchant Tools tab at the top of the My Account page.**

   If you want to create a shopping trolley, click the Shopping Cart link. For the purposes of this exercise, click Buy Now Buttons.

7. **Provide some information about the item you're selling:**

   - Enter a brief description of your sales item in the Item Name/Service box.

   - Enter an item number in the Item ID/Number Box.

   - Enter the price in the Price Of Item/Service box.

   - Choose a button that shoppers can click to make the purchase. (You can choose either the PayPal logo button or a button that you've already created.)

8. **When you're done, click the Create Button Now button.**

   You go to the PayPal – Web Accept page shown in Figure 11-1.

9. **Copy the code in the For Web Pages box and paste it onto the Web page that holds your sales item.**

   That's all there is to it.

Figure 11-1:
Copy this code to your sales catalogue Web page to enable other PayPal users to transfer purchase money to your account.

The nice thing about using PayPal is that the system enables you to accept payments through your Web site without having to obtain a merchant account. It does put a burden on your customers to become PayPal users, but chances are those who buy or sell on eBay already have one. The thing to remember is that both you and your customers place a high level of trust in PayPal to handle your money. If there is a problem with fraud, PayPal will investigate it – hopefully. Some former PayPal users detest PayPal due to what they describe as a lack of responsiveness, and they describe their unhappiness in great detail on sites like www.paypalsucks.com. You should be aware of such complaints in order to have the full picture about PayPal and anticipate problems before they arise.

Actinic

Actinic is a British multi-award winning payment software, which can help you build a payment platform for any type of business, but it specialises in small and medium-sized enterprises. Actinic's range of services is too broad to cover here, so why not just to its Web site at www.actinic.co.uk?

Micropayments

Micropayments are very small units of currency that are exchanged by merchants and customers. The amounts involved may range from a fraction of a penny to a few pounds. Such small payments enable sites to provide content for sale on a per-click basis. In order to read articles, listen to music files, or view video clips online, some sites require micropayments in a special form of electronic cash that goes by names such as *scrip* or *eCash*.

Micropayments seemed like a good idea in theory, but they've never caught on with most consumers. On the other hand, they've never totally disappeared, either. The business that proved conclusively that consumers are willing to pay small amounts of money to purchase creative content online is none other than the computer manufacturer Apple, which revolutionised e-commerce with its iPod music player and its iTunes music marketplace. Every day, users pay 99p to download a song and add it to their iPod selections. But they make such payments with their credit cards, using real pounds and pence.

In other words, iTunes payments aren't true micropayments. The micropayment system is supposed to work like this:

1. **As a vendor, you authorise a broker such as BitPass (`www.bitpass.com`) to sell content to your customers by using its payment system.**

   Typically, BitPass content is creative: cartoons, audiobooks, craft projects, and music. If a customer goes to your site and wants to purchase articles or other content, the customer has to follow a few steps.

2. **The customer first purchases a prepaid card that contains a certain amount of virtual money at face value from the broker.**

   (The purchase is made through PayPal, interestingly.)

3. **The broker then pays you, the merchant, the purchase of virtual money that the customer made, minus a service fee.**

4. **The customer is then free to make purchases from your site by clicking items that have been assigned a certain value.**

5. **The micropayment service's software causes the money to be automatically subtracted from the user's supply of scrip.**

   No credit-card numbers are exchanged in these micropayment transactions.

Fulfilling Your Online Orders

Being on the Internet can help when it comes to the final step in the e-commerce dance: order fulfilment. *Fulfilment* refers to what happens after a sale is made. Typical fulfilment tasks include the following:

- Packing up the merchandise
- Shipping the merchandise
- Solving delivery problems or answering questions about orders that haven't reached their destinations
- Sending out bills
- Following up to see whether the customer is satisfied

Order fulfilment may seem like the least exciting part of running a business, online or otherwise. But from your customer's point of view, it's the most important business activity of all. The following sections suggest how you can use your presence online to help reduce any anxiety your customers may feel about receiving what they ordered.

The back-end (or, to use the Microsoft term, BackOffice) part of your online business is where order fulfilment comes in. If you have a database in which you record customer orders, link it to your Web site so that your customers can track orders. Adobe Dreamweaver or ColdFusion can help with this process. (The most recent version, Dreamweaver 8, contains built-in commands that let you link to a ColdFusion database.)

Provide links to shipping services

One advantage of being online is that you can help customers track packages after shipment. The Parcelforce online order-tracking feature, shown in Figure 11-2, gets thousands of requests each day. If you use Parcelforce, provide a link to its online tracking page at www.parcelforce.com/portal/pw/track?catId=7500082.

The other shipping services have also created their own online tracking systems. You can link to these sites, too:

- United Parcel Service (www.ups.com/gb)
- Royal Mail (www.royalmail.co.uk)
- DHL (www.dhl.co.uk)

Figure 11-2:
Provide
links to
online
tracking
services so
that your
customers
can check
delivery
status.

Present shipping options clearly

In order fulfilment, as in receiving payment, it pays to present your clients with as many options as possible and to explain the options in detail. Because you're online, you can provide your customers with as much shipping information as they can stand. Web surfers are knowledge hounds – they can never get enough data, whether it's related to shipping or other parts of your business.

When it comes to shipping, be sure to describe the options, the cost of each, and how long each takes. (See the sidebar 'Keeping back-office functions personal', earlier in this chapter, for some good tips on when to require signatures and how to present shipping information by e-mail rather than on the Web.) Here are more specific suggestions:

✔ **Compare shipping costs.** Don't settle for a shipping provider until you've done the rounds and assessed who is the most reliable for the least cost.

✔ **Make sure that you can track.** Pick a service that lets you track your package's shipping status.

✔ **Be able to confirm receipt.** A confirmation helps everyone's peace of mind.

Many online shops present shipping alternatives in the form of a table or bulleted list of options. (*Tables,* as you probably know, are Web page design elements that let you arrange content in rows and columns, making them easier to read; refer to Chapter 5 for more on adding tables to your site.) You don't have to look very far to find an example; just visit the John Wiley & Sons Web site (www.wiley.com) and order a book from its online store. When you're ready to pay for your items and provide a shipping address, you see the bulleted list shown in Figure 11-3.

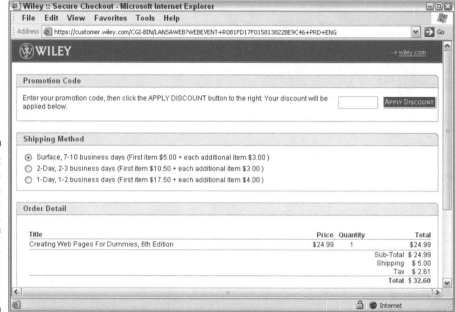

Figure 11-3:
Tables help
shoppers
calculate
costs, keep
track of
purchases,
and choose
shipping
options.

Chapter 12

Service with a Virtual Smile

● ●

In This Chapter

▶ Building a base of repeat customers through effective communication

▶ Creating forms that let shoppers talk back

▶ Encouraging contact through discussion groups

▶ Reaching out to overseas customers

▶ Finalising sales through chat-based customer service

● ●

*1*t's only human nature: Customers often wait until the last minute to request a gift or other item for a specific occasion, and that leads to an emergency for you. It may not seem fair, but a delay in responding to your customers can lead to lost business. These days, everything seems to be instant, from your porridge to your Internet connection. We take it for granted that shops no longer close on a Sunday and that they'll be open late into the evening for our convenience. Many shoppers still like to spend hours milling around the shopping centre, browsing and lunching at their leisure. But chances are that your customer is coming to you in the first place to save time as well as money. And they expect to get what they want – and fast.

Customer service is one area in which small, entrepreneurial businesses can outshine brick-and-mortar chain shops – and even larger online competitors. It doesn't matter whether you're competing in the areas of e-trading, e-music, or e-tail sales of any sort. Tools such as e-mail and interactive forms, coupled with the fact that an online commerce site can provide information on a 24/7 basis, give you a powerful advantage when it comes to retaining customers and building loyalty.

What constitutes good online customer service, particularly for a new business that has only one or two employees? Whether your customers are broadband or dialup, you need to deal with them one at a time and connect one to one. But being responsive and available is only part of the picture. This chapter presents ways to succeed with the other essential components: providing information, communicating effectively, and enabling your clientele to talk back to you online.

The Best Customer Is an Informed Customer

In a manner of speaking, satisfaction is all about managing people's expectations. If you give your customers what they're expecting or even a little bit more, they'll be happy. But how do you go about setting their level of expectation in the first place? Communication is the key. The more information you can provide up front, the fewer phone queries or complaints you'll receive later. Printed pamphlets and brochures have traditionally described products and services at length. But online is now the way to go.

Say that you're talking about a 1,000-word description of your new company and your products and/or services. If that text were formatted to fit on a 4-x-9-inch foldout brochure, the contents would cover several panels and cost an arm and a leg to print enough copies to make it worthwhile.

On the other hand, if those same 1,000 words were arranged on a few Web pages and put online, they'd probably be no more than 5K to 10K in size, so they wouldn't slow your site at all and would cost next to nothing. The same applies if you distribute your content to a number of subscribers in the form of an e-mail newsletter. In either case, you need pay only a little to publish the information.

And online publishing has the advantage of easier updating. When you add new products or services or even when you want a different approach, it takes only a little time and effort to change the contents or the look.

Why FAQs are frequently used

It may not be the most elegant of concepts, but it has worked for an infinite number of online businesspeople and it will work for you. A set of *frequently asked questions* (FAQs) is a familiar feature on many online business sites – so familiar, in fact, that Web surfers expect to find a FAQ page on every business site.

Even the format of FAQ pages is pretty similar from site to site, and this predictability is itself an asset. FAQ pages are generally presented in Q-and-A format, with topics appearing in the form of questions that have literally been asked by other customers or that have been made up to resemble real questions. Each question has a brief answer that provides essential information about the business.

But just because we're continually touting communication doesn't mean we want you to bore your potential customers with endless words that don't apply to their interests. To keep your FAQ page from getting too long, we recommend that you list all the questions at the top of the page. This way, by clicking a hyperlinked item in the list, the reader jumps to the spot down the page where you present the question that relates to them and its answer in detail.

Just having a FAQ page isn't enough. Make sure that yours is easy to use and comprehensive. Clarity and accessibility are both essential factors in successful Web sites, and your FAQ section should reflect these qualities. Check out the blueyonder user group Internet FAQs for some guidelines: www.by-users.co.uk/faqs/nontechfaq/internet/index.html.

Sure, you can compose a FAQ page off the top of your head, but sometimes getting a different perspective helps. Invite visitors, customers, friends, and family to come up with questions about your business. You may want to include questions on some of the following topics:

- ✔ **Contact information:** If I need to reach you in a hurry by mail, fax, or phone, how do I do that? Are you available only at certain hours?

- ✔ **Instructions:** What if I need more detailed instructions on how to use your products or services? Where can I find them?

- ✔ **Service:** What do I do if the merchandise doesn't work for some reason or breaks? Do you have a returns policy?

- ✔ **Value Added Tax (VAT):** Is VAT added to the cost I see on-screen?

- ✔ **Shipping:** What are my shipping options?

You don't have to use the term FAQ, either. The retailer Lands' End, which does just about everything right in terms of e-commerce, uses the term Fact Sheet for its list of questions and answers. Go to the Lands' End home page (www.landsend.co.uk) and click the About Us link to see how Lands' End presents the same type of material.

Writing an online newsletter

You may define yourself as an online businessperson, not a newsletter editor. But sharing information with customers and potential customers through an e-mail newsletter is a great way to build credibility for yourself and your business.

For added customer service (not to mention a touch of self-promotion), consider producing a regular publication, say once a fortnight or once a month, that you send out to a mailing list. Your mailing list would begin with customers and prospective customers who visit your Web site and indicate that they want to subscribe.

An e-mail newsletter doesn't happen by magic, but it can provide your business with long-term benefits that include:

- **Customer tracking:** You can add subscribers' e-mail addresses to a mailing list that you can use for other marketing purposes, such as promoting special sales items for return customers.

- **Low-bandwidth:** An e-mail newsletter doesn't require much memory. It's great for businesspeople who get their e-mail on the road via laptops, palm devices, or appliances that are designed specifically for sending and receiving e-mail.

- **Timeliness:** You can get breaking news into your electronic newsletter much faster than you can put it in print.

The fun part is to name your newsletter and assemble content that you want to include. Then follow these steps to get your publication up and running:

1. **Create your newsletter by typing the contents in plain-text (ASCII) format.**

   Optionally, you can also provide an HTML-formatted version. You can then include headings and graphics that appear in e-mail programs that support HTML e-mail messages.

   If you use a plain-text newsletter, format it by using capital letters; rules that consist of a row of equal signs, hyphens, or asterisks; or blank spaces to align elements.

2. **Save your file with the proper filename extension: `.txt` for the text version and `.htm` or `.html` if you send an HTML version.**

3. **Attach the file to an e-mail message by using your e-mail program's method of sending attachments.**

4. **Address your file to the recipients.**

   If you have lots of subscribers (many newsletters have hundreds or thousands), save their addresses in a mailing list. Use your e-mail program's address book function to do this.

5. **Send your newsletter.**

It's a good idea to consider when your newsletter will be best received by your customers. As a business journalist specialising in Web publications, Dan has sent innumerable newsletters in his time. He found that small businesses are most receptive (more of them opened their newsletters) on a Thursday afternoon. If you're a fashion retailer, for example, trying sending yours on a Friday, when most people will be at their work desks but will also be winding down for the weekend!

Managing a mailing list can be time consuming. You have to keep track of people who want to subscribe or unsubscribe, as well as those who ask for more information. You can save time and trouble by hiring a company such as ListCast (www.listcast.com) to do the day-to-day list management for you.

Mixing bricks and clicks

If you operate a bricks-and-mortar business as well as a Web-based business, you have additional opportunities to get feedback from your shoppers. Take advantage of the fact that you meet customers personally on a regular basis and ask them for opinions and suggestions that can help you operate a more effective Web site, too.

When your customers are in the checkout line (the real one with the cash till, not your online shopping trolley), ask them to fill out a questionnaire about your Web site. Consider asking questions like the following:

- Have you visited this shop's Web site? Are you familiar with it?
- Would you visit the Web site more often if you knew there were products or content there that you couldn't find in our physical location?
- Can you suggest some types of merchandise, or special sales, you'd like to see on the Web site?

Including your Web site's URL on all the printed literature in your shop is a good idea. The feedback system works both ways, of course: You can ask online customers for suggestions of how to run your bricks-and-mortar shop better, and what types of merchandise they'd like to see on your real as opposed to your 'virtual' shelves.

Helping Customers Reach You

Greg's the type of person who has an ex-directory home phone number. But being anonymous is not the way to go when you're running an online business. (He uses a different number for business calls, by the way.) Of course, you don't have to promise to be available 24/7 to your customers in the flesh. But they need to believe that they'll get attention no matter what time of day or night. When you're online, contact information can take several forms. Be sure to include

- ✔ Your snail mail address
- ✔ Your e-mail address(es)
- ✔ Your phone and fax numbers, and a free (0800) number (if you have one)

Most Web hosting services (such as the types of hosts that we describe in Chapter 3) give you more than one e-mail inbox as part of your account. So it may be helpful to set up more than one e-mail address. One address can be for people to communicate with you personally, and the other can be where people go for general information. You can also set up e-mail addresses that respond to messages by automatically sending a text file in response. (See the 'Setting up autoresponders' section, later in this chapter.)

Even though you probably won't meet many of your customers in person, you need to provide them with a human connection. Keep your site as personal and friendly as possible. A contact page is a good place to provide some brief biographical information about the people visitors can contact, namely you and any employees or partners in your company.

Not putting your contact information on a separate Web page has some advantages, of course. Doing so makes your patrons have to wait a few seconds to access it. If your contact data is simple and your Web site consists only of a few pages, by all means put it right on your home page.

Going upscale with your e-mail

These days, nearly everyone we know, including our respective parents, has an e-mail account. But when you're an online businessperson, you need to know more about the features of e-mail than just how to share a joke or exchange a recipe. The more you discover about the finer technical points of e-mail, the better you're able to meet the needs of your clients. The following sections suggest ways to go beyond simply sending and receiving e-mail messages, and utilise e-mail for business publishing and marketing.

Setting up autoresponders

An *autoresponder,* which also goes by the name *mailbot,* is software that you can set up to send automatic replies to requests for information about a product or service, or to respond to people subscribing to an e-mail publication or service.

You can provide automatic responses either through your own e-mail program or through your Web host's e-mail service. If you use a Web host to provide automatic responses, you can usually purchase an extra e-mail address that can be configured to return a text file (such as a form letter) to the sender.

Look for a Web host that provides you with one or more autoresponders along with your account. Typically, your host assigns you an e-mail address that takes the form info@mycompany.co.uk. In this case, someone at your hosting service configures the account so that when a visitor to your site sends a message to info@yourcompany.com, a file of your choice, such as a simple text document that contains background information about you and your services, automatically goes out to the sender as a reply.

Greg's own Web host and ISP, XO Communications, lets Greg create and edit an autoresponse message for each of his e-mail accounts. First, he logs on to his host's gateway, which is the service it provides customers for changing their e-mail settings. He clicks the link Edit E-mail Settings to go to the page called E-mail Settings shown in Figure 12-1. He checks the Auto Respond box to turn the feature on and then clicks Edit Autoresponse Message to set up his autoresponse text.

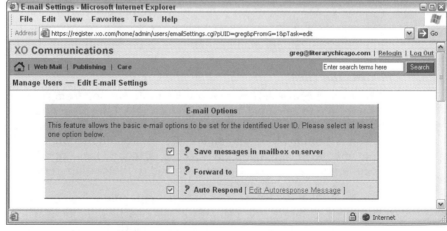

Figure 12-1:
Many Web hosts and ISPs enable users to create their own auto-response messages.

If the service that hosts your Web site does not provide this service free, you can always do it through your basic Outlook e-mail software, which comes with Microsoft Office packages. Read the walkthrough at this address to find out exactly how it's done: www.pcanswers.co.uk/tips/default.asp? pagetypeid=2&articleid=28816&subsectionid=616.

Noting by quoting

Responding to a series of questions is easy when you use *quoting* – a feature that lets you copy quotes from a message to which you're replying. Quoting, which is available in almost all e-mail programs, is particularly useful for responding to a mailing list or newsgroup message because it indicates the specific topic being discussed.

How do you tell the difference between the quoted material and the body of the new e-mail message? The common convention is to put a greater-than (>) character in the left margin, next to each line of the quoted material.

When you tell your e-mail software to quote the original message before you type your reply, it generally quotes the entire message. To save space, you can *snip* (delete) out the part that isn't relevant. However, if you do so, it's polite to type the word <snip> to show that you've cut something out. A quoted message looks something like this:

```
Mary Agnes McDougal wrote:
>I wonder if I could get some info on <snip>
>those sterling silver widgets you have for sale . . .
Hi Mary Agnes,
Thank you for your interest in our premium collector's
          line
of widgets. You can place an order online or call our
          toll-
free number, 0800-WIDGETS.
```

Attaching files

A quick and convenient way to transmit information from place to place is to attach a file to an e-mail message. In fact, attaching files is one of the most useful things you can do with e-mail. *Attaching,* which means that you send a document or file along with an e-mail message, allows you to include material from any file to which you have access. Attached files appear as separate documents that recipients can download to their computers.

Many e-mail clients allow users to attach files with a simple button or other command. Compressing a lengthy series of attachments by using software such as StuffIt or WinZip conserves bandwidth. Using compression is also a necessity if you ever want to send more than one attached file to someone whose e-mail account doesn't accept multiple attachments.

Protocols such as MIME (Multipurpose Internet Mail Extensions) are sets of standards that allow you to attach graphic and other multimedia files to an e-mail message. Recipients must have an e-mail program that supports MIME (which includes almost all the newer e-mail programs) in order to download and read MIME files in the body of an e-mail message. In case your recipient has an e-mail client that doesn't support MIME attachments, or if you aren't sure whether it does, you must encode your attachment in a format such as BinHex (if you're sending files to a Macintosh) or UUCP (if you're sending files to a newsgroup).

Creating a signature file that sells

One of the easiest and most useful tools for marketing on the Internet is called a signature file, or a sig file. A *signature file* is a text blurb that your system automatically appends to the bottom of your e-mail messages and newsgroup postings. You want your signature file to tell the readers of your message something about you and your business; you can include information such as your company name and how to contact you.

Creating a signature file takes only a little more time than putting your John Hancock on the dotted line. First, you create the signature file itself, as we describe in these steps:

1. **Open a text-editing program.**

   This example uses Notepad, which comes built in with Windows. If you're a Macintosh user, you can use SimpleText. With either program, a new blank document opens on-screen.

2. **Press and hold down the hyphen (–) or equal sign (=) key to create a dividing line that will separate your signature from the body of your message.**

   Depending on which symbol you use, a series of hyphens or equal signs forms a broken line. Don't make this line too long, or it will run onto another line, which doesn't look good; 30 to 40 characters is a safe measure.

3. **Type the information about yourself that you want to appear in the signature, pressing Enter after each line.**

   Include such information as your name, job title, company name, e-mail address, and Web site URL. A three- or four-line signature is the typical length.

   If you're feeling ambitious at this point, you can press the spacebar to arrange your text in two columns. Greg's agent (who's an online entrepreneur himself) does this with his own signature file, as shown in Figure 12-2.

Figure 12-2:
A signature
file often
uses divider
lines and
can be
arranged in
columns to
occupy less
space
on-screen.

Always include the URL to your business Web site in your signature file and be sure to include it on its own line. Why? Most e-mail programs will recognise the URL as a Web page by its prefix (http://www.) and suffix (.com, .co.uk, and so on). When your reader opens your message, the e-mail program displays the URL as a clickable hyperlink that, when clicked, opens your Web page in a Web browser window.

4. **Choose File⇨Save.**

   A dialog box appears, enabling you to name the file and save it in a folder on your hard drive.

5. **Enter a name for your file that ends in the filename extension .txt.**

   This extension identifies your file as a plain text document.

6. **Click the Save button.**

   Your text file is saved on your computer's hard drive.

Now that you've created a plain-text version of your electronic signature, the next step is to identify that file to the computer programs that you use to send and receive e-mail and newsgroup messages. Doing so enables the programs to make the signature file automatically appear at the bottom of your messages. The procedure for attaching a signature file varies from program to program; the following steps show you how to do this by using Microsoft Outlook Express 6:

1. **Start Outlook Express and choose Tools⇨Options.**

   The Options dialog box opens.

2. **Click the Signatures tab.**

3. **Click New.**

   The options in the Signatures and Edit Signature sections of the Signatures tab are highlighted.

4. **Click the File button at the bottom of the tab and then click Browse.**

   The Open dialog box appears. This standard Windows navigation dialog box lets you select folders and files on your computer.

5. **Locate the signature file that you created in the previous set of steps by selecting a drive or folder from the Look In drop-down list. When you locate the file, click the filename and then click the Open button.**

   The Signature File dialog box closes, and you return to the Options dialog box. The path leading to the selected file is listed in the box next to File.

6. **Click the Add Signatures to All Outgoing Messages check box and then click OK.**

   The Options dialog box closes, and you return to Outlook Express. Your signature file is now automatically added to your messages.

To test your new signature file, choose File⇨New⇨Mail Message from the Outlook Express menu bar. A new message composition window opens. Your signature file should appear in the body of the message composition window. You can compose a message by clicking before the signature and starting to type.

Creating forms that aren't formidable

In the old days, people who heard 'here's a form to fill out' usually started to groan. Who likes to stare at a form to apply for a job or for financial aid or, even worse, to figure out how much you owe in taxes? But as an online businessperson, forms can be your best friends because they give customers a means to provide you with feedback as well as essential marketing information. Using forms, you can find out where customers live, how old they are, and so on. Customers can also use forms to sound off and ask questions.

Forms can be really handy from the perspective of the customer as well. The speed of the Internet enables them to dash off information right away. They can then pretty much immediately receive a response from you that's tailored to their needs and interests.

Forms consist of two parts, only one of which is visible on a Web page:

- ✔ The visible part includes the text-entry fields, buttons, and check boxes that an author creates with HTML commands.
- ✔ The part of the form that you don't see is a computer script that resides on the server that receives the page.

The script, which is typically written in a language such as Perl, AppleScript, or C++, processes the form data that a reader submits to a server and presents that data in a format that the owner or operator of the Web site can read and use.

Getting the data to you

What exactly happens when customers connect to a page on your site that contains a form? First, they fill out the text-entry fields, radio buttons, and other areas you have set up. When they finish, they click a button, often marked Submit, in order to transmit, or *post,* the data from the remote computer to your Web site.

A computer script called a Common Gateway Interface (CGI) program receives the data submitted to your site and processes it so that you can read it. The CGI may cause the data to be e-mailed to you, or it may present the data in a text file in an easy-to-read format.

Optionally, you can also create a CGI program that prompts your server to send users to a Web page that acknowledges that you have received the information and thanks them for their feedback. It's a nice touch that your customers are sure to appreciate.

Writing the scripts that process form data is definitely in the field of webmasters or computer programmers and is far beyond the scope of this book. But you don't have to hire someone to write the scripts: You can use a Web page program (such as Microsoft FrontPage or Adobe Dreamweaver) that not only helps you create a form but also provides you with scripts that process the data for you. (If you use forms created with FrontPage, your Web host must have a set of software called FrontPage Server Extensions installed. Call your host or search the host's online Help files to see whether the extensions are present.)

Some clever businesspeople have created some really useful Web content by providing a way for nonprogrammers such as you and us to create forms online. Appropriately enough, you connect to the server's Web site and fill out a form provided by the service in order to create your form. The form has a built-in CGI that processes the data and e-mails it to you. See the 'Free Forms Online' section of the Internet Directory (on this book's Web site) to find some free form creation and processing services.

Using FrontPage to create a form

You can use the Form Page Wizard that comes with Microsoft FrontPage to create both parts of forms: the data-entry parts (such as text boxes and check boxes), as well as the behind-the-scenes scripts, called *WebBots,* that process form data. Creating your own form gives you more control over how it looks and a greater degree of independence than if you use a ready-made forms service.

The first step in setting up a Web page form is determining what information you want to receive from someone who fills out the form. Your Web page creation tool then gives you options for ways to ask for the information you want. Start FrontPage and choose Insert⇨Form, and a submenu appears with many options. The most commonly used options are the following:

- **Textbox:** Creates a single-line box where someone can type text.
- **Text Area:** Creates a scrolling text box.
- **File Upload:** Lets the user send you a text file.
- **Checkbox:** Creates a check box.
- **Option Button:** Creates an option button, sometimes called a radio button.
- **Drop-Down Box:** Lets you create a drop-down list.
- **Picture:** Lets you add a graphic image to a form.

Figure 12-3 shows the most common form fields as they appear in a Web page form that you're creating.

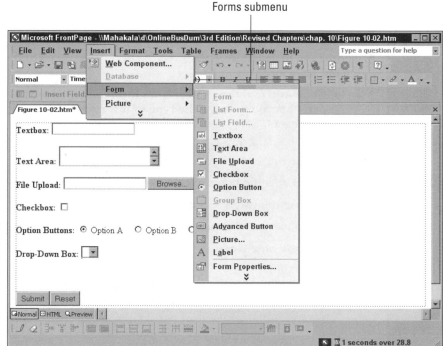

Figure 12-3: FrontPage provides you with menu options for creating form elements.

When you choose Insert⇨Form, FrontPage inserts a dashed, marquee-style box in your document to signify that you're working on Web page form fields rather than normal Web page text.

The Form Page Wizard is a great way to set up a simple form that asks for information from visitors to your Web site. It lets you concentrate on the type of data you want to collect rather than on the buttons and boxes needed to gather it. We show you how to create such a form in the following steps. (These steps are for FrontPage 2002; version 2003 requires similar steps, but provides you with more options.)

1. **Choose Start⇨Programs⇨Microsoft FrontPage.**

   FrontPage starts and a blank window appears.

2. **Choose File⇨New⇨Page Or Web.**

   The New Page or Web task pane appears.

3. **Click Page Templates.**

   The Page Templates dialog box appears.

4. **Double-click Form Page Wizard.**

   The first page of the Form Page Wizard appears. (You can click Finish at any time to see your form and begin editing it.)

5. **Click Next.**

6. **Follow the instructions presented in succeeding steps of the wizard to create your form.**

   a. **Click Add and then select from the set of options that the wizard presents you with for the type of information you want the form to present.**

      This data may include account information, ordering information, and so on.

   b. **Select specific types of information you want to solicit.**

   c. **Choose the way you want the information to be presented.**

      You have options such as a bulleted list, numbered list, and so on.

   d. **Identify how you want the user-submitted information to be saved.**

      You can choose to save information as a text file, a Web page, or with a custom CGI script if you have one.

7. **Click Finish.**

   The wizard window closes, and your form appears in the FrontPage window.

When you finish, be sure to add your own description of the form and any special instructions at the top of the Web page. Also add your copyright and contact information at the bottom of the page. Follow the pattern you've set on other pages on your site. You can edit the form by using the Forms submenu options if you want to.

Be sure to change the background of the form page from the boring default grey that the wizard provides to a more compelling colour. See Chapter 5 for more specific instructions on changing the background of Web pages you create.

Making Customers Feel That They Belong

In the old days, people went to the market often, sometimes on a daily basis. The shopkeeper was likely to have set aside items for their consideration based on individual tastes and needs. More likely than not, the business transaction followed a discussion of families, politics, and other village gossip.

Good customer service can make your customers feel like members of a community that frequent a family bakery – the community of satisfied individuals who regularly use your goods and services. In the following sections, we describe some ways to make your customers feel like members of a group, club, or other organisation who return to your site on a regular basis and interact with a community of individuals with similar interests.

Putting the 'person' into personal service

How often does an employee personally greet you as you walk through the door of a shop? On the Web as well as in real life, people like a prompt and personal response. Your challenge is to provide someone on your Web site who's available to provide live customer support.

Some Web sites do provide live support so that people can e-mail a question to someone in real-time (or close to real-time) Internet technologies, such as chat and message boards. The online auction giant eBay.co.uk has a New Users Board, for example, where beginners can post questions for eBay support staff, who post answers in response.

An even more immediate sort of customer support is provided by *chat*, in which individuals type messages to one another over the Internet in real time. One way to add chat to your site is to start a Yahoo! group, which we describe later in this chapter.

Adding the personal touch that means so much

Sarah-Lou Reekie started her business out of an apartment in London in 1997. She developed an herbal insect repellent called Alfresco while working in a botanical and herbal research centre. Since then, sales have grown quickly — often doubling each year. One key to Reekie's quick success is that no products directly competed with her lotion. Another key component is her personal approach to serving her customers, who include movie stars on location and other prominent entertainers like Sir Paul McCartney.

Reekie's Web site (www.alfresco.uk.com), shown in the accompanying figure, nearly doubled sales, but she stuck to basic business practices and focused on cultivating the customer base she had already developed through selling her product by word of mouth. She started a fan club for Alfresco, and she has personally visited some of her best customers.

Q. How have you been able to keep a steady flow of business amid the ups and downs of the world economy?

A. We have built up a bigger and bigger customer base by constantly giving good service to customers. We send out special editions for frequent buyers, have a fan club, and encourage customers to make recommendations. We bring out new and exciting products; we care and look after our customers.

Q. What are the one or two most important things people should keep in mind if they are starting an online business these days?

A. It is not necessary to spend a fortune to set it up. Find a host that has been in business a number of years. (There *are* experts now.) A clean database that really works for you is vital, as your customers are the most precious things a business can have. Keep in touch with them. Treat them with care and respect.

Q. What's the single best improvement you've made to your site to attract more customers or retain the ones you've had?

A. Putting on a special code that only special customers or fan club members can access for discounts, and so on. For example, Royal Bank of Scotland employees have a special code dedicated to them.

Q. Is this a good time to start an online business?

A. I actually feel it is a great time to start an e-commerce biz for a number of reasons, not least being that the technical support is now well and truly in place. Let's just say more people know what they are doing than in earlier years. Secondly, most new customers are not as concerned about credit-card security, as there really has been hardly any fraud.

Q. What advice would you give to someone thinking of starting a new business on the Web?

A. Your customer is King, Queen, Prince, and Princess. Whatever you would like yourself is what you should aim to offer. 'Do as you would like to be done by' should be your motto. Expose yourself any which way and as often as is acceptable to as many well-targeted customers as possible. Most of all, keep a positive attitude. Sir Paul McCartney once said to me when I felt depressed and almost ready to give up, 'Always have faith.' I'm glad I listened to him!

LivePerson (`www.liveperson.com`) provides a simpler alternative that allows small businesses to provide chat-based support. LivePerson is software that enables you to see who is connected to your site at any one time and instantly lets you chat with them, just as if you're greeting them at the front door of a bricks-and-mortar shop.

LivePerson works like this: You install the LivePerson Pro software on your own computer (not the server that runs your site). With LivePerson, you or your assistants can lead the customer through the process of making a purchase. For example, you may help show customers what individual sale items look like by sending them an image file to view with their Web browsers. You can try LivePerson Pro for free for 30 days and then pay around $50 per month thereafter.

Not letting an ocean be a business barrier

You're probably familiar with terms such as *global village* and *international marketplace*. But how do you extend your reach into the huge overseas markets where e-commerce is just beginning to come into its own? Making sure that products are easily and objectively described with words as well as clear images and diagrams, where necessary, is becoming increasingly important. There are other ways to effectively overcome language and cultural barriers, some of which are common sense while others are less obvious.

Keep in mind the fact that shoppers in many developing nations still prefer to shop with their five senses. So that foreign customers never have a question on how to proceed, providing them with implicit descriptions of the shopping process is essential. You should make information on ordering, payment, execution, and support available at every step.

Customer support in Asia is, in many ways, a different creature than in the West. While personalisation still remains critical, language and translation gives an e-commerce site a different feel. You may have to replace a Western site that works well by looking clean and well organised with the more chaotic blitz of characters and options that's often found more compelling by Eastern markets. In Asia, Web sites tend to place more emphasis on colour and interactivity. Many e-commerce destinations choose to dump all possible options on the front page, instead of presenting them in an orderly, sequential flow.

Having a discussion area can enhance your site

Can we talk? Even Greg's pet birds like to communicate by words as well as squawks. A small business can turn its individual customers into a cohesive group by starting its own discussion group on the Internet. Discussion groups work particularly well if you're promoting a particular type of product or if you and your customers are involved in a provocative or even controversial area of interest.

The three kinds of discussion groups are

- **A local group:** Some universities create discussion areas exclusively for their students. Other large companies set aside groups, sometimes called *intranets,* that are restricted to their employees. Outsiders can't gain access because the groups aren't on the Internet but rather are on a local server within the organisation.

- **A Usenet newsgroup:** Individuals are allowed to create an Internet-wide discussion group in the `alt` or `biz` categories of Usenet without having to go through the time-consuming application and approval process needed to create other newsgroups.

✔ **A Web-based discussion group:** Microsoft FrontPage includes easy-to-use wizards that enable you to create a discussion area on your business Web site. Users can access the area from their Web browsers without having to use special discussion-group software. Or, if you don't have FrontPage, you can start a Yahoo! group, which we describe in the section named (surprise!) 'Starting a Yahoo! group'.

Of these three alternatives, the first isn't appropriate for your business purposes. The following sections focus on the last two types of groups.

In addition to newsgroups, many large corporations host interactive chats moderated by experts on subjects related to their areas of business. But small businesses can also hold chats, most easily by setting up a chat room on a site that hosts chat-based discussions. But the hot way to build goodwill and establish new connections with customers and interested parties is an interactive Web-based diary called a *blog* (short for Web log); find out more about blogs in Chapter 4.

Starting an alt discussion group

Usenet is a system of communication on the Internet that enables individual computer users to participate in group discussions about topics of mutual interest. Internet newsgroups have what's referred to as a hierarchical structure. Most groups belong to one of seven main categories: `comp`, `misc`, `news`, `rec`, `sci`, `soc`, and `talk`. The name of the category appears at the beginning of the group's name, such as `rec.food.drink.coffee`. In this section, we discuss the `alt` category, which is just about as popular as the seven we just mentioned and which enables individuals – like you – to establish their own newsgroups.

In our opinion, the `biz` discussion groups aren't taken seriously because they are widely populated by unscrupulous people promoting get-rich-quick schemes and egomaniacs who love the sound of their own voices. The `alt` groups, although they can certainly address some wild and crazy topics, are at least as well known and often address serious topics. Plus, the process of setting up an `alt` group is well documented.

The prefix `alt` didn't originally stand for *alternative,* although it has come to mean that. The term was an abbreviation for Anarchists, Lunatics, and Terrorists, which wasn't so politically incorrect back in those days. Now, `alt` is a catchall category in which anyone can start a group, if others show interest in the creator's proposal.

The first step to creating your own `alt` discussion group is to point your Web browser to Google Groups (`groups.google.com`) or launch your browser's newsgroup software. To start the Outlook Express newsgroup software, click the plus sign next to the name of the newsgroup software in the program's Folders pane (both options assume you've already configured Outlook Express to connect to your ISP's newsgroup server) and access the group called `alt.config.newgroups`. This area contains general instructions on starting your own Usenet newsgroup. Also look in `news.answers` for the message 'How to Start a New Usenet Newsgroup'.

To find out how to start a group in the `alt` category, go to Google (`www.google.com`), click Groups, and search for the message 'How to Start an Alt Newsgroup'.) Follow the instructions contained in this message to set up your own discussion group. Basically, the process involves the following steps:

1. **You write a brief proposal describing the purpose of the group you want to create and including an e-mail message where people can respond with comments.**

   The proposal also contains the name of your group in the correct form (`alt.groupname.moreinfo.moreinfo`). Try to keep the group name short and official looking if it's for business purposes.

2. **You submit the proposal to the newsgroup `alt.config`.**

3. **You gather feedback to your proposal by e-mail.**

4. **You send a special message called a *control message* to the news server that gives you access to Usenet.**

   The exact form of the message varies from server to server, so you need to consult with your ISP on how to compose the message correctly.

5. **Wait a while (a few days or weeks) as news administrators (the people who operate news servers at ISPs around the world) decide whether to adopt your request and add your group to their list of newsgroups.**

Before you try to start your own group, look through the Big Seven categories (`comp`, `misc`, `news`, `rec`, `sci`, `soc`, and `talk`) to make sure that someone else isn't already covering your topic.

Starting a Yahoo! group

When the Internet was still fresh and new, Usenet was almost the only game in town. These days, the Web is pretty much (along with e-mail) the most popular way to communicate and share information. That's why starting a discussion group on the Web makes perfect sense. A Web-based discussion group is somewhat less intimidating than others because it doesn't require a participant to use newsgroup software.

Yahoo! groups are absolutely free to set up. The service exists only on the .com version of Yahoo! and not the .co.uk one as yet, but then that's the great thing about the Internet: It's not confined by national borders. (To find out how to set up a group, just go to the FAQ page, help.yahoo.com/help/us/groups/index.html and click the How Do I Start a Group? link.) They not only enable users to exchange messages, but they can also communicate in real time by using chat. And as the list operator, you can send out e-mail newsletters and other messages to your participants, too.

Simply operating an online shop isn't enough. You need to present yourself as an authority in a particular area that is of interest. The discussion group needs to concern itself primarily with that topic and give participants a chance to exchange views and tips on the topic. If people have questions about your shop, they can always e-mail you directly – they don't need a discussion group to do that.

Creating a Web discussion area with FrontPage

The reason that Microsoft FrontPage is such a popular tool for creating Web sites is that it enables you to create Web page content that you would otherwise need complicated scripts to tackle. One example is the program's Discussion Group Wizard, which lets you create Web pages on which your members (as opposed to customers, remember?) can exchange messages and carry on a series of back-and-forth responses (called *threads*) on different topics. Newcomers to the group can also view articles that are arranged by a table of contents and accessible by a searchable index.

Follow these steps to set up your own discussion group with Microsoft FrontPage:

1. **Start FrontPage by choosing Start⇨All Programs⇨Microsoft FrontPage.**

   The FrontPage window opens.

   You can create a new discussion *web* (that is, a group of interlinked documents that together comprise a Web site) of Web pages by using one of the built-in wizards that comes with FrontPage.

2. **To use the FrontPage Discussion Group Wizard, choose File⇨New⇨ Page Or Web.**

   The New Page Or Web task pane appears.

3. **Click Web Site Templates.**

   The Web Site Templates dialog box appears.

4. **Select Discussion Web Wizard and then click OK.**

   A dialog box appears, stating that the new discussion web is being created. Then the first of a series of Discussion Web Wizard dialog boxes appears.

5. **Click Next.**

   The second dialog box lets you specify the features you want for your discussion web. If this is the first time you've created a group, leave all the options checked.

6. **Click Next.**

   A dialog box appears that lets you specify a title and folder for the new discussion web. Enter a title in the box beneath Enter a descriptive title for this discussion. You can change the default folder name `_disc1` if you want.

7. **Click Next.**

   The dialog box that appears lets you choose one of three options for the structure of your discussion:

   - Select Subject, Comments if you expect visitors to discuss only a single topic.

   - Select Subject, Category, Comments if you expect to conduct discussions on more than one topic.

   - Select Subject, Product, Comments if you want to invite discussions about products you produce and/or sell.

   After you select one of these options, the next Discussion Web Wizard dialog box appears. Go through this and the subsequent dialog boxes, answering the questions they present you with in order to determine what kind of discussion group you're going to have. At any time, as you go through the series of Discussion Web Wizard pages, you can click the Finish button to complete the process.

8. **When you're finished, the preset pages for your discussion web appear in the FrontPage Explorer main window.**

The middle column of the FrontPage window shows the arrangement of the discussion documents. The right side of the window is a visual map that shows how the discussion group is arranged and how the pages are linked to each other.

When you set up a discussion area with FrontPage, you have the option of designing your pages as a *frameset,* or a set of Web pages that has been subdivided into separate frames. To find out more about frames, see Chapter 5.

Editing the discussion pages

After you use the Discussion Group Wizard to create your pages, the next step is to edit the pages so that they have the content you want. With your newly created pages displayed in the FrontPage window, you can start editing by double-clicking the icon for a page (such as the Welcome page, which has a filename such as `disc_welc.htm`) in your discussion web. Whatever page you double-click opens in the right column of the FrontPage window.

For example, you may add a few sentences to the beginning of the Welcome page that you have just created in order to tell participants more about the purpose and scope of the discussion group. You can add text by clicking anywhere on the page and typing.

To edit more pages in your discussion group, choose File⇨Open. The Open File dialog box appears with a list of all the documents that make up your discussion group. You can double-click a file's name in order to edit it. When you finish editing files, choose File⇨Save to save your work.

To see how your discussion pages look, use the FrontPage Preview feature. Choose File⇨Preview In Browser, and the page you've been editing appears in your browser window.

Posting your discussion area

The final step is to transfer your discussion web of pages from your own computer to your Web host's site on the Internet. Many Web-hosting services support one-step file transfers with Microsoft FrontPage. If you plan to use FrontPage often, we recommend locating a host that offers this support. (If your host doesn't support such transfers, you need to use an FTP program such as Fetch or WS_FTP to transfer your files.)

With one-step file transfers, you simply connect to the Internet, choose File⇨Publish Web from the FrontPage menu bar, and enter the URL of your directory on your host's Web server where your Web pages are published. Click OK, and your files are immediately transferred.

Chapter 13

Search Engines: What You Need to Know

*T*he other day, Greg took some old radios to a local repair shop. The shop has been in business for more than three decades but never seemed to be busy. This time, however, the owner told Greg he was overwhelmed with hundreds of back orders and wouldn't be able to get to Greg's jobs for several weeks. His shop had just been featured on a television show, and now people were driving long distances to bring him retro audio equipment to fix.

If you can get your business mentioned in just the right place, customers will find you more easily. On the Web, search engines are the most important places to get yourself listed. One of the key requirements for any business is the ability to match up your products or services with potential customers and to ensure that your company shows up in lots of search results and that your site is near the top of the first page. You do have a measure of control over the quality of your placement in search results, and this chapter describes strategies for improving it.

Search engines have created a huge industry for themselves and the search engine optimisation businesses that feed off them. People around the world lodge billions of search enquiries every month, which lead to billions of results. You can see why it's easy for your Web site to get lost in the jumble of businesses who are vying for attention.

Understanding How Search Engines Find You

Have you ever wondered why some companies manage to find their way to the top of a page of search engine results – and occasionally pop up several times on the same page – while others get buried deep within pages and pages of Web site listings? In an ideal world, search engines would rank e-commerce sites by their design, functionality, and whether the businesses behind them give the best possible deals. But with so many millions of Web sites crowding the Internet, the job of processing searches and indexing Web site URLs and contents has to be automated. Because it's computerised, you can perform some magic with the way your Web pages are written that can help you improve your placement in a set of search results.

Your site doesn't necessarily need to appear right at the top of the first search results page. The important thing is to ensure that your site appears before that of your competition. You need to think like a searcher, which is probably easy because you probably do plenty of Web-based searches yourself. How do you find the Web sites you want? Two things are of paramount importance: keywords and links.

Keywords are key

A *keyword* is a word describing a subject that you enter in a search box in order to find information on a Web site or on the wider Internet. Suppose that you're trying to find a source for an herbal sleep aid called Nightol. You'd naturally enter the term *Nightol* in the search box on your search service of choice, click a button called Search, Search Now, Go, or something similar, and wait a few seconds for search results to be gathered.

When you send a keyword to a search service, you set a number of possible actions in motion. One thing that happens for sure is that the keyword is processed by a script on a Web server that is operated by the search service. The script makes a request (which is called, in computerspeak, a *query*) to a database file. The database contains contents culled from millions (even billions, depending on the service) of Web pages.

The database contents are gathered from two sources. In some cases, search services employ human editors who record selected contents of Web pages and write descriptions for those pages. But Web pages are so ubiquitous and changeable that most of the work is actually done by computer programs that automatically scour the Web. These programs don't record every word on every Web page. Some take words from the headings; others index the first 50 or 100 words on a Web site. Accordingly, when Dan did a search for Twix on Google.co.uk, the sites that were listed at the top of the first page of search results had two attributes:

- ✔ Some sites had the brand name Twix in the URL, such as `www.twix.com` or `en.wikipedia.org/wiki/Twix`.
- ✔ Other sites had the word Twix mentioned several times at the top of the home page.

A service called Wordtracker (`wordtracker.com`) does daily surveys of the keyword queries made to various search engines. It creates lists of what it finds to be the most popular search terms. It's not likely those terms apply to your own e-commerce Web site, of course. But if you want to maximise the number of visits to your site, or just make your site more prominent in a list of search results, you may do well to know what's trendy and write your text accordingly.

Adding your site's most important keyword to the URL is one solution to better search placement. But you can't always do this. When it comes to keywords, your job is to load your Web site's headings with as many words as you can find that are relevant to what you sell. You can do so by:

- ✔ Registering your site with one or more of the services (see the 'Going Gaga over Google' section, later in this chapter).
- ✔ Burying keywords in the <META> tag in the HTML for your home page so that they aren't visible to your visitors but appear to the spider programs that index Web pages (see the 'Adding keywords to your HTML' section, later in this chapter).
- ✔ Adding keywords to the headings and initial body text on your pages, as described in the 'Adding keywords to key pages' section, later in this chapter.

A keyword doesn't have to be a single word. You can also use a phrase containing two or more words. Think beyond single words to consider phrases people may enter when they're trying to find products or services you're offering.

Links help searchers connect to you

Keywords aren't the only things that point search services to Web sites. Services like Google keep track of the number of links that point to a site. The greater the number of links, the higher that site's ranking in a set of Google search listings. It's especially good if the URLs that form the links make use of your keywords.

Suppose that your ideal keywords are 'Dan's Shoe Shop'. The ideal URL would be www.dansshoesshop.co.uk, www.dansshoeshop.com, and so on. You can create the following HTML link to your e-commerce Web site on a personal Web page, or an eBay About Me page (see Chapter 10):

```
<a href='http://www.dansshoeshop.com'> Visit Dan's Shoe
          Shop </a>
```

Such a link would be doubly useful: A search service such as Google.co.uk would find your desired keywords ('Dan's Shoe Shop') in the visible, clickable link on your Web page, as well as in the HTML for the link.

Don't forget the human touch

We don't want to suggest that search engines work solely by means of computer programs that automatically scour Web pages and by paid advertisements. Computer programs are perceived to be the primary source, but the human factor still plays a role. Yahoo!, one of the oldest search engines around, originally compiled its directory of Web sites by means of real live employees. These days, its Web directory is hard to spot on Yahoo.co.uk. But editors still index sites and assign them to a category called New and Notable Sites, which includes sites that are especially cool in someone's opinion.

There's almost no way to make sure that a human editor indexes your Web site. The only thing you can do is to make your site as unique and content rich as possible, which helps your business not only show up in directories and search results but also drum up more paying customers for you, too.

Taking the initiative: Paying for ads

You can't get much better placement than right at the top of the first page of a set of search results, either at the top of the page or in a column on the right-hand side. It's even better if your site's name and URL are highlighted in a colour.

Unfortunately, the only way to get such preferred treatment is to pay for it. And that's just what a growing number of online businesses are doing – paying search engines to list their sites in a prominent location. See the 'Paying for search listings can pay off' sidebar, later in this chapter, for more information.

Knowing who supplies the search results

Another important thing to remember about search engines is that they often gather results from *other* search services. You may be surprised to find out that, if you do a search of the Web on AOL, your search results are primarily gathered from Google. That's because AOL has a contract from Google to supply such results. The same applies to thousands of major Web sites that have taken advantage of Google's powerful search capabilities (Myspace.com being another example). Not only that, but many search services are owned by parent search services.

Just what are the most popular search services in the world? A rundown appears in Table 13-1. The services are presented in rank order, beginning in the first row with Google, which is No. 1. Rankings were reported by Nielsen NetRatings in July 2006.

Table 13-1	Internet Search Services	
Search Service	*URL*	*Proportion of searches*
Google	`www.google.com`	49.2%
Yahoo!	`www.yahoo.com,`	23.8%
MSN Search	`search.msn.com`	9.6%
AOL Search,	`search.aol.com`	6.3%
Ask.com	`www.ask.com`	2.6%
Others	none	8.5%

These search services are by no means the only ones around. Note that the 'other' search engines focus on Web sites and Internet resources in specific countries and account for 8.5 per cent of global searches. You can find more of them at `www.searchenginewatch.com/links/article.php/2156121`.

Going Gaga over Google

When it comes to search engines, Google is at the top of the heap. A few years ago, it was Yahoo! that was setting the pace, but Google's lightening quick searches and its comprehensive documenting of the Web has made it favourite.

Google is a runaway success thanks to its effectiveness. You're simply more likely to find something on Google, more quickly, than you are on its competitors. Any search engine placement strategy has to address Google first and foremost. But that doesn't mean you should ignore Google's competitors, such as Yahoo! and MSN.

Googling yourself

If you want to evaluate the quality of your search results placement on Google, you have to start by taking stock of where you currently stand. That's easily done: Just go to Google's UK home page (www.google.co.uk) and 'Google' yourself. (In other words, do a search for your own name or your business's name – a pastime that has also been called *egosurfing*.) See where your Web site turns up in the results and also make note of which other sites mention yours.

Next, click Advanced Search or go directly to www.google.co.uk/advanced_search?hl=en. Under the heading Page-Specific Search, enter the URL for your e-commerce site in the Links text box and then click Search. The results that appear in a few seconds consist of Web sites that link to yours. The list should suggest to you the kinds of sites you should approach to solicit links. It should also suggest the kinds of informational Web sites you may create for the purpose of steering business to your Web site. (See the 'Maximising links' section, later in this chapter, for a specific example.)

Playing Google's game to reach No. 1

Not long ago, some bloggers got together and decided to play a game called *Google bombing*. The game is simple: It consists of making links to a particular Web site in an attempt to get that site listed on Google. The more links the site has pointing to it, the higher that site appears in a set of search results. Of course, the links that are made all have to be connected with a particular keyword or phrase. In the game we're recalling, one phrase used was 'miserable failure'. The words 'miserable failure' were hyperlinks pointing to the Web site of the White House. The story went that if you went to Google, typed the words *miserable failure,* and clicked the I'm Feeling Lucky button, you would be taken to President Bush's biography on the White House Web site – this still worked at time of writing. (Incidentally, if you type those words and click Google Search rather than I'm Feeling Lucky, the No. 2 hit takes you to Jimmy Carter's biography on the White House Web site; and the No. 3 hit takes you to a story about search engine manipulation on the BBC News Web site and the No.4 hit brings up Michael Moore's Web site.) You can find out more about this interesting pastime on a Web site called The Word Spy (www.wordspy.com/words/Googlebombing.asp).

The Google game applies to your e-commerce Web site, too. Suppose that you sell yo-yos, and your Web site URL is www.yoyoplay.com. The game is to get as many other Web sites as possible to link to this URL. The terms that a visitor clicks to get to this URL can be anything: *Yo-Yos, Play Yo-Yos,* and so on. The more links you can make, the better your search results will be.

Leaving a Trail of Crumbs

In order to improve your site's search placement, you need to make it easy for searchers to find you. You leave a trail of digital crumbs. You add keywords to the HTML for your Web pages, and you make sure that your site is included in the databases of the most popular services.

Keep in mind that most Web surfers don't enter single words in search boxes. They tend to enter phrases. Combinations of keywords are extra effective. If you sell tools, don't just enter *tools* as a keyword. Enter keywords such as *tool box, power tool, tool caddy, pneumatic tool, electric tool,* and so on.

Adding keywords to your HTML

What keywords should you add to your site? Take an old-fashioned pencil and paper and write down all the words you can think of that are related to your site, your products, your services, or you – whatever you want to promote, in other words. You may also enlist the help of a printed thesaurus or the one supplied online at Dictionary.com (www.dictionary.com). Look up one term associated with your goods or services, and you're likely to find a number of similar terms.

After you have a set of keywords, you need to add them to the HTML for your Web pages. Keywords and Web site descriptions are contained within HTML commands that begin with <META>. If you type the commands by hand using a text editor, you need to locate the commands in between the <HEAD> and </HEAD> tags at the head of the document. They look like this:

```
<META NAME='description'>
<META NAME='keywords'>
```

Some Web page editors make this user friendly for you: You can type your information in specially designated boxes. Figure 13-1 shows Adobe Dreamweaver's commands, which are accessed by opening the Objects panel, clicking Keywords, and then typing the words in the Keywords dialog box.

Keywords already present in HTML   Click here to add keywords

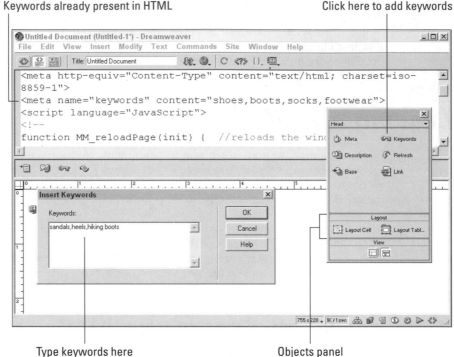

Figure 13-1:
Some Web
page editors
make it easy
to add
keywords
and
descriptions
for search
services
to find.

Type keywords here   Objects panel

You can also spy on your competitors' Web sites to see whether they have added any keywords to their Web pages by following these steps:

1. **Go to your competitor's home page and choose View➪Source if you're using Internet Explorer.**

   A new window opens with the page source supplied.

2. **Scroll through the code, looking for the `<META>` tags if they're present. (Press Ctrl+F, enter META, and click the Find button if you can't find them on your own.)**

   If the page's author used <META> tags to enter keywords, you'll see them on-screen.

3. **Make a note of the keywords supplied and see whether any may be applied to your own Web site.**

Keywords, like Web page addresses, are frequently misspelled. Make sure that you type several variations on keywords that may be subject to typos: for example, **Aberdeen, Abberdeen, Aberdeene**, and so on. Don't worry about getting capitalisation just right, however; most searchers simply enter all lowercase characters and don't bother with capital letters at all.

Spying on the Web searchers

If you've ever wondered what people search for every day on the Internet, you're in luck. A site called Metaspy (`www.metaspy.com`) lets visitors look 'behind the scenes' at a list of keywords that visitors to its search service, MetaCrawler, are entering in near-real time. (The list of search services is refreshed every 15 seconds.) It doesn't help you make your e-commerce site more visible, but it does tell you how diverse the topics are that are searched on Web sites. If nothing else, it makes you aware that some of your keywords need to be general and universal as well as topic specific.

Besides keywords, the <META> tag is also important for the Description command, which enables you to create a description of your Web site or Web page that search engines can index and use in search results. Some search services also scan the description for keywords, too, so make sure that you create a description at the same time you type your keywords in the <META> tags.

Registering your site with Google.co.uk

Google has a program that automatically indexes Web pages all over the Internet. The program actually has a name: Googlebot. However, you don't have to wait for Googlebot to find your site: You can fill out a simple form that adds your URL to the sites that are indexed by this program. Go to `www.google.co.uk/addurl.html`, enter your URL and a few comments about your site, and click the Add URL button. That's all there is to it. Expect to wait a few weeks for your site to appear among Google's search results if it doesn't appear there already.

Getting listed in the Yahoo! index

Yahoo! won't guarantee to list just any Web site, but don't fret, there are two ways to give yourself a fighting chance. One is building a vibrant and content rich Web site; the other is buying your way into its search pages.

For £60, Yahoo! sets you up with a pay-per-click search package. That means you pay Yahoo a small amount of money every time someone finds your Web pages through its search engine. To start with, this charge comes out of your initial £60 deposit; when that runs out, you can decide to top it up and continue to get your Web site listed prominently, or you can simply stop there. Follow this link for more information: `searchmarketing.yahoo.com/en_GB/arp/srch.php?o=GB0176`.

Search Engine Watch (`searchenginewatch.com`) is a great place to go for tips on how search engines and indexes work, and how to get listed on them. The site includes an article about one company's problems getting what it considers to be adequate Yahoo! Coverage.

What else can you do to get listed on Yahoo!? We have a three-step suggestion:

1. **Make your site interesting, quirky, or somehow attention grabbing.**

   You never know; you may just stand out from the sea of new Web sites and gain the attention of Yahoo's indexing software.

2. **Submit your Web site to the search engine.**

   a. **Go to www.yahoo.co.uk, and click the How To Suggest A Site link at the very bottom of the page.**

   The Yahoo! Submit Your Site page appears.

   b. **Click the Submit Your Site For Free button.**

   c. **Input your main domain name and the address of one other page you'd like people to go to.**

   d. **Press the Submit URL button.**

3. **Try a local Yahoo! index.**

   Yahoo! Local, like Google Local, aims to document all the useful bricks-and-mortar businesses around the UK. If you have a physical shop, you can do worse than getting listed with the search service. Go to `uk.local.yahoo.com` and click the Help link at the top right-hand corner of the page. You're asked to contact Yahoo! with your new business listing. Click the Contact Us link, and you're presented with a form to fill in. When you're finished, submit the form by simply clicking the Send button at the bottom of the page.

Getting listed with other search services

Search services can steer lots of business to a commercial Web site, based on how often the site appears in the list of Web pages that the user sees and how high the site appears in the list. Your goal is to maximise your site's chances of being found by the search service.

Paying for search listings can pay off

Listing with search sites is growing more complex all the time. Many sites are owned by other sites. AltaVista is part of the Yahoo! Search Marketing network. You tell Yahoo! how much you'll pay if someone clicks your listing when it appears in a list of search results. The higher you bid, the better your ranking in the results. In exchange for the fees you pay to Yahoo!, your search listings appear in multiple search sites. The same system applies with Google.

Some search services are part of the Overture network, but they still allow individuals to submit their sites for consideration. Here's a quick example that shows how to submit your site (for consideration) to one of the search engines that still gives you the do-it-yourself option:

1. **Connect to the Internet, start your Web browser, and go to AltaVista at `uk.altavista.com`.**

   The AltaVista home page appears.

2. **Click the Submit A Site link.**

   The AltaVista Submit A Site page appears.

3. **Click the Click Here link (under the heading Basic Submit).**

   The Yahoo! Search Sign In page appears. Confused? AltaVista gets its search results from Yahoo!. Therefore, you have to register Yahoo! in order to have people find you on AltaVista.

4. **Enter your Yahoo! ID and password. (If you don't have them yet, click the Sign Up Now link on the same page to obtain them.) Then click Sign In.**

   The Yahoo! Submit Your Site page appears.

5. **In the box labelled Enter the URL, type the URL for your site's home page and then click the Submit URL button.**

   Your page is added to the list of pages that Yahoo!'s 'crawler' program indexes. As the note on the Submit Your Site page says, you can expect the process to take several weeks.

Businesses on the Web can get obsessed with how high their sites appear on the list of search results pages. If a Web surfer enters the exact name of a site in the Excite search text box, for example, some people just can't understand why that site doesn't come back at the top – or even on the first page – of the list of returned sites. Of the millions of sites listed in a search service's database, the chances are good that at least one has the same name as yours (or something close to it) or that a page contains a combination of the same words that make up your organisation's name. Don't be overly concerned with hitting the top of the search-hit charts. Concentrate on creating a top-notch Web site and making sales.

Adding keywords to key pages

Earlier in this chapter (see 'Adding keywords to your HTML'), we show you how to add keywords to the HTML for your Web pages. Those keywords aren't ones that visitors normally see, unless they view the source code for your Web page. Other keywords can be added to parts of your Web page that are visible – parts of the page that those programs called *crawlers* or *spiders* scan and index:

- ✔ **The title:** Be sure to create a title for your page. The title appears in the title bar at the very top of the browser window. Many search engines index the contents of the title because it appears not only at the top of the browser window, but at the top of the HTML, too.

- ✔ **Headings:** Your Web page's headings should be specific about what you sell and what you do.

- ✔ **The first line of text:** Sometimes, search services index every word on every page, but others limit the amount of text they index. So the first lines may be indexed, while others are not. Get your message across quickly; pack your first sentences with nouns that list what you have for sale.

The best way to ensure that your site gets indexed is to pack it with useful content. We're talking about textual content: Search programs can't view photos, animations, or sounds. Make sure that your pages contain a significant amount of text as well as these other types of content.

Web sites that specialise in search-engine optimisation talk about something called *keyword density:* the number of keywords on your page, multiplied by the number of times each one is used. Keyword density is seen as a way to gain a good search engine ranking. In other words, if you sell shoes and you use ten different terms once, you won't get as good of a ranking compared to the use of six of seven words that appear twice, or a handful of well-chosen keywords used several times each.

Take the following passage taken from the home page of Startups.co.uk, which Dan used to be the editor of. It serves people who are considering starting a business, or those who have just taken the plunge. Notice how many times *business, start,* and *entrepreneur* are used. (The actual text is a lot longer, and the words are repeated several more times.)

'Whether you are a budding entrepreneur ready to start a business for the first time or you are an established entrepreneur looking to do it a second time, we have all the news and information you need to get your business starting on the right foot.'

Don't make your pages hard to index

Sometimes, the key to making things work is simply being certain that you aren't putting roadblocks in the way of success. The way you format Web pages can prevent search services from recording your text and the keywords you want your customers to enter. Avoid these obvious hindrances:

- ✔ **Your text begins too far down the page.** If you load the top of your page with images that can't be indexed, your text will be indexed that much slower, and your rankings will suffer.

- ✔ **Your pages are loaded with Java applets, animations, and other objects that can't be indexed.** Content that slows down the automatic indexing programs will reduce your rankings, too.

- ✔ **Your pages don't actually include the ideal keyword phrase you want your searchers to use.** If you have a business converting LP records to CDs, you want the phrase 'LP to CD' or 'convert LPs to CDs' somewhere on your home page and on other pages as well.

Every image on your Web page can potentially be assigned a textual label (also known as *ALT text* because the ALT element in HTML enables it to be used). The immediate purpose of the label is to tell visitors what the image depicts in case it cannot be displayed in the browser window. As a trick to produce more keyword density, you can assign keywords or keyword phrases to these names instead.

Maximising links

Along with keywords, hyperlinks are what search engines use to index a site and include it in a database. By controlling two types of links, you can provide search services with that much more information about the contents of your site:

- ✔ The hyperlinks contained in the bodies of your Web pages
- ✔ The links that point to your site from other locations around the Web

The section 'Links help searchers connect to you', earlier in this chapter, mentions the links in the bodies of your own Web pages. One of the most effective tricks for increasing the number of links that point to your online shop is to create several different Web sites, each of which points to that shop. That's just what Lars Hundley did with his main e-commerce site, Clean Air Gardening (`www.cleanairgardening.com`).

'Creating my own network of gardening sites that provide quality information helps me rise to the top of the search engines in many categories,' says Lars. 'People find the content sites sometimes and click through to Clean Air Gardening to buy related products.'

It's true: Do an Advanced Search on Google for sites that link to `www.cleanairgardening.com`, and you'll find links in the following locations. First, the ones that are run by Lars:

- Organic Pest Control (`www.organicgardenpests.com`)
- Guide to Using a Reel Mower (`www.reelmowerguide.com`)
- Organic Garden Tips (`www.organicgardentips.com`)
- CompostGuide.com (`www.compostguide.com`)
- Rain Barrel Guide (`www.rainbarrelguide.com`)

Next, just a sampling of the many sites that link to Clean Air Gardening and that aren't run by Lars:

- National Gardening Association (`garden.garden.org`)
- GardenToolGuide.com (`www.gardentoolguide.com`)
- Master Composter (`www.mastercomposter.com`)
- Organic Gardening (`www.organicgardening.com`)

For the sites that Lars doesn't run himself, he solicits links. 'I also exchange links with other high-ranking related sites, both in order to improve my rankings, and to provide quality links for my visitors. If you stick with quality links, you can never go wrong.'

Some companies may offer you *SEO in a box* – in other words, search engine optimising software. This software has its benefits but is probably not worth the money. If you're really serious about optimising your online visibility, try a consultancy like Oyster Web (`www.oyster-web.co.uk`). Either way, always make sure that you've exhausted all the free channels of search optimisation before you shell out any cash. A free online guide like the one at the following address is a good place to start: `www.makemetop.co.uk/what_is_seo`.

Monitoring Traffic: The Science of Webanalytics

How do you improve the number of times your site is found by search engines? One way is to analyse the traffic that comes to your site, a practice often called *Webanalytics*. When it comes to search engine placement, the type of research you need to perform is called *log file analysis,* which can tell you exactly what keywords already have been used to find your site. You can then combine those words into new keyword phrases, hopefully helping even more people find your site. You can get software that will do the analysis for you, or you can do it yourself:

✔ **Software options:** Some software options are specifically designed to help improve search engine optimisation. OptiLink (www.optilinksoftware. com/download.html) counts the number of keywords on a Web page. It analyses the links that point at the page and helps you analyse what the best keywords are, where they need to be located, and what specific text will make the links rank higher in Google's search results.

✔ **Do-it-yourself options:** The other, more labour-intensive way to analyse what drives visitors to your Web site is through analysis of log files. A *log file* is an electronic document that a Web server compiles as a record of every visit made to a Web page, image, or other object on a site. Most Web-hosting services let you look at the log file for your Web site. The log file gives you a rough idea of where your visitors are from and which resources on your Web site are the most visited. By focusing on particular types of log file data, you can evaluate how visitors find your site and which search services are doing the best job of directing visitors to you.

If you look at log file information in its raw text form, you're probably mystified by page after page of numbers and techie gibberish. Log files typically record information such as the IP address and the domain name of the computer that accesses a Web page. They don't tell you the name and address of the person using the machine at the time. They give you an idea of where the computer is located geographically, based on the suffix at the end of a domain name (such as .de for Germany or .fr for France). You'll probably need to make use of a log file analyser such as ClickTracks.com (www.clicktracks.com) or WebTrends (www.webtrends.co.uk), which present the data in a format that is easy to interpret.

When you're viewing log files, one important thing to track is *referrer reporting,* which gives you the site the visitor was viewing just before coming to yours. This report tells you what sites are directing visitors to yours. Make note of the search engines that appear most frequently; these are the ones you need to work on when it comes to improving your placement in sets of search results.

Part IV
The Necessary Evils: Law and Accounting

In this part . . .

*B*efore you can start raking in the big (or at least moderate) bucks on the Web, you've got to get your ducks in a row. Along with the flashy parts of an online business – the ads, the Web pages, the catalog listings – you have to add up numbers and obtain the necessary licenses.

This part addresses the aspects of doing business online that have to be covered in order to pay taxes, take deductions, and observe the law. You may think of them as necessary evils that help you avoid trouble, but they're also ways to help you boost your bottom line and help you stand out from your competitors, too. In this part, you read about taxes, licensing, accounting, copyright, and other scintillating legal and financial must-haves for your online business.

Chapter 14

Making It All Legal

As the field of e-commerce becomes more competitive, e-patents, e-trademarks, and other means of legal protection multiply correspondingly. The courts are increasingly being called upon to resolve smaller e-squabbles and, literally, lay down the e-law.

For example, when Google purchased the video-sharing Web site YouTube for $1.65 billion, it was forced to pull large numbers of video files from its archive. Why? Because users were uploading all sorts of copyrighted material that they had no licence to broadcast. Now, some commentators think that YouTube is less valuable, because, for example, you can no longer get sneak previews of up-and-coming films unless it has been okayed by the film companies themselves.

In an earlier example, in April 2002, the popular search service Overture sued another popular search service, Google, for allegedly stealing its patented system of presenting search results based on bids placed by advertisers and Web sites.

In 2003, the US WIPO Arbitration and Mediation Center was confronted with 1,100 domain name disputes – an average of 3 per day. Many of these were filed by large corporations seeking to gain control over domain names that were allegedly being held by small business cybersquatters. In summer 2004, Microsoft settled a lawsuit it had filed in US district court by paying $20 million to stop a company called Lindows.com from infringing on its trademarked name Windows.

As a new business owner, you need to remember that ignorance is not an excuse. This area may well make you nervous because you lack experience in business law and you don't have lots of money with which to hire lawyers and accountants. You don't want to be discovering for the first time about copyright or the concept of intellectual property when you're in the midst of a dispute. In this chapter, we give you a snapshot of legal issues that you can't afford to ignore. Hopefully, this information can help you head off trouble before it occurs.

Thinking about Trade Names and Trademarks

A *trade name* is the name by which a business is known in the marketplace. A trade name can also be *trademarked,* which means that a business has taken the extra step of registering its trade name so that others can't use it. At the same time, it's important to realise that a trade name can be a trademark even though it hasn't been registered as such. Specifically, a trademark is a word, phrase, symbol, or design that identifies and distinguishes the source of your goods or services. Big corporations protect their trade names and trademarks jealously, and sometimes court battles erupt over who can legally use a name.

Although you're unlikely to ever get involved in a trademark battle yourself, and you may never trademark a name, you need to be careful which trade name you pick and how you use it. Choose a name that's easy to remember so that people can associate it with your company and return to you often when they're looking for the products or services that you provide. Also, as part of taking your new business seriously and planning for success, you may want to protect your right to use your name by registering the trademark, which is a relatively easy and inexpensive process.

Take the example of SoOrganic, a Web Site run by managing director Samantha Burlton, which sells organic and ethically sourced food, clothes, toys, and household products. Do a Google.co.uk search for her Web site, and you'll see her described as the 'real' SoOrganic. Why? Because Sainsbury's supermarket chain has launched a line of organic foods by the same name. They currently sit No. 1 and 2 on the Google search ranking, so you can see why some conflict may occur!

You can trademark any visual element that accompanies a particular tangible product or line of goods, which serves to identify and distinguish it from products sold by other sources. In other words, a trademark is not necessarily just for your business's trade name. In fact, you can trademark letters, words, names, phrases, slogans, numbers, colours, symbols, designs, or shapes. For example, take a look at the cover of the book you're reading right now. Look closely and see how many ™ or ® symbols you see. The same trademarked items are shown at the Dummies Web site, as you can see in Figure 14-1. Even though the *For Dummies* heading doesn't bear a symbol, it's a trademark – believe us.

For most small businesses, the problem with trademarks is not so much protecting your own as it is stepping on someone else's. Research the name you want to use to make sure that you don't run into trouble. A good place to start is by checking out Companies House's Web site (`www.companieshouse.co.uk`), which is the definite list of businesses operating (and recently folded) in the UK. It'll tell you what company names are currently taken, and which you can use – you can also register your own business name through the site, at a cost of £20.

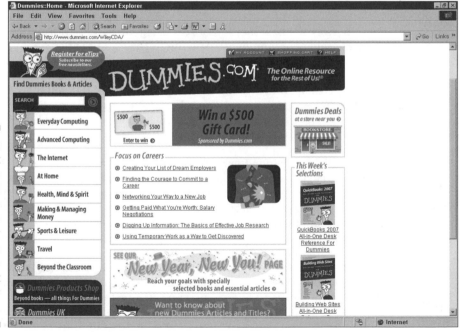

Figure 14-1:
You don't have to use special symbols to designate logos or phrases on your Web site, but you may want to.

Determining whether a trademark is up for grabs

To avoid getting sued for trademark infringement and having to change your trade name or even pay damages if you lose, you should conduct a trademark search before you settle on a trade name. The goal of a trademark search is to discover any potential conflicts between your trade name and someone else's. Ideally, you conduct the search before you actually use your trade name or register for an official trademark.

We spoke to David Adler of the law firm David M. Adler, Esq. & Associates (www.ecommerceattorney.com). Based in Chicago, in the United States, Adler knows a thing or two about copyright law. (Far more cases of infringement are contested in the United States every year than in the UK.) He says, 'If you don't have a registered trademark, your trade name becomes very difficult to protect. It's a good idea to do a basic search on the Internet. But keep in mind that just because you don't find a name on the Internet doesn't mean it doesn't exist. Follow that up with a trademark search. You don't want to spend all the money required to develop a brand name only to find that it isn't yours.'

Far and away the best method of searching for patent information is to do a search online, or simply call or write to the Patent Office (www.patent.gov.uk). The Patent Office has all the information you could possibly need about how to avoid infringing other people's copyrighted material and how to protect your own. You can also check out one of the helpful online business magazines, such as www.realbusiness.co.uk or www.startups.co.uk, for more information and examples of how people and businesses have protected themselves in practice.

Cyberspace goes beyond national boundaries. A trademark search in your own country may not be enough. Most industrialised countries, including the United Kingdom, have signed international treaties that enable trademark owners in one country to enforce their rights against infringement by individuals in another country. Conducting an international trademark search is difficult to do yourself, so you may want to pay someone do the searching for you.

The consequences of failing to conduct a reasonably thorough trademark search can be severe. In part, the consequences depend on how widely you distribute the protected item – and on the Internet, you can distribute it worldwide. If you attempt to use a trademark that has been registered by someone else, you could go to court and be prevented from using the trademark again. You may even be liable for damages and solicitor's fees. So it's best to be careful.

Protecting your trade name

The legal standard is that you get the rights to your trade name when you begin using it. You get the right to exclude others from using it when you register your trademark with the Patent Office. But when you apply to register a trademark, you record the date of its first use. Effectively, then, the day you start using a name is when you actually obtain the rights to use it for trade.

After researching your trade name against existing trademarks, you can file an application with the Patent and Trademark Office online by following these steps:

1. **Connect to the Net, start up your browser, and go to the Patent Office home page (www.patent.gov.uk), shown in Figure 14-2.**

2. **Click on Trade marks and then, on the Trade marks page, click the link entitled How To Apply.**

   Read this section thoroughly; it gives you all your options when applying for protection.

3. **If you think applying online is the best way forward, click Making Your Application Online.**

   Again read this section thoroughly; it tells you how to avoid making mistakes that may delay your application.

4. **At the bottom of the page click the link Electronic Trade Mark Application Form.**

   Fill the form in as prompted and click the Send button. If you need any further guidance, simply scroll to the bottom of the page and click the Help Filling In This Form link.

Be prepared for a lengthy approval process after you file your application. Trademark registration can take months, and it's not uncommon to have an application returned. Sometimes, an applicant receives a correspondence that either rejects part of the application or raises a question about it. If you receive such a letter, don't panic. You need to go to a lawyer who specialises in or is familiar with trademark law and who can help you respond to the correspondence. In the meantime, you can still operate your business with your trade name.

Costs vary (from £50 to £200) depending on what *class* of trademark you want to apply for. It's too complicated to go into here – but you can get all the information you need by logging on to www.patent.gov.uk, clicking Trade Marks, and checking out the Costs and Timeline section.

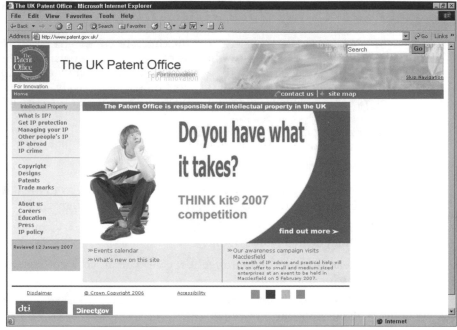

Trademarks are listed in a searchable register called GB esp@cenet (accessible through `www.patent.gov.uk`), last for ten years, and are renewable. You don't have to use the ™ or ® symbol when you publish your trademark, but doing so impresses upon people how seriously you take your business and its identity.

Ensuring that your domain name stays yours

The practice of choosing a domain name for an online business is related to the concept of trade names and trademarks. By now, with cybersquatters and other businesspeople snapping up domain names since 1994 or so, it's unlikely that your ideal name is available in the popular `.com` or `.co.uk` domain. It's also likely that another business has a domain name very similar to yours or to the name of your business. There are two common problems:

✔ Someone else has already taken the domain name related to the name of your existing business.

✔ The domain name you choose is close to one that already exists or to another company with a similar name. (Check out the Microsoft Windows/Lindows.com dispute detailed at the beginning of this chapter.)

If the domain name that you think is perfect for your online business is already taken, you have options. You can contact the owner of the domain name and offer to buy it. Alternatively, you can choose a domain name with another suffix. If a `.com` name isn't available, try the old standby alternatives, `.co.uk` (which, in theory at least, is for nonprofit organisations) and `.net` (which is for network providers).

You can also choose one of the new Top-Level Domains (TLDs), a new set of domain name suffixes that have been made available, which include the following:

- ✔ `.biz` for businesses
- ✔ `.info` for 'information' or general use
- ✔ `.name` for personal names
- ✔ `.tv` for Web site audio and video feeds
- ✔ `.eu` for Web sites aimed at European Union countries

You can find out more about the new TLDs at the nominet Web site (`www.nominet.org.uk`), the official register of UK Web domains, and in Chapter 8.

You can always get around the fact that your perfect domain name isn't available by changing the name slightly. Rather than `treesurgeon.com`, you can choose `tree-surgeon.com` or `treesurgery.com`. But be careful, lest you violate someone else's trademark and get into a dispute with the holder of the other domain name.

Practising Safe Copyright

What's the difference between a trademark and a copyright? Trademarks are covered by trademark law and are distinctive words, symbols, slogans, or other things that serve to identify products or services in the marketplace. *Copyright,* on the other hand, refers to the creator's ownership of creative works, such as writing, art, software, video, or cinema (but not names, titles, or short phrases). Copyright also provides the owner with redress in case someone copies the works without the owner's permission. Copyright is a legal device that enables the creator of a work the right to control how the work is to be used.

Although copyright protects the way ideas, systems, and processes are embodied in the book, record, photo, or whatever, it doesn't protect the idea, system, or process itself. In other words, if William Shakespeare were writing Romeo and Juliet today, his exact words would be copyrighted, but the general ideas he expressed would not be.

Fair use . . . and how not to abuse it

Copyright law doesn't cover everything. According to Business Link (www.businesslink.gov.uk), the government group that gives advice to businesses, you can make *limited use* of copyrighted material without the author's permission in the following circumstances:

✔ For use as teaching material

✔ For criticising and reviewing

✔ For news reporting

✔ When it applies to court proceedings

Fair use, as this is sometimes referred to as, has some big grey areas that can be traps for people who provide information on the Internet. Don't fall into one of these traps. Shooting off a quick e-mail asking someone for permission to reproduce his or her work isn't difficult. Chances are that person will be flattered and will let you make a copy as long as you give him or her credit on your site. Fair use is entirely dependent on the unique circumstances of each individual case, and this is an area where, if you have any questions, you should consult a solicitor.

Even if nobody ever called you a nerd, as a businessperson who produces goods and services of economic value, you may be the owner of intellectual property. *Intellectual property* refers to works of authorship as well as certain inventions. Because intellectual property may be owned, bought, and sold just like other types of property, it's important that you know something about the copyright laws governing intellectual property. Having this information maximises the value of your products and keeps you from throwing away potentially valuable assets or finding yourself at the wrong end of an expensive lawsuit.

Copyright you can count on

Everything you see on the Net is copyrighted, whether a copyright notice actually appears. Copyright exists from the moment a work is fixed in a tangible medium, including a Web page. For example, plenty of art is available for the taking on the Web, but look before you grab. Unless an image on the Web is specified as being copyright free, you'll be violating copyright law if you take it. HTML tags themselves aren't copyrighted, but the content of the HTML-formatted page is. General techniques for designing Web pages aren't copyrighted, but certain elements (such as logos) are.

Keep in mind that it's okay to use a work for criticism, comment, news reporting, teaching, scholarship, or research. That comes under the *fair use* limitation. (See the nearby sidebar 'Fair use . . . and how not to abuse it' for more information.) However, we still contend that it's best to get permission or cite your source in these cases, just to be safe.

Making copyright work for you

A copyright – which protects original works of authorship – costs nothing, applies automatically, and lasts more than 50 years. When you affix a copyright notice to your newsletter or Web site, you make your readers think twice about unauthorised copying and put them on notice that you take copyright seriously. Check out Dan's Web site at `www.infozoo.co.uk` and notice the copyright notice subtly included at the bottom of the every page.

Creating a good copyright notice

Even though any work you do is automatically protected by copyright, having some sort of notice expresses your copyright authority in a more official way. Copyright notices identify the author of a given work (such as writing or software) and then spell out the terms by which that author grants others the right (or the licence) to copy that work to their computer and read it (or use it). The usual copyright notice is pretty simple and takes this form:

```
Copyright 2007 [Your Name] All rights reserved
```

You don't have to use the © symbol, but it does make your notice look more official. In order to create a copyright symbol that appears on a Web page, you have to enter a special series of characters in the HTML source code for your page. For example, Web browsers translate the characters `&copy;` as the copyright symbol, which is displayed as © in the Web browser window. Most Web page creation tools provide menu options for inserting special symbols such as this one.

Copyright notices can also be more informal, and a personal message can have extra impact. On its 100% Design conference Web site (`www.100percent design.co.uk`), Reed Exhibitions includes both the usual copyright notice plus a very detailed message about how others can use its design elements (`www.100percentdesign.co.uk/page.cfm/Link=2/t=m`).

Protecting with digital watermarks

In traditional offset printing, a *watermark* is a faint image embedded in stationery or other paper. The watermark usually bears the name of the paper manufacturer, but it can also identify an organisation for whom the stationery was made.

Watermarking has its equivalent in the online world. Graphic artists sometimes use a technique called *digital watermarking* to protect images they create. This process involves adding copyright or other information about the image's owner to the digital image file. The information added may or may not be visible. (Some images have copyright information added, not visible in the body of the Web page but in the image file itself.) Other images, such as the one shown in Figure 14-3, have a watermark pasted right into the visible area, which makes it difficult for others to copy and reuse them.

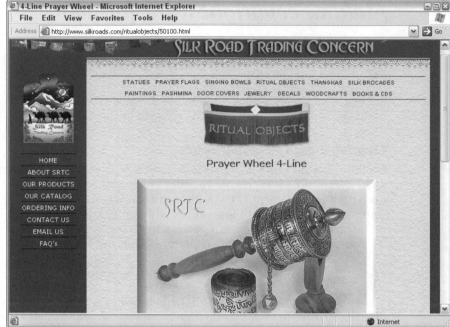

Figure 14-3:
If your products are particularly precious, such as unique works of art, assert your copyright over them on your Web site.

Digimarc (www.digimarc.com), which functions as a plug-in application with the popular graphics tools Adobe Photoshop (www.adobe.com) and Paint Shop Pro 7 (www.corel.com), is one of the most widely used water-marking tools.

Doing the paperwork on your copyright

There is no official copyright registrar in the UK, because copyright is automatic, but a number of unofficial companies will log your claim to a copyright for you. That step will help if you ever have the misfortune of falling into a dispute with another party, but you should think very carefully before handing over your hard-earned cash. You can guard copyrighted material for a much lower cost in several other ways.

The most common method is to send material to yourself via recorded delivery, and not open the package when you receive it. That gives a clear date before which the material must have been created. When it comes to digital information, designs, logos, and so on, you can protect your copyright by printing screen grabs of your work and following the process from there.

Understanding Legal Basics

The UK prides itself on the ease with which you can start a business. If you know what you're doing, it can take just a couple of days compared to weeks and months elsewhere in the world. That's not to say you can just set up shop and start trading, however. To start with, restrictions regulate the selling of certain types of products, such as food and agricultural products, and your own software, as well as running businesses where you are responsible for the well-being of others (say, if you ran a paintball business, where you teach your customers how to use the guns, you oversee games, or where you may need to use basic first aid).

You must also register your business with Her Majesty's Revenue and Customs (HMRC), an organisation which takes a close interest in any money you make from the business. If your business is successful, you soon have to register for Value Added Tax (VAT). But even at the very beginning, you have to register yourself as self-employed for tax purposes – even if your business is part-time or you have a nine-to-five job, too. It means you have to start filling in your own self-assessment tax forms annually and must declare your earnings each year.

So, you need accounting software to keep track of your finances and a business bank account that is separate from your current account. These elements, along with any special qualifications you may require to start your business, are essential. They're as important as your product, promotional material, and informing the tax authorities; all are required before you start a business.

Business Link, part of the Department for Trade and Industry, is a service dedicated to helping businesses get off the ground. In our opinion, the best thing about Business Link is its Web site (`www.businesslink.gov.uk`), which has a huge budget and numerous staff dedicated to keeping track of the evolving rules and regulations about starting up, as well as a whole range of hints, tips, and straight-talking advice on how you can give yourself the best chance of success.

We can't cover every small legal detail applying to every type of business here, but the Business Link Web site does, plus it offers links to industry specific organisations that can help you further. Our advice is to read all the information relevant to you as thoroughly as possible and check out links to organisations that cover your sector well before you start your own business venture. Remember: Forewarned is forearmed!!

Your Business in the Eyes of the Law

It's true that no two businesses are alike, but you have the option of picking not only your product, marketing material, and Web design, but also the legal form that your business takes. You have a number of options from which to choose, and the choice can affect the amount of taxes you pay and your liability in case of loss. The following sections describe your alternatives.

If you're looking for more information, Colin Barrow explores the legal and financial aspects of launching and operating a small business in *Starting a Business For Dummies* and Paul Barrow's *Bookkeeping For Dummies* (both by Wiley) is also useful.

Sole trader

If you're a *sole trader,* you're the only boss. You make all the decisions, and you get all the benefits. On the other hand, you take all the risk, too. This setup is the simplest and least expensive type of business because you can run it yourself. You don't need an accountant or lawyer to help you form the business, and you don't have to answer to partners or stockholders, either. To become a trader, you just have to declare yourself as such with Her Majesty's Revenue and Customs (www.hmrc.gov.uk).

Partnership

In a *partnership,* you share the risk and profit with at least one other person. Ideally, your partners bring skills to the endeavour that complement your own contributions. One obvious advantage to a partnership is that you can discuss decisions and problems with your partners. All partners are held personally liable for losses. The rate of taxes that each partner pays is based on his or her percentage of income from the partnership.

If you decide to strike up a partnership with someone, drawing up a *partnership agreement* is a good idea. Although you aren't legally required to do so, such an agreement clearly spells out the duration of the partnership and the responsibilities of each person involved. In the absence of such an agreement, the division of liabilities and assets is considered to be equal, regardless of how much more effort one person has put into the business than the other.

Statutory business entity

A *statutory business entity* is a business whose form is created by statute, such as a corporation or a limited liability company. If sole traders and partnerships are so simple to start up and operate, why would you consider incorporating? After all, you almost certainly need a lawyer to help you incorporate. Besides that, you may undergo a type of *double taxation:* If your corporation earns profits, those profits are taxed at the corporate rate, and any shareholders have to pay income tax, too.

Despite these downsides, you may want to consider incorporation for the following reasons:

- ✔ If you have employees, you can deduct any health and disability insurance premiums that you pay.
- ✔ You can raise money by offering stock for sale.
- ✔ Transferring ownership from one shareholder to another is easier.
- ✔ The company's principals are shielded from liability in case of lawsuits.

Limited company

The main difference between a limited liability company and a partnership is that the liabilities of the business are not passed on to the owners. You are only liable for any debt you incurred (say, if the founders jointly took out a loan), but you don't have liability for the company's taxes. Similarly to a partnership, some form of written agreement is essential here. Overseen by an impartial witness (preferably a lawyer), the operating agreement shows who holds what position in the business, what roles they perform, and how much of the business they own for tax purposes.

A limited liability company gets taxed twice, once for income and once for profits. The owners work out how much tax they have to pay and then submit a self-assessment form to HM Revenue & Customs.

Corporation

When you think of a corporation, your head may be filled with multibillion pound making entities like BP, Nike, and Coca-Cola. This is fair enough, but it doesn't reflect the whole picture. (For starters, only very few corporations make profits in the billions!) In terms of structure, all corporations are alike: They have their own names, bank accounts, and taxes to file. They are legal entities (much like people are) that are created for the sole purpose of doing business. Because of this legal status, they are the biggest and most complex form of business you will come across, and the vast majority of startups don't have to worry about becoming incorporated for some time yet (if at all).

Corporations pay corporation tax (duh!); how much you pay depends on

- How much profit you make
- Whether you keep that profit to yourself or invest it straight back into developing the business

Top whack corporation tax is 30 per cent of earnings, or *profits*. That applies to profits of more than £1.5 million (wowza!), but the government offers taper relief so that smaller profits are taxed proportionately. Corporation tax is precisely nought if you make less than ten grand and plough the whole lot into the business.

Because our venerable Chancellor keeps tinkering with the tax system, in order to close loopholes and get his hands on all your lovely wonga, there's an ongoing debate whether it's better to incorporate your business or not. The truth is, incorporation depends on your personal circumstances, type of business, profits, and plans for the future. Ask an accountant what he or she thinks before you take action. Try an online business forum, such as the one on RealBusiness.co.uk (www.realbusiness.co.uk), and see whether anyone's prepared to give you some free advice.

Keeping Out of Legal Trouble

A big part of keeping your online business legal is steering clear of so-called business opportunities that can turn into big problems. In the following list, we highlight some areas to watch out for.

- **Get it in writing!** Perhaps the most important way to avoid legal trouble is to get all your agreements in writing. (Notice how lawyers always do that?) Even if the parties involved type and sign a simple one-page sheet describing what is to be done and what is to be paid, that's far better than a verbal agreement. It's also better than an e-mail message – an e-mail doesn't enable signatures, and a single message doesn't clearly point out that both parties have actually agreed to something. A qualified lawyer can help you prepare contracts that you can send to both suppliers and customers who engage your services.

The other important things to get in writing are *policy statements:* statements that spell out how a customer is to use your goods or services, or statements as to how you manage your customers' personal information. Such statements build trust among your clientele. But remember that when you publish a policy statement on your Web site, you need to actually follow what it prescribes; you can be sued if you violate it.

✔ **Ever thought of health and safety?** It may come as a surprise, but as soon as you set up and register your online business, you must create a safe and risk free environment for your employees (even if the only employee is you!). It sounds silly, but the Health & Safety Executive is taking no chances – it's ultimately responsible for the welfare of British workers and is charged with keeping accidents and illnesses down. Follow this link to the HSE Web site (www.hse.gov.uk/businesses.htm) for the lowdown on your responsibilities.

✔ **Remember the red tape or form-filing.** A lot is made in the UK about red tape (for example, the various regulations defining what you can and can't do). Businesspeople tell Dan that it's not the rules themselves, or even the taxes, that are the main problem; it's the reams of forms that you have to fill in to show you've complied. Take Dan's pals who run a husband-and-wife window-cleaning company, number of employees: two. They recently had to fill in a form describing the demographic makeup of their business. In other words they had to declare that their business was 50 per cent men (the husband) and 50 per cent female (the wife), that the business was exclusively made up of British people, and that all the staff were in their 40s.

Of course, in a business of two people, you'd be forgiven for employing only 40-something Brits, but that doesn't apply to larger businesses. You can scoff at these documents, but (unfortunately) you still have to fill them in and return them to the authorities.

✔ **Adult content is risky business.** Be careful if you provide so-called adult content. There's no doubt about it: Cyberspace is full of X-rated sites, many of which do make money. (Porn is one of the Net's most successful industries!) But this area is risky.

If you do sell adult items online, consider working with a blocking company, such as CyberPatrol (www.cyberpatrol.com) or Net Nanny (www.netnanny.com/home/home.asp), which can prevent minors from visiting your site. Always put up a front page warning users that entering the site will expose them to adult content, and in general do all you can to protect youngsters – you have been warned.

✔ **What you don't know about acceptable use policies can hurt you.** Be aware of acceptable use policies set up by agencies that control what goes out online. Usually, the company that hosts your Web site has a set of acceptable use guidelines spelling out what kind of material you can and can't publish. For example, AOL has its own policies for its members who create home pages using its platform.

Another important kind of acceptable use policy that you need to know about is the acceptable use policy issued by your Internet service provider. The most common restriction is one against *spamming* (sending unsolicited bulk mailings). Not following your Web host's or your ISP's guidelines can get you kicked off the Internet, so make sure that you're aware of any restrictions by reading the guidelines posted on your ISP's or Web host's site.

Chapter 15

Online Business Accounting Tools

Some people have a gift for keeping track of expenses, recording financial information, and performing other fiscal functions. Unfortunately, we, and many of you, do not have these rare skills. Yet we know (and you should know) the value of accounting procedures, especially those that relate to an online business.

Without having at least some minimal records of your day-to-day operations, you won't have any way – other than the proverbial gut feeling – of knowing whether your business is truly successful. Besides that, banks and the taxman don't put much stock in gut feelings. When the time comes to ask for a loan or to pay taxes, you'll regret not having water-tight records close at hand.

In this chapter, we introduce you to simple, straightforward ways to handle your online business's financial information – and all businesspeople know that accurate record keeping is essential when revenues dwindle and expenses must be reduced. In this chapter, you discover the most important accounting practices and find out about software that can help you tackle the essential fiscal tasks that you need to undertake to keep your new business viable. (For more information on these topics, also see *Bookkeeping For Dummies,* published by Wiley.)

ABCs: Accounting Basics for Commerce

We can summarise the most important accounting practices for your online business as follows:

> ✔ **Deciding what type of business you're going to be:** Are you going to be a sole trader, partnership, limited business, or corporation? (See more about determining a legal form for your business in Chapter 14.)
>
> ✔ **Establishing good record-keeping practices:** Record expenses and income in ways that will help you at tax time.
>
> ✔ **Obtaining financing when you need it:** Although getting started in business online doesn't cost a lot, you may want to expand someday, or borrow money to buy stock, and good accounting can help you do it.

There's nothing sexy about accounting (unless, of course, you're married to an accountant; in that case, you have a financial expert at hand and can skip this chapter anyway!). Then again, there's nothing enjoyable about unexpected cash shortages or other problems that can result from bad record keeping.

Good accounting is the key to order and good management for your business. How else can you know how you're doing? Yet many new businesspeople are intimidated by the numbers game. Use the tool at hand – your computer – to help you overcome your fear: Start keeping those books!

Choosing an accounting method

Accepting that you have to keep track of your business's accounting is only half the battle; next, you need to decide how to do it. The point at which you make note of each transaction in your books and the period of time over which you record the data make a difference not only to your accountant but also to agencies such as HM Revenue & Customs (HMRC). Even if you hire someone to keep the books for you, you need to know what options are open to you.

Consult the HMRC Web site (www.hmrc.gov.uk) and check out the section on Businesses & Corporations. It's got a whole host of information telling you how and when accounting procedures come into play. You may also want to check out the Chartered Institute of Taxation (www.tax.org.uk) or an accountancy firm like TaxAssist Accountants (www.taxassist.co.uk).

Cash-basis versus accrual-basis accounting

Don't be intimidated by the terms in this section: They're simply two methods of totalling up income and expenses. Exactly where and how you do the recording is up to you. You can take a piece of paper, divide it into two columns labelled *Income* and *Expenses,* and do it that way. (We describe some more high-tech tools later in this chapter.) These methods are just two standard ways of deciding when to report them:

✔ **Cash-basis accounting:** You report income when you actually receive it and write off expenses when you pay them. This is the easy way to report income and expenses, and probably the way most new small businesses do it.

✔ **Accrual-basis accounting:** This method is more complicated than the cash-basis method, but if your online business maintains an inventory, you must use the accrual method. You report income when you actually receive the payment; you write down expenses *when services are rendered* (even though you may not have made the cash payment yet). For example, if a payment is due on December 1, but you send the cheque out on December 8, you record the bill as being paid on December 1, when the payment was originally due.

Accrual-basis accounting creates a more accurate picture of a business's financial situation. If a business is experiencing cash flow problems and is extending payments on some of its bills, cash-basis accounting provides an unduly rosy financial picture, whereas the accrual-basis method would be more accurate.

Choosing an accounting period

The other choice you need to make when it comes to deciding how to keep your books is the accounting period you're going to use. Here, again, you have two choices:

✔ **Calendar year:** The calendar year ends on December 31. This is the period with which you're probably most familiar and the one most small or home-based businesses choose because it's the easiest to work with.

✔ **Fiscal year:** In this case, the business picks a date other than December 31 to function as the end of the fiscal year. Many large organisations pick a date that coincides with the end of their business cycle. Some pick March 31 as the end, others June 30, and still others September 30.

If you use the fiscal-year method of accounting, you must file your tax return three and a half months after the end of the fiscal year. If the fiscal year ends on June 30, for example, you must file by October 15.

Knowing what records to keep

When you run your own business, it pays to be meticulous about recording everything that pertains to your commercial activities. The more you understand what you have to record, the more accurate your records will be – and the more deductions you can take, too. Go to the office supply retailer and get a financial record book (or *journal*), which is set up with columns for income and expenses.

Tracking income

Receiving cheques, bank transfers, and credit-card payments for your goods or services is the fun part of doing business, and so income is probably the kind of data that you'll be happiest about recording.

You need to keep track of your company's income (or, as it is sometimes called, your *gross receipts*) carefully. Not all the income your business receives is taxable. What you receive as a result of sales (your *revenue*) is taxable, but loans that you receive aren't. Be sure to separate the two and pay tax only on the sales income. But keep good records: If you can't accurately report the source of income that you didn't pay taxes on, the HRMC will label it *unreported income,* and you'll have to pay taxes, and possibly fines, on it.

Just how should you record your revenue? For each item, write down a brief, informal statement. This statement is a personal record that you may make on a slip of paper or even on the back of a cancelled cheque. Be sure to include the following information:

- ✔ Amount received
- ✔ Type of payment (credit card, electronic cash, or cheque)
- ✔ Date of the transaction
- ✔ Name of client or customer
- ✔ Goods or services you provided in exchange for the payment

Collect all your cheque stubs and revenue statements in a folder labelled *Income* so that you can find them easily at tax time.

Assessing your assets

Assets are resources that your business owns, such as your office and computer equipment. *Equity* refers to your remaining assets after you pay your creditors.

Any equipment you have that contributes to your business activities constitutes your assets. Equipment that has a life span of more than a year is expected to help you generate income over its useful life; therefore, you must spread out (or, in other words, *expense*) the original cost of the equipment over its life span. Expensing the cost of an asset over the period of its useful life is called *depreciation.* In order to depreciate an item, you estimate how many years you're going to use it and then divide the original cost by the number of years. The result is the amount that you report in any given year. For example, if you purchase a computer that costs £900 and you expect to use it in your business for three years, you expense £300 of the cost each year.

You need to keep records of your assets that include the following information:

- ✔ Name, model number, and description
- ✔ Purchase date
- ✔ Purchase price, including fees
- ✔ Date the item went into service
- ✔ Amount of time the item is put to personal (as opposed to business) use

File these records in a safe location along with your other tax-related information.

Recording payments

Even a lone entrepreneur doesn't work in a vacuum. An online business owner needs to pay a Web host, an ISP, and possibly Web page designers and other consultants. If you take on partners or employees, things get more complicated. But in general, you need to record all payments in detail as well.

Your accountant is likely to bring up the question of how you pay the people who work for you. You have two options: You can treat them either as full- or part-time employees or as independent contractors. HMRC uses a stringent series of guidelines to determine who is a contractor and who is a full-time employee. Check out the following link, which describes the legal difference between contractors and employees: www.yourpeoplemanager.com/ YUgHntBoivVsHw.html.

Hiring independent contractors rather than salaried workers is far simpler for you: You don't have to pay benefits to independent contractors, for one thing, plus you don't have to schedule their holidays, pension payments, or life insurance policies. Just be sure to get invoices from any independent contractor who works for you. If you have full-time employees whom you pay an hourly wage or annual salary, things get more complicated, and you had best consult an accountant to help you set up the salary payments.

Listing expenses

Get a big folder and use it to hold any receipts, contracts, cancelled cheques, credit-card statements, or invoices that represent expenses. It's also a great idea to maintain a record of expenses that includes the following information:

- ✔ Date the expense occurred
- ✔ Name of the person or company that received payment from you
- ✔ Type of expense incurred (equipment, utilities, supplies, and so on)

Recalling exactly what some receipts are for is often difficult a year or even just a month after the fact. Be sure to jot down a quick note on all cancelled cheques and copies of receipts to remind you of what the expense involved.

Understanding the Ps and Qs of P&Ls

You're likely to hear the term *profit-and-loss statement* (also called a P&L) thrown around when discussing your online business with financial people. A P&L is a report that measures the operation of a business over a given period of time, such as a week, a month, or a year. The person who prepares the P&L (either you or your accountant) adds up your business revenues and subtracts the operating expenses. What's left are either the profits or the losses.

Most of the accounting programs listed later in this chapter include some way of presenting profit and loss statements and enable you to customise the statements to fit your needs.

Accounting Software for Your Business

The well-known commercial accounting packages, such as Microsoft Money, QuickBooks, and Sage, let you prepare statements and reports and even tie into a tax preparation system. Stick with these programs if you like setting up systems such as databases on your computer. Otherwise, go for a simpler method and hire an accountant to help you.

Whatever program you choose, make sure that you're able to keep accurate books and set up privacy and backup schemes that prevent your kids from zapping your business records.

If your business is a relatively simple one – say, if you're a sole trader – you can record expenses and income on a spreadsheet or by hand and add them up at tax time. Then input them into a HMRC tax return. Alternatively, you can record your entries and turn them over to a tax advisor who can prepare a profit and loss statement and tell you the balance due on your tax payment.

If you're looking to save a few quid and want an extra-simple accounting program that you can set up right now, look no further than Microsoft's own Excel spreadsheet software, which comes with standard Microsoft Office package. It can help you tot up your earnings and deduct tax, but you'll need some practice to get it right.

Turbo Cash 7 (www.turbocashuk.com),is a step up from a spreadsheet, but so simple that even financially impaired people like us can pick it up quickly. Turbo Cash is *open source* (meaning anyone can use it under the terms of the General Public Licence) and is designed to enable people with no prior accounting experience to keep track of income and expenses. Go to the Web site to see how it stands up against more established players like QuickBooks and Sage.

Another popular, basic, and cheap accounting tool is Owl Simple Business Accounting. The following steps illustrate how easy it is to start keeping books with SBA. These instructions assume that you have downloaded and installed the software from the Owl Software Web site (`www.owlsoftware.com/sba.htm`).

1. **Choose Start➪All Programs➪OWL Business Apps➪SB Accounting 2.**

   The main Owl Simple Business Accounting window appears, as shown in Figure 15-1.

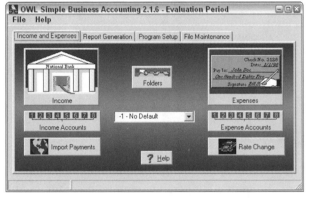

Figure 15-1: SBA uses folders to contain income and expense data that you report.

TIP

The program comes with a set of sample data already entered to help you get accustomed to its features. Choose Help➪Help to open the SBA User's Guide help files. Click the topic Getting Started if you want an overview of how the program operates.

2. **Click the Program Setup tab to bring it to the front and than make any custom changes you may want:**

   • If you want to operate in a fiscal year different from the pre-entered January 1, enter the number for the new month that you want to set as the beginning of your fiscal year.

   • If you want your on-screen and printed reports to be in a different font than the pre-selected one (MS Sans Serif), click the Report Font button, choose the font you want, and then click OK to close the Font dialog box. Times New Roman is usually a good choice because it's relatively compact.

3. **Click the File Maintenance tab to bring it to the front and then click the Erase Data button. When asked whether you want to erase expense data or other information, click OK.**

   This step erases the sample data that was pre-entered to show you how the program works.

4. **Select the Income and Expenses tab to bring it to the front and then click the Folders button to create folders for your business data.**

   The PickFol dialog box appears, as shown in Figure 15-2. This dialog box lists any folders that have been created.

Figure 15-2:
Use this dialog box to add, delete, or edit folders that hold your business data.

5. **Click New.**

   The Folder Definition dialog box appears.

6. **Enter a new name in the Description box and click Save.**

   A Confirm dialog box appears, asking whether you want to add another folder.

7. **If you do, click Yes and repeat Step 6; when you're done, click No.**

   The Folder Definition dialog box closes, and you return to the PickFol dialog box, where your renamed folder or folders appear.

   You may want to create separate folders for your personal or business finances, for example. After your folders are set up, you can record data as the following steps describe.

8. **Click Exit.**

   The PickFol dialog box closes and you return to the main OWL Simple Business Accounting window.

9. **Select the Income and Expenses tab to bring it to the front and then click either the Income Accounts or Expense Accounts button to create an Income or Expense Account.**

   The Select Account dialog box appears.

10. **Click New.**

    The Account Definition dialog box appears.

11. **Enter a name for the account in the Description dialog box and then click Save.**

    A dialog box appears, asking whether you want to create another account.

12. **If you do, click Yes and repeat Step 11; when you're done, click No.**

    The Select Account dialog box appears, listing the items you just created.

13. **Click Exit.**

    You return to the main OWL Simple Business Accounting window.

14. **When you've created Income and Expense Accounts, click either the Income button or the Expense button, depending on the type of data you want to enter.**

    Depending on the button you clicked, the Select Income or Select Expense dialog box appears.

15. **Click New to enter a new item.**

    A dialog box named either Income or Expense appears, depending on the button you selected in Step 14.

16. **Enter the amount and description in the appropriate fields and click Save.**

    The Confirm dialog box appears, asking you to confirm that you either want to add or delete a record.

17. **Click No.**

    You return to the Income or Expense dialog box, where you can make more entries.

18. **When you finish, click Save.**

    You return to the Select Item dialog box, where you can review your changes.

19. **Click Exit.**

    You return to the Income and Expenses options.

20. **When you're all finished, choose File⇨Exit to exit the program until your next accounting session.**

After entering some data, you can select the Report Generation tab, run each of the reports provided by SBA, and examine the output. When running the reports, be sure to select a reporting period within the current calendar year.

The Taxman Cometh: Concerns for Small Business

After you make it through the startup phase of your business, it's time to be concerned with taxes. Here, too, a little preparation up front can save you lots of headaches down the road. But as a hard-working entrepreneur, time is your biggest obstacle.

Successive surveys reveal that a large number of entrepreneurs leave filing their taxes until the last minute. A few return their tax returns late and incur fines from HM Revenue and Customs. Planning is really important for taxes. In fact, HMRC rules state that businesses must keep records appropriate to their trade or business for several years after the transactions are made. HMRC has the right to view these records if it wants to audit your business's (or your personal) tax return. If your records aren't to HMRC's satisfaction, the penalties can be serious.

Should you charge VAT?

Here's one of the most frequently asked questions we receive from readers: Should I charge sales tax for what I sell online? The short answer is that, as always, it depends. VAT is a tax that applies to the transfer of goods and services. You have to register for VAT when your turnover reaches £61,000 per year, but you can register before your business gets to this stage.

Once you've registered, you must charge varying levels of VAT, depending on what you sell. You must also keep records of what you charge for what products or services. This is called your *output tax*. There's a comprehensive guide to VAT on the HMRC Web site. Follow these steps to find it.

1. **Log on to www.hmrc.gov.uk.**

   Look toward the top right-hand corner of the home page and locate the VAT link under Businesses & Corporations. Clicking the link takes you to the VAT home page.

2. **Locate the navigation panel on the left-hand side.**

   This features click-throughs to online forms, rates, and codes, but also Information & Guides. Click this link.

3. **Click Introduction To VAT and scroll down to the What Is VATable link.**

   This step brings up a guide to the various rates of VAT (including the zero rate), what you can charge (and be charged) VAT on, and where to go for more information.

It's a good idea to familiarise yourself with this and other guides on the Web site, because they help shed light on seemingly complex issues. Bookmark this section and refer back to it when you need to.

Remembering other business taxes

There's a whole range of taxes that you have to consider, if not always pay. As your business grows, the number and complexity of taxes you must deal with grows, too. That's why businesses often start up using accountancy software, then hire a part-time bookkeeper, then a full-time accountant, and then eventually an accounts department and outsourced consultants.

To start with, however, you just need to think about taxable income. Anything you make money from is taxable in theory, but the authorities don't get interested until your making a few thousand pounds a year (which, of course, you must make to survive). That's where income or corporation tax comes in, depending on the business model you choose to adopt. (See Chapter 14 for more on the types of businesses you can start.)

Another area that adds to tax considerations is the business costs you incur, many of which are tax deductible. Then there's business rates, or council tax, the level of which depends on the size and location of your premises, as well as staff pay – it's down to you to organise their income tax and national insurance contributions.

 Happily, this confusing sounding series of taxes is nicely summarised on Business Link's Web site (www.businesslink.gov.uk), where you can find accessible information on what you have to pay and what you don't.

Deducing your business deductions

One of the benefits of starting a new business, even if the business isn't profitable in the beginning, is the opportunity to take business deductions and reduce your tax payments. Always keep receipts from any purchases or expenses associated with your business activities. Make sure that you're taking all the deductions for which you're eligible.

For example, if you work at home (and we're assuming that, as an entrepreneur, you do), set aside some space for a home office. This space isn't just a territorial thing. It can result in some nifty business deductions, too.

Say that you have your office in your spare bedroom. Paint the room, and you can claim money back on the paint you use. The same applies to equipment and furniture. Again, Business Link's Web site (www.businesslink.gov.uk) has a full rundown of what you can claim tax-back against. To find it, click the following link path from the site's home page: Taxes⇨Returns and Payroll⇨ Business Expenses⇨Business Expenses and Dispensations.

Part V
The Part of Tens

'Hey, honey, I've just bought a little old place
in England called Cornwall from a guy
called Charlie Windsor.'

In this part . . .

If you're like us, you have one drawer in the kitchen filled with utensils and other assorted objects that don't belong anywhere else. Strangely enough, that's the place we can almost always find something to perform the task at hand.

Part V of this book is called The Part of Tens because it's a collection of miscellaneous secrets arranged in sets of ten. Filled with tips, cautions, suggestions, and examples of new ways to make money online, this part presents many kinds of information that can help you plan and create your own business presence on the Internet.

Chapter 16

Ten Must-Have Features for Your Web Site

● ●

*Y*ou can put any number of snazzy features on your Web site. If you ever meet with a Web design firm, you're sure to hear about all the cool scripts, animations, and other interactive add-ons that can go on your pages. Some pizzazz isn't a bad thing, especially if you're just starting out and need to set yourself apart from the competition. Interactive features and a well-designed Web site give you an air of competence and experience, even if your online business is brand new.

But the Web site features that count toward your bottom line are the ones that attract and retain customers and entice them back to you regularly. Along with the bells and whistles, your business home on the Web needs to have some basic must-haves that shoppers expect. Make sure that your site meets the minimum daily requirements: It needs to be easy to find, loaded with content, include content and background information about you, and include features that make shopping (if that's what you do) easy and secure. This chapter describes ten specific features that help you achieve these objectives.

Secure Easy-to-Remember URLs

Names are critical to the success of any business. A name becomes identified with a business, and people associate the name with its products and its level of customer service. When a small company developed a software product called Lindows, giant Microsoft sued initially, but eventually paid $20 million to stop the infringement on its well-known trademarked product Windows.

Write down five or six names that are short and easy to remember and that would represent your business if included in an URL. Do a domain name search and try to find the one you want. (A good place to search is Network Solutions, `www.networksolutions.com/whois/index.jsp`). Try to keep your site's potential name as short and as free of elements like hyphens as possible. A single four- to ten-character name in between the `www.` and the `.com` or `.co.uk` sections of the URL is easy to remember.

Domain names are cheap, especially if you're able to lock them up for several years at a time. Names in the .com and .co.uk domains are still the most desirable type of URL suffixes because they're the ones that most consumers expect to see when they're trying to find your Web site's URL. Even if you are able to get a .com name, you should purchase domain names in other popular domains such as .net and .org.uk. That way, you protect your URL from being 'poached' by competitors who are trying to copy you. If your URL is easily misspelled, consider purchasing a domain name that represents a common misspelling. That way, if shoppers make a typing error, they're still directed to your site.

Provide a Convenient Payment Method

Shoppers go online for many reasons, but those reasons don't include a desire for things to be complex and time consuming. No matter how technically complex it may be to get one's computer on the Internet, shoppers still want things to be quick and seamless. At the top of the list of seamless processes is the ability to pay for merchandise purchased online.

You don't have to get a merchant account from a bank to process your own credit-card payments. You don't need to get point-of-sale hardware, either. The other day, Greg paid for a heater from a company that sent him to PayPal's Web site. PayPal (www.paypal.com) began as an independent company, but it became so popular among members of the auction site eBay that eBay eventually purchased it. Chances are that many of your prospective customers already have accounts with PayPal if they use eBay. Greg did, so his purchase process was completed in less than a minute. Set yourself up as a seller with PayPal and BidPay and accept money orders and personal cheques. If you can take the additional step of getting a shopping trolley and a credit-card payment system, so much the better.

Promote Security, Privacy, and Trust

Even shoppers who have been making purchases online for years at a time still feel uncertainty when they type their credit-card number and click a button labelled Pay Now, Purchase, or Submit to a commercial Web site. We're speaking from personal experience.

What promotes trust? Information and communication. Shoppers online love getting information that goes beyond what they can find in a printed catalogue. Be sure to include one or more of the following details that can make shoppers feel good about pressing your Buy Now button:

- An endorsement from an organisation that is supposed to promote good business practices, such as Investors in People, Business in the Community, or by your own customers

- A privacy statement that explains how you're going to handle customers' personal information

- Detailed product descriptions that show you're knowledgeable about a product

Another thing that promotes trust is information about who you are and why you love what you do, as described in the 'Blow Your Own Trumpet' section, later in this chapter.

Choose Goods and Services That Buyers Want

Every merchant would love to be able to read the minds of his or her prospective customers. On the Internet, you have as much chance of reading someone's mind as you have of meeting that person face to face. Nevertheless, the Internet does give potential buyers several ways to tell you what they want:

- Come right out and ask them. On your Web site, invite requests for merchandise of one sort or another.

- After a purchase, ask customers for suggestions about other items they'd like to buy from you.

- Visit message boards, newsgroups, and Web sites related to the item you want to sell.

- Make a weekly (remember that Saturdays and Sundays are the best days for auctions to end) search of eBay.co.uk's completed auctions to see what has sold, and which types of items have fetched the highest prices.

An article called 'Is your Web site up to scr@tch' (`www.realbusiness.co.uk/ARTICLE/Is-your-website-up-to-scr@tch/69.aspx`) contains lots of best practices: Decide why you want to sell something online; identify what constitutes success for your sales efforts; back your decisions with information; run promotions and launch sales that are intended to achieve your goals; track the way customers use your site; evaluate what works and what doesn't; and adjust your sales effort accordingly.

Have a Regular Influx of New Products

With a printed catalogue, changes to sales items can be major. The biggest problem is the need to physically reprint the catalogue when inventory changes. One of the biggest advantages associated with having an online sales catalogue is the ability to alter your product line in a matter of minutes, without sending artwork to a printer. You can easily post new sales items online each day, as soon as you get new sales figures.

One reason to keep changing your products on a regular basis is that your larger competitors are doing so. Lands' End, which has a well-designed and popular online sales catalogue (www.landsend.co.uk), puts out new products on a regular basis and announces them in an e-mail newsletter to which loyal customers can subscribe.

Be Current with Upkeep and Improvements

Do you have a favourite blog, comic strip, or newspaper columnist that you like to visit each day? We certainly do. If these content providers don't come up with a new material on a regular basis, you get discouraged. Your loyal customers will hopefully feel the same way about your Web site, eBay shop, or other sales venue.

We know what you're thinking: You've got so many things to do that you can't possibly be revisiting your Web site every day and changing headings or putting new sales online. You have to get the kids off to school, pack up merchandise, run to the post office, clean the house – the list goes on and on. You can't be two places at once. But two people can. Hire a student or friend to run your site and suggest new content for you. In a five-minute phone conversation, you can tell your assistant what to do that day, and you can go on to the rest of your many responsibilities.

Personally Interact with Your Customers

The fact that personal touch counts for so much in Internet communication is a paradox. With rare exceptions, you never meet face to face with the people with whom you exchange messages. Maybe it's the lack of body language and visual clues that make shoppers and other Web surfers so hungry for attention. But the fact is that impersonal, mass e-mail marketing messages (in other words, *spam*) are reviled while quick responses with courteous thank-yous are eagerly welcomed.

You can't send too many personal e-mail messages to your customers, even when they're only making an enquiry and not a purchase. Not long ago, Greg asked some questions about a heater he was thinking of buying online. He filled out the form on the company's Web site and submitted his questions. The representative of the company got right back to him.

'First of all, let me thank you for your interest in our product,' the letter began. She proceeded to answer his questions and then finished with another thank-you and 'If you have any further questions, please don't hesitate to ask.' Greg didn't hesitate: He asked more questions, she answered and again said, 'Don't hesitate to ask' at the end. It's possible it was all 'form letter' material, added to the beginning and end of every enquiry, but it makes a difference. Greg eventually purchased the item.

Don't be afraid to pour on the extra courtesy and provide complete answers to every question: Just tell yourself each answer is worth an extra pound or two in sales. It probably is.

Post Advertisements in the Right Places

When most people think about advertising on the Internet, they automatically think about banner advertisements placed on someone else's Web page. A banner advertisement is only one kind of online ad, and possibly the least effective. Make use of all the advertising options going online brings you, including the following:

- **Use word of mouth:** Bloggers use this method all the time: One person mentions something in another blog, that blogger mentions someone else, and so on.

- **Exchange links:** 'You link to my Web site, and I'll link to yours', in other words. This option is especially effective if you're linking to a business whose products and services complement your own.

✔ **Multiply Web sites:** If you have three Web sites, you immediately have two sites linking to each one of yours. Your ability to exchange links with other Web sites triples, too.

✔ **Get listed in search engines:** Make sure that your site is listed in the databases maintained by Google and the other search engines (see Chapter 13 for more information).

Make sure that your home page contains keywords in text and headings that search engines can use to index it and add it to your database. The more keywords you add, the better your chances of having your site turn up in search results.

Blow Your Own Trumpet

Sam Walton founded Wal-Mart, and the Walton family still runs it, but 99 per cent of the shoppers who flock to the megastores every day don't know or care about that fact. Wal-Mart is a well-established brand with a physical presence. Your fledgling online business has neither of those advantages. You need to use your Web site to provide essential background about yourself, why you started your business, and what your goals are.

Your immediate aim is to answer the question that naturally arises when a consumer visits your online business: 'Who are these people?' or 'Who is this guy?' The indirect goal is to answer a question that the shopper doesn't necessarily ask consciously, but that is present nonetheless: 'Why should I trust this place?' Be sure to tout your experience, your background, your family, or your hobbies – anything to reassure online shoppers that you're a reputable person who is looking out for their interests.

Create a Well-Organised Web Site

A well-organised Web site isn't quite as essential as it used to be, because you can establish a regular income on eBay without having any Web site at all. But even if you become a well-established eBay seller, you're going to want a Web site at some point or another. How do you make your site well organised? Make sure that your site incorporates these essential features:

✔ **Navigation buttons:** Consumers who are in a hurry (in other words, almost all consumers) expect to see a row of navigation buttons along the top or one of the sides of your home page. Don't make them hunt; put them there.

- ✔ **A site map:** A page that leads visitors to all areas of your site can prevent them from going elsewhere if they get lost.

- ✔ **Links that actually work:** Nothing is more frustrating than clicking a link that's supposed to lead to a photo and/or a bit of information that you really want and to come up with the generic `Page not found` error message.

- ✔ **Links that indicate where you are on the site:** Such links are helpful because, like a trail of breadcrumbs, they show how the customer got to a particular page. Here's an example:

```
Clothing > Men's > Sportswear > Shoes > Running
```

When your site grows to contain dozens of pages and several main categories, links that look like this one can help people move up to a main category and find more subcategories.

Be the first to visit your Web site and test it to make sure that the forms, e-mail addresses, and other features function correctly. If someone sends you an e-mail message only to have it 'bounce back', you'll probably lose that customer, who may well conclude that you aren't monitoring your Web site or your business. At the very least, open your site in both Microsoft Internet Explorer and Firefox browsers to make sure that your text and images load correctly.

Chapter 17

Ten Hot Ways to Be an Ontrepreneur

• •

*N*ot so long ago, starting an online business primarily meant creating a Web site and organising it in a businesslike manner. You'd create a catalogue, add a shopping trolley and payment system, and hope customers would find you.

These days, you don't have to create a full-fledged Web site to sell online. The hottest ways to make money are to sign up with an online service that helps individuals get their content online and market themselves or their products and services before the public. You may have to pay a small monthly hosting fee or a sales commission. But the benefits are huge: You don't have to do all the work of creating a catalogue and payment system because your host does the work for you. It may mean signing up with a company that streamlines the process of setting up a blog or creating a shop on eBay.

This chapter presents ten innovative approaches to making money online. By following one or more of these relatively simple options, you can start generating income quickly and painlessly. You may not make a fortune, but you focus attention on yourself and your business that can brighten your life even as it puts extra cash in your pocket.

Start a Blog

In many cases, adding the personal touch separates the successful businesses shops from soulless warehouses. Nowadays, however, you're likely to be greeted with a cheery hello even when you wander into a pound shop. The precedent has definitely been set for mixing the family into business. With a blog of the sort described in Chapter 4, you can combine the personal and business areas of your life into a single Web page.

The advantage of a blog is that you can give customers a window into your mind. A blog can build trust, which in turn can build business. You may not want to define yourself with your strong religious preferences or passionate view on the results of the latest election, but it can be a definite asset to post a few photos of your children or pets. You can also include a narrative of your latest family holiday. On a slightly more businesslike side, consider a link to the text of a paper you presented at the latest professional conference you attended. Of even more relevance may be a series of photos showing the happy day that the new press was delivered to your printing plant, accompanied by examples of new brochures that feature the results of its bells and whistles. Whatever the subject, the goal is to keep the tone of the text upbeat and breezy, friend to friend.

Turn Your Hobby into a Business

Both your authors are perfect example of people who were able to start a new career thanks to the Internet. We both started when the World Wide Web was new, and lots of people who were previously not all that comfortable with the computer were trying to go online. Nowadays, there's not such a need for beginners' books, especially now that modern babies seem to be born with computer mice in their hands. So we're not recommending that you follow in our exact footsteps. But the point is that you should take anything you love and are good at and turn it into a Web site.

Greg once wrote about a woman named Kim Corbin who loves to skip. She started a Web site called iSkip.com (www.iskip.com). She now goes around the country, giving seminars on skipping and inspiring others to improve their mood and get some exercise by doing the same. The gothic rock star Marilyn Manson sells his artwork on his Web site (www.marilynmansonartworkonline.com). One of Greg's favourite online people, a Wisconsin woman who calls herself The Butter Cow Lady and who has gained local fame through her butter sculptures, sells her life story on her site (www.thebuttercowlady.com). On the Web, you're limited only by your imagination as to what you can sell. Take what you know and love and run with it.

Get Other People to Contribute

Many Web sites work by soliciting contributions from interested visitors. If you build a Web site, others will come. The most obvious example is eBay: The site's success is due almost entirely to content submitted by sellers around the world.

You can emulate eBay's success on a smaller scale. Say that you'd like to sell greeting cards. You might post the images of folks who take photographs of scenery, make block prints of jungle animals, or collect drawings and paintings. Or quilting may be your passion. Why not set up a Web site that offers the work of those who create different patterns, use different fabrics, collect antique quilts, or do repairs? The Web is the perfect place to bring like-minded individuals together, and contributions from others can keep your site current and successful while giving you time to focus on design and marketing issues.

Sites like Lulu.com (`www.lulu.com`) allow unpublished authors to have their work bound in an attractive fashion and put up for sale. Once the cost of creating the books is paid by the customer, he or she can then sell books through Lulu.com. Money earned is split 80/20 between the author and Lulu.com itself respectively. Slashdot (`slashdot.org`), a popular news-and-views site for computer nerds, depends on those very same nerds for many of its stories and reviews and gains credibility for welcoming opinions from far and wide.

Inspire Others with Your Thoughts

Sometimes, you end up making a huge change in your life without really trying. You put something online that's sincere, heartfelt, and that you think may help some other people. You find out that tons of people out there feel the same way.

Salam Pax, an Iraqi citizen writing under a pseudonym, also known as the 'Baghdad Blogger', didn't use his writing to make money online initially, yet his words were read the world over. He wrote a personal account of the goings on in Iraq during the war with Britain and America in 2003. The blog was popular because it cut through media and political spin and told readers exactly what was happening on the ground, as well as how the war was affecting ordinary families.

Despite not setting out to enrich himself, Pax later converted his blog into a column on the Guardian Unlimited Web site and has landed a film and book deal. It just goes to show what you can achieve if you capture people's imagination.

Offer Your Services on a Directory

If you say the phrase 'making money online', what comes to the minds of most people is selling small, easily transportable objects. But merchandise is only one type of product you can make available in the marketplace; you can also market your services and your knowledge. Place an ad on your local version of Craigslist (www.craigslist.org) or Gumtree (www.gumtree.com). Then register with a directory like the one on RealBusiness.co.uk (www.realbusiness.co.uk).

Simply purchasing a domain name for your Web site and then creating a simple one-page advertisement that points people to your offices and explains your qualifications can help. Check out e-commerce attorney David Adler's Web site (www.ecommerceattorney.com).

Ask for Contributions

You can earn money through the Web in more than one way, and you don't necessarily have to 'charge' for services rendered. Relying on the kindness of strangers, as sites like Wikipedia do, is one way of earning an income without demanding cash upfront.

This model is less reliable than the standard 'money for products' approach, and you have to be pretty special to get people to part with their money voluntarily, but in some cases it can earn you some extra cash.

eBay and Amazon would struggle if they asked for contributions, because they already have healthy takings. The sites that are most likely to get people reaching for their wallets are expert blogs, sources of accurate information (like Wikipedia), or those that display artistic works (like pictures, novels, or poetry).

Give Out Not-So-Free Advice

The Internet has always been a great place to get questions answered. Over the years, the newsgroups that populate Usenet have been the primary resources for answers and support. You can also start a Web site on which you offer your consulting services. You can gather tips, tricks, and instructions pertaining to your field of interest: Rod Stephens does just that on his VB Helper site (www.vb-helper.com) where he gathers information on the programming language Visual Basic. He also solicits donations (see the preceding section).

Turn to Your Pets for Help

We're not kidding. As an online businessperson, you're looking for something you're passionately interested in and that other people love just as much. Practically everybody has a pet of some sort that they love. Pets, pet care, and related products and services abound on the Web. If you breed pets, you can start up a Web site and take orders. You can create pet toys and sell them online. If you're a photographer, you can take photos of pets. If you're a Web site designer, you can create Web sites for pampered pets that describe training. Just think about the animals you love and that live close to you, and you're bound to come up with ideas that will have them and their owners eating out of your hand.

Become a Mine of Information

What's that you say? You don't have a pet, you can't draw, you don't have any products to sell, and you aren't a professional contractor? Never fear. On the Web, information sells. Chances are you have a mine of information about one topic in particular. You know a lot about your family history, you know everything there is to know about collecting coins, you're a genius with identifying rocks, or you're an avid birdwatcher. Create a Web site in which you put every bit of information you have online. Make your site the one and only greatest resource ever devoted to this topic.

Follow the example of the Urban Legend Reference Pages (www.snopes.com), a Web site started back in 1995 by a husband-and-wife team living in California. The site collects urban legends of all sorts and reports on whether or not they're actually true; it makes enough money from ads to keep it going. But the main thing is that it's a labour of love for its creators.

Need Income? Just Ask!

It sounds odd, but if you present yourself in the right way on the Web, and you simply ask for money, you just might get it. The most famous case is that of Karyn Bosnak. When she found herself buried in £10,000 of credit-card debt, she created a Web site called SaveKaryn.com (www.savekaryn.com). She asked for donations to help her out of debt. In just 20 weeks, her site received nearly two million visits, and she wasn't in debt any more – especially because her book *Save Karyn* (Corgi Adult) was published in several languages, too.

When blogger Andrew Sullivan was in need of funds to keep his blog online, faithful readers donated more than £35,000. Sullivan was well established by that time; people knew he'd use the money to keep providing them with the opinions and insights they were used to. Present yourself in an open, positive manner, and readers will respond to you, too.

Be advised that the field of virtual panhandling is already very crowded. Just check the Google directory at `directory.google.com/Top/Society/People/Requesting_Help/Debt_Reduction`. These people have created Web sites seeking donations so that they can get out of debt. You'll have to find a way to distinguish yourself from the crowd if you want attention for your financial needs.

Expand Your Existing Business to the Web

Expanding your business to the Web isn't new, of course. But a surprising number of established businesspeople haven't done it yet. Some that have make do with boring static sites that do more harm than good. Many of the lawyers we know have no idea what to do with the Web. The same goes for other service providers, from dentists to plumbers to car mechanics. It can be as simple as listing a fee chart, your hours, and where to park when customers come to your facility. Or you can expand a bit to include references from satisfied customers.

The point is that these days a large percentage of the population is sitting at the computer already hooked up to the Internet. When they suddenly realise that they need their suit pressed for a meeting the next day or that their kids need school supplies, they're more likely to call up information on service providers by using a search engine than they are to flip through the phone book and make a call to find out locations and hours.

Chapter 18

Ten Must-See Web Sites
for Online Entrepreneurs

● ●

*Y*ou're starting an online business, so it's important that you understand the Internet and all it has to offer. You should know by now that it's a great learning resource and it can teach you an awful lot about how to run your own Web business.

The following are ten of the best and most useful Web sites available to you as you research your idea and learn how to piece it into a fully-functioning business. These sites will help you get your business up and running and to grow it from a small start-up to a flourishing online success story. Now get surfing!

Realbusiness.co.uk

In need of some inspiration? One of Dan's Web sites, Realbusiness.co.uk, is the Web site of Real Business Magazine (www.realbusiness.co.uk), and it's the place to start your journey. It's full of great features, profiles and interviews with entrepreneurs from all walks of life. There's an online forum where you can ask questions or express your views, a news blog (written by Dan), podcasts, vodcasts; everything you need to understand who entrepreneurs are, what they strive for and what you can achieve too.

Google.co.uk

Well, before you start your online business, you'll need to do plenty of research. Take your knock-out business idea and consider whether others are doing something similar - is there room for your idea in the market? You must work out who will build your Web siteWeb site: Will it be you, a friend or a professional company? You also have to think about who'll will host your Web siteWeb site, how you'll promote it and how will you make it visible amongst all the other Web-based businesses out there.

Google.co.uk (`www.google.co.uk`) is your ally in this research. The great thing about finding reputable businesses to help you is that they are likely to have a higher Google rating (ie they will appear on the first page of a search on the Web site). A company providing search engine optimisation and online marketing, for example, should be easy to find in a Web search. If they are not, then they're not very good at their job, and you should leave them well alone.

UKWDA.org

Google.co.uk's great for finding businesses that care about (and spend money on) marketing; but it doesn't *guarantee* 100 per cent that you'll find your ideal service provider. You should always ask for customer references from businesses before you sign on the dotted line. If possible, you should also see if they are members of accredited bodies. For web designers the relevant body is the UK Web Design Association (`www.ukwda.org`).

If you are employing a company to do the design work for your web site, then make sure they are accredited in some way. Members of UKWDA must abide by a code of conduct, giving you an extra level of assurance compared with unaccredited companies.

Businesslink.gov.uk

Your one stop shop for information on the mechanics of starting a business is Business Link's Web site (`www.businesslink.gov.uk`). The Web site offers hundreds of official guides that are updated constantly. It's not just rules and regulations that are covered, but advice on how to start your business, how to maintain it and how to grow it. Business Link is funded by the Department of Trade and Industry, so you know that the guides are accurate and up-to-date. It's without doubt the best source of practical business advice online.

HMRC.gov.uk

Like Business Link, HM Revenue & Customs is a government organisation, meaning that the content on its Web site (`www.hmrc.gov.uk`) is trustworthy and chimes with UK rules and regulations. It doesn't have the same number of guides as Business Link, nor does it offer as much advice. But it's the ideal source of information on your business' tax commitments.

The chances are you're not a tax expert; you just have a good business idea that you think could earn you some money and perhaps develop into something big. But you do need a grasp of what you must pay back to the government; the amounts vary depending on the nature of your business and the amount of money you make. This Web site will tell you everything you need to know to get started.

Ebay.co.uk

In today's ultra-competitive world, the customer really is king. Sites like `www.play.com`, `www.cdwow.com` and `www.firebox.com` force down the price of items that cost a lot more in high street stores. Their profit margins are pretty tight, but they shift so much stock that they can earn a tidy living for their directors.

Further more, price comparison Web sites like `www.kelkoo.com` and `www.pricerunner.co.uk` let consumers know exactly where they can find the cheapest brands. You have to be sure that you can either offer products cheaper (very unlikely nowadays) or that you offer a bespoke service and good customer care.

Apart from the sites listed above, the best way to assess whether your business will sink or swim is to check out the competition on eBay.co.uk (`www.ebay.co.uk`). Study your competitors like a hawk. What makes them professional? How much do their products usually sell for and how can you improve on the customer's experience? If you can't do it cheaper or better, then maybe it's not worth doing at all!

Startups.co.uk

Startups.co.uk (`www.startups.co.uk`) is another great information resource for people thinking about starting a business (of course, Dan would say that, because he's partly responsible for creating it). Arguably the best thing about the site is not its daily small business newsfeed, or its large mine of 'how-to' guides. The best thing is its real life start-up stories and its busy online forum where you can ask questions and make suggestions to its many users, some of whom are lawyers, accountants and other advisers who give their advice away for free.

Guardian Technology

It's vitally important to keep up with the times when you start your online business. There's nothing worse than trawling through a site that feels like it was developed in 1996. Innovative super sites like Youtube (www.youtube.com), Google (www.google.co.uk), and Bebo (www.bebo.com) are distant cousins of your own site and you must pay attention to the jazzy new tools they keep producing.

Keep track of redesigns, new services and product ideas, and try to apply them to your own Web site. But instead of trawling around the internet all day waiting for sites to do something new, keep track through a news service like the Guardian's Technology Web site (http://technology.guardian.co.uk) or one of the many blogs on the subject such as Techcrunch (www.techcrunch.com).

Idiottoys.com

There are two ways of understanding where the bar is set in terms of quality products and services. As we explained above, you can check out the Web success stories and learn from them, but it's also a good idea to learn from other people's mistakes (this can be fun too!).

For tips on what not to do, take a look at Idiottoys.com (www.idiottoys.com). It's a funny, yet sometimes very useful site dedicated to the worst ideas in technology. For more tips, take a look at www.thisisbroken.com, which gives examples of failed marketing campaigns, silly competitions and nonsensical promotional text.

Order-order.com

Writing a blog (or web log) is a good way of keeping your Web site fresh with new, hopefully daily, content. But it only works if you're any good at writing, or if you have something useful to say, otherwise who's gonna want to read it? Luckily, there are some excellent blogs to help you gauge your own blog writing abilities. There's Dan's Real Business blog (www.realbusiness.co.uk), which needless to say comes highly recommended, and a host of others. Try political agitator Guido Fawkes' diary at www.order-order.com, or marketing guru Seth Godin's superb blog at http://sethgodin.typepad.com.

Index

using personal information manager, 208–210

businesses. *See also specific businesses*
expanding to Web, 338
types of, 306–308

Buy It Now (BIN) prices, 221

Buying Online For Dummies (Lowery), 202

• C •

calendar year, selecting as accounting period, 313
cash-basis accounting, versus accrual-basis accounting, 312–313
categories, choosing for eBay listings, 226–227
CD-RW/DVD±RW drive, understanding, 58
cellular phones, selling services/products for, 102–103
certificates
encrypting e-mail messages with, 178–179
using and obtaining, 174–176
CGI scripts
creating Web page forms with, 156, 264
included as Web hosting service, 84
need for with search boxes, 148
chat
encouraging customer communication/community with, 97
providing customer service with, 267
cheapness, differentiating oneself with, 13
checking out, software packages facilitating options for, 76
The Chocolate Farm, growth and changes of, 33
clip art
highlighting sale items with, 201
using on Web pages, 123
CoffeeCup HTML Editor, overview, 89
colocation, advantages of, 212
colour artifacts, reducing in digital photos, 61
colour, using for effective wallpaper, 119–121
commercial Web sites, types of, 39–40
communication
advantage of online versus print, 254

encouraging customer, 96–97
facilitating efficient business, 208–210
importance of personal with customers, 329
using advanced e-mail features to improve, 258–263
using FAQs for, 254–255
value of online newsletters for, 255–257
community
Craigslist as, 109
creating among customers, 97
creating through Web sites, 29–30
creating with discussion areas, 270–271
creating with feedback, 153–161
for sellers, 108
using for market research, 110–111
as value proposition, 108
competitors
researching, 13
spying on for added keywords, 284–285
ComponentControl, 213
computers
considerations for selecting, 55–56
planning for online business purchases, 55
protecting against theft, 168
safely having multiple users of, 164–165
selling online, 44
understanding CD-RW/DVD±RW drive on, 58
understanding hard drive storage requirements, 57–58
understanding processor speed of, 56–57
connections
dialup versus broadband Internet, 62–63
types of server, 85
consumer products. *See* products
contact details, including on Web site, 38
contact information, providing comprehensive, 258
content
adding keywords to, 288
appropriate to business personality, 150
blogging for, 103–104
differentiating oneself with, 13
filling Web sites with, 23–24
finding endorsements, 150–151
including expert information, 151

• E •

• *K* •

FOR DUMMIES®

Do Anything. Just Add Dummies

PROPERTY

UK editions

Buying and Selling a Home	Renting Out Your Property	Buying a Property in Eastern Europe
0-7645-7027-7	0-470-02921-8	0-7645-7047-1

PERSONAL FINANCE

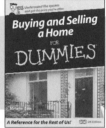

Investing	Bookkeeping	Sorting Out Your Finances
0-7645-7023-4	0-470-05815-3	0-7645-7039-0

BUSINESS

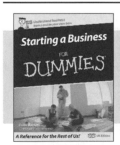

Starting a Business	Marketing	Business Plans
0-7645-7018-8	0-7645-7056-0	0-7645-7026-9

Answering Tough Interview Questions For Dummies
(0-470-01903-4)

Arthritis For Dummies
(0-470-02582-4)

Being the Best Man For Dummies
(0-470-02657-X)

British History For Dummies
(0-470-03536-6)

Building Confidence For Dummies
(0-470-01669-8)

Buying a Home on a Budget For Dummies
(0-7645-7035-8)

Children's Health For Dummies
(0-470-02735-5)

Cognitive Behavioural Therapy For Dummies
(0-470-01838-0)

Cricket For Dummies
(0-470-03454-8)

CVs For Dummies
(0-7645-7017-X)

Detox For Dummies
(0-470-01908-5)

Diabetes For Dummies
(0-7645-7019-6)

Divorce For Dummies
(0-7645-7030-7)

DJing For Dummies
(0-470-03275-8)

eBay.co.uk For Dummies
(0-7645-7059-5)

European History For Dummies
(0-7645-7060-9)

Gardening For Dummies
(0-470-01843-7)

Genealogy Online For Dummies
(0-7645-7061-7)

Golf For Dummies
(0-470-01811-9)

Hypnotherapy For Dummies
(0-470-01930-1)

Irish History For Dummies
(0-7645-7040-4)

Neuro-linguistic Programming For Dummies
(0-7645-7028-5)

Nutrition For Dummies
(0-7645-7058-7)

Parenting For Dummies
(0-470-02714-2)

Pregnancy For Dummies
(0-7645-7042-0)

Retiring Wealthy For Dummies
(0-470-02632-4)

Rugby Union For Dummies
(0-470-03537-4)

Small Business Employment Law For Dummies
(0-7645-7052-8)

Starting a Business on eBay.co.uk For Dummies
(0-470-02666-9)

Su Doku For Dummies
(0-470-01892-5)

The GL Diet For Dummies
(0-470-02753-3)

The Romans For Dummies
(0-470-03077-1)

Thyroid For Dummies
(0-470-03172-7)

UK Law and Your Rights For Dummies
(0-470-02796-7)

Winning on Betfair For Dummies
(0-470-02856-4)

FOR DUMMIES®

Do Anything. Just Add Dummies

HOBBIES

0-7645-5232-5

0-7645-6847-7

0-7645-5476-X

Also available:

Art For Dummies
(0-7645-5104-3)

Aromatherapy For Dummies
(0-7645-5171-X)

Bridge For Dummies
(0-471-92426-1)

Card Games For Dummies
(0-7645-9910-0)

Chess For Dummies
(0-7645-8404-9)

Improving Your Memory
For Dummies
(0-7645-5435-2)

Massage For Dummies
(0-7645-5172-8)

Meditation For Dummies
(0-471-77774-9)

Photography For Dummies
(0-7645-4116-1)

Quilting For Dummies
(0-7645-9799-X)

EDUCATION

0-7645-7206-7

0-7645-5581-2

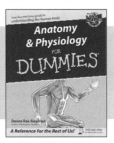
0-7645-5422-0

Also available:

Algebra For Dummies
(0-7645-5325-9)

Algebra II For Dummies
(0-471-77581-9)

Astronomy For Dummies
(0-7645-8465-0)

Buddhism For Dummies
(0-7645-5359-3)

Calculus For Dummies
(0-7645-2498-4)

Forensics For Dummies
(0-7645-5580-4)

Islam For Dummies
(0-7645-5503-0)

Philosophy For Dummies
(0-7645-5153-1)

Religion For Dummies
(0-7645-5264-3)

Trigonometry For Dummies
(0-7645-6903-1)

PETS

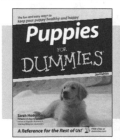
0-470-03717-2

0-7645-8418-9

0-7645-5275-9

Also available:

Labrador Retrievers
For Dummies
(0-7645-5281-3)

Aquariums For Dummies
(0-7645-5156-6)

Birds For Dummies
(0-7645-5139-6)

Dogs For Dummies
(0-7645-5274-0)

Ferrets For Dummies
(0-7645-5259-7)

Golden Retrievers
For Dummies
(0-7645-5267-8)

Horses For Dummies
(0-7645-9797-3)

Jack Russell Terriers
For Dummies
(0-7645-5268-6)

Puppies Raising & Training
Diary For Dummies
(0-7645-0876-8)

FOR DUMMIES®

The easy way to get more done and have more fun

LANGUAGES

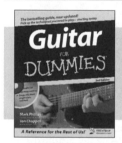

Spanish FOR DUMMIES
0-7645-5194-9

French FOR DUMMIES
0-7645-5193-0

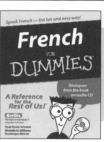

Italian FOR DUMMIES
0-7645-5196-5

Also available:

Chinese For Dummies
(0-471-78897-X)

Chinese Phrases
For Dummies
(0-7645-8477-4)

French Phrases For Dummies
(0-7645-7202-4)

German For Dummies
(0-7645-5195-7)

Italian Phrases For Dummies
(0-7645-7203-2)

Japanese For Dummies
(0-7645-5429-8)

Latin For Dummies
(0-7645-5431-X)

Spanish Phrases
For Dummies
(0-7645-7204-0)

Spanish Verbs For Dummies
(0-471-76872-3)

Hebrew For Dummies
(0-7645-5489-1)

MUSIC AND FILM

Guitar FOR DUMMIES
0-7645-9904-6

Filmmaking FOR DUMMIES
0-7645-2476-3

Piano FOR DUMMIES
0-7645-5105-1

Also available:

Bass Guitar For Dummies
(0-7645-2487-9)

Blues For Dummies
(0-7645-5080-2)

Classical Music For Dummies
(0-7645-5009-8)

Drums For Dummies
(0-471-79411-2)

Jazz For Dummies
(0-471-76844-8)

Opera For Dummies
(0-7645-5010-1)

Rock Guitar For Dummies
(0-7645-5356-9)

Screenwriting For Dummies
(0-7645-5486-7)

Songwriting For Dummies
(0-7645-5404-2)

Singing For Dummies
(0-7645-2475-5)

HEALTH, SPORTS & FITNESS

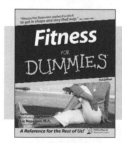

Fitness FOR DUMMIES
0-7645-7851-0

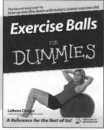

Exercise Balls FOR DUMMIES
0-7645-5623-1

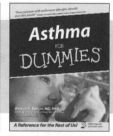

Asthma FOR DUMMIES
0-7645-4233-8

Also available:

Controlling Cholesterol
For Dummies
(0-7645-5440-9)

Dieting For Dummies
(0-7645-4149-8)

High Blood Pressure
For Dummies
(0-7645-5424-7)

Martial Arts For Dummies
(0-7645-5358-5)

Menopause For Dummies
(0-7645-5458-1)

Power Yoga For Dummies
(0-7645-5342-9)

Weight Training
For Dummies
(0-471-76845-6)

Yoga For Dummies
(0-7645-5117-5)

FOR DUMMIES®

Helping you expand your horizons and achieve your potential

INTERNET

0-7645-8996-2

0-471-77084-1

0-7645-7327-6

Also available:

eBay.co.uk
For Dummies
(0-7645-7059-5)
Dreamweaver 8
For Dummies
(0-7645-9649-7)
Web Design
For Dummies
(0-471-78117-7)

Everyday Internet
All-in-One Desk Reference
For Dummies
(0-7645-8875-3)
Creating Web Pages
All-in-One Desk Reference
For Dummies
(0-7645-4345-8)

DIGITAL MEDIA

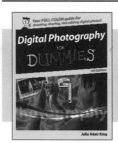

0-7645-9802-3

0-471-74739-4

0-7645-9803-1

Also available:

Digital Photos, Movies, &
Music GigaBook
For Dummies
(0-7645-7414-0)
Photoshop CS2
For Dummies
(0-7645-9571-7)
Podcasting
For Dummies
(0-471-74898-6)

Blogging
For Dummies
(0-471-77084-1)
Digital Photography
All-In-One Desk Reference
For Dummies
(0-7645-7328-4)
Windows XP Digital Music For
Dummies
(0-7645-7599-6)

COMPUTER BASICS

0-7645-8958-X

0-470-05432-8

0-7645-7326-8

Also available:

Office XP 9 in 1
Desk Reference
For Dummies
(0-7645-0819-9)
PCs All-in-One Desk
Reference For Dummies
(0-471-77082-5)
Pocket PC For Dummies
(0-7645-1640-X)

Upgrading & Fixing PCs
For Dummies
(0-7645-1665-5)
Windows XP All-in-One Desk
Reference For Dummies
(0-7645-7463-9)
Macs For Dummies
(0-470-04849-2)
